Small-Group Reading Instruction

A Differentiated Teaching Model for Intermediate Readers, Grades 3–8

BEVERLY TYNER

Chattanooga, Tennessee, USA

SHARON E. GREEN

Emporia State University
Emporia, Kansas, USA

INTERNATIONAL
Reading Association
800 BARKSDALE ROAD, PO BOX 8139
NEWARK, DE 19714-8139, USA
www.reading.org

The International Reading Association attempts, through its publications, to provide a forum for a wide spectrum of opinions on reading. This policy permits divergent viewpoints without implying the endorsement of the Association.

Director of Publications Dan Mangan
Editorial Director, Books and Special Projects Teresa Curto
Managing Editor, Books Shannon T. Fortner
Acquisitions and Developmental Editor Corinne M. Mooney
Associate Editor Charlene M. Nichols
Production Editor Amy Messick
Associate Editor, Books Elizabeth C. Hunt
Books and Inventory Assistant Rebecca A. Zell
Permissions Editor Janet S. Parrack
Assistant Permissions Editor Tyanna L. Collins
Production Department Manager Iona Muscella
Supervisor, Electronic Publishing Anette Schütz
Senior Electronic Publishing Specialist R. Lynn Harrison
Electronic Publishing Specialist Lisa M. Kochel
Proofreader Stacey Lynn Sharp

Project Editor Charlene M. Nichols

Art Cover Design, Linda Steere; Photos, Fred Carr; Interior Reproducible Illustrations, Sharon K. Lauman

Web addresses in this book were correct as of the publication date but may have become inactive or otherwise modified since that time. If you notice a deactivated or changed Web address, please e-mail books@reading.org with the words "Website Update" in the subject line. In your message, specify the Web link, the book title, and the page number on which the link appears.

Library of Congress Cataloging-in-Publication Data

Tyner, Beverly.
   Small-group reading instruction : a differentiated teaching model for
intermediate readers, grades 3-8 / Beverly Tyner, Sharon E. Green.
      p. cm.
   Includes bibliographical references and index.
   ISBN 0-87207-574-5
   1. Reading (Elementary) 2. Group reading. 3. Reading--Remedial
teaching.   I. Green, Sharon E., 1970-   . II. Title.
   LB1573.T97 2005
   372.41'62--dc22
                                                                    2005013828

To our precious children: Leslie, Susan, Jennifer, Harrison, Jack, and Benjamin. They are truly our greatest gifts and our most important students.

CONTENTS

First and foremost, we believe all children have the right to quality reading instruction. In order to become successful in today's society, all students must become competent readers and writers. With the pressure of high-stakes assessments and heightened demands through state and federal guidelines, the quest for effective reading instruction is at the forefront of education. Although there has been unprecedented focus on and funding for early literacy development, little has been done to enhance reading instruction for upper elementary and middle school students. In most instances, the intermediate years are the last opportunity for students to receive focused reading instruction and, therefore, are critical.

Teaching reading above the primary grades brings the added pressure of content area mandates, which present a daunting task for many upper elementary and middle school teachers. Traditional whole-class instruction for these students fails for much of the same reason as it does in the primary grades: Within any classroom, there are multiple levels of readers. If we are serious in our desire to make all students competent readers, we, as educators, must provide differentiated reading instruction geared to the specific needs of students as they matriculate through the upper grades.

For most intermediate readers, the transition from "learning to read" to "reading to learn" marks the beginning of an important milestone. Left unsupported, these readers may fail to develop the critical skills necessary to pave the way to more advanced reading levels. Intermediate readers vary in their levels of literacy learning and, as such, reading instruction must be differentiated to meet these needs. *Differentiation* as it relates to this text is reading instruction based on the developmental needs of the reader. Differentiating instruction may not always be convenient or easy, but it is a necessity if we are to provide quality reading instruction for all students. Unfortunately, "one-size-fits all" instruction is not effective because there is no one standard student profile. Rather, all readers can be readily identified by their reading characteristics and distinct predicable stages through which all readers pass. Simply stated, we must be able to assess a student's literacy knowledge and be prepared to provide focused reading instruction based on those identified needs.

This book presents a small-group differentiated teaching model with effective teaching strategies for growth in fluency; word study, including phonics and vocabulary; and comprehension—areas that have been identified in the National Reading Panel Report of 2000 (National Institute of Child Health and Human Development [NICHD]) as critical to the reading process. Key to this entire book is the focus on differentiated instructional practices within a small group, which ultimately results in better instruction for all children.

Intermediate teachers often do not have the time to select materials and develop appropriate instruction to meet the needs of all their students. This book is intended for those teachers. We provide both the research base and the practical implementation model to assist in meeting the literacy needs for all intermediate students. While research-based strategies are now mandated throughout the United States, our intention is not to provide extensive research reviews. Rather, this book presents a step-by-step model for teachers, in which the research has been carefully reviewed and is reflected.

Our goal in writing this book is to provide a guide for systematic, research-based, differentiated reading instruction. This book will offer teachers, administrators, staff developers, and teacher educators a practical, powerful, instructional model that will help to empower teachers with effective reading instruction. These intermediate students must continue to be supported in literacy development as they grow toward reading independence.

Acknowledgments

First, we would like to thank the many teachers and students who unknowingly have provided the motivation for this book. We are especially grateful to our husbands, Paul and Brian, for their steadfast support as we have completed this book—which has sometimes meant doing more than their part with household and parental duties. We would like to give special thanks to the administrators and staffs of the Cleveland City School District, Cleveland, Tennessee, USA; Clifton Hills Elementary School, East Lake Elementary School, and Hillcrest Elementary School, Hamilton County School District, Chattanooga, Tennessee, USA; Prairie Park Elementary School, Lawrence Public Schools, Kansas, USA; and Ascension Catholic School, Overland Park, Kansas, USA. We also would like to thank the preservice teachers at Emporia State University, Emporia, Kansas, USA.

Without the support of the International Reading Association, this endeavor never would have been possible. We thank Corinne Mooney and Charlene Nichols for their patience, valuable input, and talents in editing and publishing this book.

Please send comments and questions about this book. Beverly will be happy to answer your questions about the book, the accompanying video series, or the Small-Group Differentiated Teaching Model. A link to Beverly's e-mail can be found at smallgroupreading.com.

CHAPTER 1

Intermediate Reading Instruction and the Small-Group Differentiated Reading Model

In the current climate of the No Child Left Behind (NCLB) Act of 2001 (2002), there is unprecedented accountability for educators to ensure that all students can read proficiently by the time they leave third grade. The NCLB Act was designed to help all students meet high academic standards by requiring that states create annual assessments to measure academic proficiency in grades 3 through 8. Unfortunately, thus far, most of the resources associated with NCLB have been earmarked for early childhood (K–3) programs. In 2003, 37% of fourth graders and 26% of eighth graders were reading on a basic proficiency level (National Center for Education Statistics [NCES], 2003). Obviously, the needs of the intermediate (grades 3–8) students are not currently being addressed. We, as educators, cannot continue to ignore the number of intermediate students who are still struggling with their reading skills as they progress to the upper grades.

Currently, the culture of the upper elementary and middle school classrooms is primarily one of standards-driven, whole-class instruction. Little attention is given to the notion of differentiating reading instruction as a way to meet the needs of all students. However, there is a great deal of attention being paid to differentiated instruction with regard to providing multiple ways of presenting information to students (Tomlinson, 1999). This book specifically discusses differentiated instruction as it relates to the developmental needs of readers and reading instruction.

Many of the intermediate teachers with whom we have worked voice their frustration as they strive to meet the mandates dictated by high-stakes assessments. We are continually told comments such as, "I don't know how to teach reading. I am a science teacher and I have all these kids who can't read the textbook. So how am I supposed to teach my content?" With the increased pressure to succeed, teachers and administrators are scrambling to find the "quick fix" that will have all students reading on grade level. This mindset leads to a frenzy in the purchasing of scripted, neatly boxed, standards-based reading programs for teachers to implement. However, without the necessary knowledge of the reading process and a developmental model, these programs will continue to fall short of expectations. The bottom line is that teachers—not programs—teach students to read.

In order to meet the needs of their students, intermediate teachers need to be better prepared for this challenge. Historically, these teachers have had minimal coursework and training in reading development. In fact, most teacher education programs only require one content area reading course for those seeking middle school certification. Additionally, there is a lack of research and resources available that address the reading needs of intermediate students. Yet, teachers still have the formidable task of teaching the diverse readers in their classrooms. Without a practical model for implementation and a knowledge base in reading development, teachers will continue to struggle in their efforts to provide effective reading instruction for all of their students.

Accompanying these accountability issues is the mandate that *all* students must show adequate gains in reading. Research supports that instruction within a student's zone of proximal development (Vygotsky, 1934/1978) is necessary for growth to occur. The zone of proximal development refers to the level at which a student is "ripe for instruction" or, more specifically, "the distance between the actual developmental level as determined by individual problem solving and the level of potential development as determined through problem solving under adult guidance or in collaboration with more capable peers" (p. 86). Thus, students need repeated opportunities to read instructional level text. Instructional level text refers to the text that a student can read and understand with explicit instruction and support from the teacher. In order to provide these opportunities for all students, the teacher must differentiate instruction in a small-group setting bringing together homogeneously grouped readers. This book provides both the theoretical knowledge base and practical application model necessary to implement small-group differentiated reading instruction in the intermediate grades.

The Small-Group Differentiated Reading Model

Development of the Model

We became intrigued with the idea of small-group instruction in the intermediate grades through our work with both preservice and inservice teachers in grades 3–8. Beverly, a former classroom teacher, district-level administrator, and graduate professor, recognized the need for effective classroom reading instruction that was differentiated based on the needs of these intermediate readers. Sharon, a former classroom and special education teacher, also recognized these needs. After a chance meeting, we started to talk about our experiences with these readers and the dire need to support intermediate teachers in their efforts to develop proficient readers.

Our interest in developing a specific small-group model for intermediate grades resulted in our mutual association with the work of Darrell Morris (1999), who developed the Howard Street tutoring program in Chicago, Illinois, USA (this later became known as Early Steps). Using Morris's work, Francine Johnston, Marcia Invernizzi, and Connie Juel created Book Buddies (1998), a volunteer tutoring program in Charlottesville, Virginia, USA.

As evidenced by recent research, both programs have shown steady improvement with the populations they serve (Allington & Cunningham, 2002; Invernizzi, Juel, & Rosemary, 1997; Morris & Slavin, 2003; Morris, Tyner, & Perney, 2000; Santa & Hoien, 1999; Wasik, 1997). An important component of the aforementioned programs is the use of a balanced approach in their tutoring lessons. Rather than choosing a purely phonetic or whole-language approach, Early Steps and Book Buddies programs merged both methodologies into a practical model. Research by Snow, Burns, and Griffin (1998) proves that the successful teaching of reading requires skill instruction, including phonics (word study) and phonemics, in conjunction with stimulating, meaningful reading and writing experiences. This balanced perspective is fundamental to producing well-rounded readers.

Although both of the tutoring programs were highly successful with individual students, it became apparent that this kind of effective instruction was lacking in most regular classroom settings. Using the components of Early Steps, Beverly created the Small-Group Differentiated Reading Model that addressed the needs of beginning and struggling readers in the regular classroom setting (Tyner, 2004). This model provided a framework for instructing beginning and struggling readers. She based the model on research that supports reading, writing, and spelling as integrated processes (Bear, 1991; Bear, Invernizzi, Templeton, & Johnston, 2004; Moats, 2000). Further, she took into consideration the stages of development through which readers progress and differentiated the model and subsequent instruction, based on the developmental needs of the reader. At the same time, Sharon experienced success with a similar model as her graduate students completed a one-on-one tutoring program with remedial readers above grade 3. Using this model, the students showed significant progress (Green & Massengill, 2005).

As news of the model's success spread, upper elementary and middle school teachers cried out for help because they were frustrated by the lack of such a model in the intermediate grades. It became apparent to us that the model needed to be extended. We knew that the needs of the teachers and the students at this level were not different from those in the primary grades. The one-size-fits-all curriculum traditionally seen in grades 3–8 is simply not effective much for the same reason that it is not effective in the primary grades. As a sequel to the first book *Small-Group Reading Instruction: A Differentiated Teaching Model for Beginning and Struggling Readers* (Tyner, 2004), this book includes the later stages of reading development as well as the model for implementing small-group differentiated reading instruction in the intermediate classroom.

Differentiating the Stages of Reading Development

Most researchers agree that reading acquisition occurs in a stage-like progression (Chall, 1983). Just as children naturally pass through developmental milestones in physical development, they move through reading stages toward the goal of becoming an advanced reader. Understanding the differences between these reading stages is critical because it allows for the differentiation of instruction based on readers' needs within each particular stage.

Differentiated is defined as both "the development of the simple to the complex" and "a difference between individuals of the same kind" (*Webster's Ninth New Collegiate Dictionary*, 1984, p. 205). Typically in an intermediate classroom, readers are often grouped together with little discrimination between abilities. However, this discrimination is critical when it comes to providing effective reading instruction and should not be overlooked.

In most intermediate classrooms, there are some students who struggle with reading, others who read well above grade level, and the rest fall somewhere in between. Small-group differentiated reading instruction allows teachers to accommodate the diverse needs of heterogeneously grouped students. This model takes into account the developmental stages of reading through which the reader progresses and adapts the instruction and strategies necessary to support the reader at any given stage.

To effectively guide the reading process, there first must be an understanding of the developmental reading stages and the print demands readers encounter at these varying stages. For example, in the beginning reading stages, there is a stronger emphasis on decoding than on comprehension. As readers progress, this focus shifts to a stronger emphasis on comprehension due to readers' increased word recognition abilities within more complex text. In effect, readers are able to spend more of their mental energy on what the words mean rather than on what the words are. Table 1 details the five stages in beginning reading development discussed in the aforementioned book. Table 2 shows the subsequent three stages of intermediate reading development discussed in this book.

The Stages of Intermediate Reading

Chall (1979) was one of the first reading researchers to discuss the developmental stages through which a reader passes. Her research was based on the work of developmental psychologists as they described the typical psychological development of a child. Since Chall's first publication, many other researchers have followed in her footsteps and developed similar stages of reading development (e.g., Fountas & Pinnell, 1996; Gunning, 2002). Delineation and names of reading stages vary from researcher to researcher. The stages presented in this text reflect our philosophy.

An intermediate reader is best described as one who has made the transition, or is in the process of making the transition, from "learning to read" to "reading to learn." Intermediate reading can be further broken down into the following stages: evolving reader, maturing reader, and advanced reader. Combined, these stages typically cover grades 3–8. It also is important to note that these stages build upon one another in a continuum. In doing so, the beginning and endpoints of the stages are not always clearly defined. Rather, there is some overlap. For example, the maturing reader may be able to comprehend text on a higher level; however, he or she may still need some practice with ambiguous vowel patterns, which is a word study feature generally studied in the evolving reader stage. Therefore, we examine these stages in terms of typical, grade-level development and expectations. In our experience with intermediate students who show deficits, particularly in the area of word study, they did not receive appropriate developmental instruction in this area in the earlier grades. It is, therefore, critical as students reach the intermediate grades that teachers are aware of these deficits and adjust their instruction accordingly. In the following sections, we introduce

T A B L E 1
Stages of Beginning Reading Development

Stage	Appropriate Grade Level	Beginning Student Characteristics	Major Focuses
1 Emergent Reader	Pre-K/K	• Knows less than half the alphabet • Has no concept of word • Has little phonemic awareness • Recognizes a few sight words	• Using memory and pictures • Recognizing and reproducing letters of the alphabet • Tracking print • Distinguishing beginning consonant sounds • Recognizing 10 sight words
2 Beginning Reader	Late K/Early First Grade	• Knows three quarters or more of the alphabet • Is beginning to track print • Is able to hear some sounds • Recognizes 10 sight words	• Completing alphabet recognition and production • Using beginning and ending consonant sounds • Recognizing 50 sight words • Reading simple text • Using sentence context and pictures or word recognition cues to decode
3 Fledgling Reader	Early/Mid First Grade	• Confirms with beginning and ending consonant sounds • Recognizes 50+ sight words • Reads simple text	• Recognizing and using word families in reading and writing • Recognizing 100+ sight words • Reading more complex text • Developing fluency • Developing comprehension strategies • Self-correcting errors
4 Transitional Reader	Mid/Late First Grade	• Recognizes word families in isolation and in texts • Recognizes 100+ sight words • Reads developed text	• Using word patterns in reading and writing • Developing independent reading using decoding and comprehension strategies • Developing fluency
5 Independent Reader	Early/Late Second Grade	• Reads and writes independently • Uses strategies to figure out new words • Reads fluently • Uses word patterns in reading and writing	• Developing diverse comprehension strategies • Using complex word patterns • Developing fluency in a variety of texts • Responding to text in a variety of ways

T A B L E 2
Stages of Intermediate Reading Development

Stage/Grade Level	Beginning Student Characteristics	Major Focuses
Evolving Late 2nd–Late 4th Grade	**Reading** • Has an extensive sight vocabulary • Begins to read more fluently and expressively • "Chunks" unknown words • Depends less upon finger pointing and subvocalizing (these strategies phase out during the stage) **Word Study (spelling)** • Knows most short vowels; blends and digraphs are correct • Recognizes common long-vowel patterns in text • Begins to make connections between spelling and vocabulary • Begins to learn about the meaning connections of simple prefixes and suffixes	**Fluency** • Developing smooth, quick, accurate, automatic word recognition while using expression to interpret the author's meaning **Word Study (spelling)** • Learning common, uncommon, and complex vowel patterns in one-syllable words, contractions, complex digraphs and blends, homophones and homographs, and compound words, as well as simple prefixes and suffixes **Comprehension** • Learning and experimenting with before-, during-, and after-reading strategies
Maturing Early 4th–Late 6th Grade	**Reading** • Reads fluently • Reads longer text in a variety of genres • Uses a variety of strategies to comprehend text **Word Study (spelling)** • Spells most one-syllable words • Continues to study the meaning connection of spelling and vocabulary • Understands meaning changes when prefixes and suffixes are added to words	**Fluency** • Transitioning to independent practice for fluency **Word Study (spelling)** • Learning about syllable patterns and syllable stress in multisyllabic words • Mastering the principle of preserving short- or long-vowel patterns as a syllable is added; learning more difficult affixes as the spelling–meaning connection is explored **Comprehension** • Developing and expanding before-, during-, and after-reading strategies
Advanced Late 6th–Early 8th Grade	**Reading** • Fluent, often avid readers • Develops competency with knowing when and how to use effective comprehension strategies based on text structure **Word Study (spelling)** • Understands basic and more complex syllable patterns	**Fluency** • Independently practicing for fluency **Word Study (spelling)** • Mastering additional complex syllable patterns • Learning polysyllabic words with Latin and Greek roots **Comprehension** • Developing independent use of strategies and developing critical insight

the three intermediate stages and provide an overview of the beginning characteristics of each stage and the instructional focus for the teacher in the areas of fluency, word study, and comprehension.

Evolving Reader Stage

According to *Webster's Tenth New Collegiate Dictionary* (2000), *evolutionary* is defined as "a process of change in a certain direction" (p. 397). This epitomizes the state of the evolving reader who moves from being a basic decoder of text to a comprehender of text. Fluency development is critical as the evolving reader makes this transition. Although the evolving reader typically is found in grades 3 and 4, readers at this stage may include higher level second graders as well as lower level fifth or sixth graders. The first section in Table 2 presents an overview of characteristics and major instructional focuses for the evolving reader.

Maturing Reader Stage

The maturing reader is best characterized as one who has successfully completed the foundational stages of reading development and is continuing to grow in his or her abilities to understand and evaluate text. The maturing reader requires less directed teacher support than an evolving reader and is developing the critical behavioral characteristics necessary to be considered an advanced reader. The second section of Table 2 outlines characteristics and instructional focuses that are representative of the maturing reader.

Advanced Reader Stage

The final stage in the Small-Group Differentiated Reading Model for intermediate readers is the advanced reader stage. Advanced readers have well-developed reading skills and are able to comprehend and critique a variety of texts and genres. The teacher's role is increasingly one that involves modeling and facilitating the critical thinking skills necessary to evaluate complex text. The final section of Table 2 displays the advanced reader characteristics and instructional focuses.

Lesson Plan Components

The components of the Small-Group Differentiated Reading Model include fluency instruction, word study instruction, and comprehension instruction. Although we advocate for the integration of comprehension and writing activities, process writing and grammar instruction should not take place during small-group reading instruction due to time constraints.

Research supports that fluency, word study, and comprehension are integrated processes (Bear, 1991; Bear et al., 2004; Moats, 2000). Bear (1991) states, "When one sees that learning to read and write are integrated, developmental processes, then the battles over the methods become absurd" (p. 156). Thus, effective reading instruction must include a balanced focus supporting reading, writing, and spelling. With proper instruction, these three processes develop in unison (Bear et al., 2004).

Fluency

Fluency refers to the ability to read smoothly, accurately, quickly, and with expression. Even though a student might be able to accurately decode the words in a given text, if the student cannot read those words automatically and with expression, he or she cannot fully understand the author's message. Fluency instruction helps build automatic word recognition so that the text can be read effortlessly and the reader can focus on meaning rather than word recognition. Research suggests that faster, accurate readers tend to have better comprehension and, therefore, are more proficient readers (Rasinski, 2000). Fluency instruction requires practice with independent level text, which refers to text that a student can read and understand without teacher support. Fluency development is best accomplished through the repeated reading of selected texts (Samuels, 1979), which leads to improvement in decoding, reading rate, expression, and comprehension.

Word Study

Word study is the systematic, developmental study of words (Bear et al., 2004; Ganske, 2000; Henderson, 1990). Based on the stages of developmental spelling, word study addresses the needs of phonics, spelling, and vocabulary development for all students. Typically, word study for an intermediate reader includes studying features such as long and ambiguous vowel patterns, syllabication, Greek and Latin affixes (prefixes and suffixes), and morphemic units (root words).

A developmental spelling approach allows students to internalize word features rather than memorize rules. Thus, students can take the information beyond the isolated classroom lesson and transfer it meaningfully to text. Using the word study approach, students categorize words, which enables them to compare and contrast similar features in words. Further, they are able to generalize these word patterns when they are faced with reading or spelling an unknown word. This approach is particularly helpful for intermediate students when they are studying specialized content-specific vocabulary.

Comprehension

Simply stated, comprehension is the ability to understand text. Good readers have a purpose for reading, and they are active participants in the thinking processes that make understanding text possible. In other words, skillful readers are able to think critically as they navigate a text.

The goal of reading is to understand and learn from text, not to merely identify words. Students do not automatically know how to comprehend information—they have to be taught through systematic, guided instruction in meaningful text (Fielding & Pearson, 1994; Keene, 2002). This allows students to more fully understand the text and make higher level thinking connections. Effective comprehension strategies include generating questions, evaluating text structure, activating background knowledge or schema, making predictions, visualizing, summarizing, and inferencing.

For many educators, the terms *strategy* and *comprehension* seem to be synonymous. In fact, the two are very different. Comprehension is the ability to understand a text. A strategy is a tool used to help a reader understand the text. We use comprehension strategies to achieve a specific reading objective. For example, if a teacher wants to activate prior knowledge, he or she may choose K-W-L (Ogle, 1986) as the strategy to achieve this comprehension goal. Creating a K-W-L chart is used to activate prior knowledge by asking students what they Know about a given topic, to establish a purpose for reading by asking students what they Want to know about a given topic, and to summarize knowledge gained by asking students what they have Learned about a given topic. Comprehension strategies can be divided into those tools that are utilized before reading, during reading, and after reading. All are important to ensure a reader understands a given text.

Gaps in Other Small-Group Reading Models

Guided reading is a common term used to describe small-group reading instruction, especially in grades K–2. Guided reading is gaining popularity in the intermediate grades; unfortunately, many models do not offer the explicit, systematic instruction in word study and comprehension that we feel are essential components of small-group instruction. In the intermediate grades, we often find that guided reading is replaced with literature circles. This change is problematic because although literature circles may be useful in motivating students and generating student discussion, they do little to support or provide explicit teacher instruction. Daniels (1994) describes literature circles as student directed, rather than teacher directed. In our opinion, literature circles alone do not typically provide the basic teacher instruction necessary to guide and develop proficient readers. Students often are given the freedom to choose and independently read a book for the purpose of small-group discussion. While this may motivate some students to read more challenging texts, students are often left with texts that are either too easy or too difficult. However, students make optimal gains only when paired with instructional level text supported by the teacher. The fact is, students are motivated to read when they *can* read their text.

In reality, we realize that small-group reading instruction might not be able to take place every day. On those days when small groups do not meet, student-directed literature circles could serve as an alternative activity but only if the students are reading books that are at their independent level. Small-group differentiated reading instruction attempts to provide explicit, teacher-directed instruction in the components identified as critical to literacy development. Table 3 compares the characteristics of literature circles and the Small-Group Differentiated Reading Model.

TABLE 3
Comparing Literature Circles and the Small-Group Differentiated Reading Model

	Literature Circles	Small-Group Differentiated Reading
Role of the Teacher/Students	Students leading/teacher facilitating discussion	Teacher directing instruction
Grouping Configuration	Students grouped according to personal book choice	Students grouped according to reading level and word study level
Text Selections	Personal text selection	Leveled books including fiction and nonfiction selections
Focus of Instruction	Student-selected discussion	Transition from systematic decoding to systematic comprehension instruction
Word Study Component	Not included	Systematic and explicit through a developmental approach

The Balanced Literacy Model for Intermediate Readers

Although this book focuses on small-group differentiated reading instruction and its importance, additional whole-class instruction that makes up the remainder of a balanced literacy model cannot be overlooked. Small-group differentiated reading is a critical part of a balanced literacy program, which, when implemented effectively, gives every student the opportunity to become a more successful reader.

A balanced literacy program is more than the combination of phonics and whole-language methodologies. It also includes different venues for teachers and students practicing reading and writing skills. In this balanced literacy model, reading, writing, and motivation are critical components. The reading and writing components include teacher modeling and sharing reading and writing experiences with students. These components also provide guided instruction geared to meet students' needs as well as promote independent reading and writing opportunities. These components work together to provide instruction in terms of what is best taught in small groups, in whole groups, or practiced independently. Reading and writing assessments guide instruction in both of these areas. Another important component in the intermediate grades is motivation for readers. Together, these components provide a powerful model for effective literacy instruction. Figure 1 shows the balanced literacy components in the intermediate classroom.

FIGURE 1
Balanced Literacy Instruction in the Intermediate Classroom

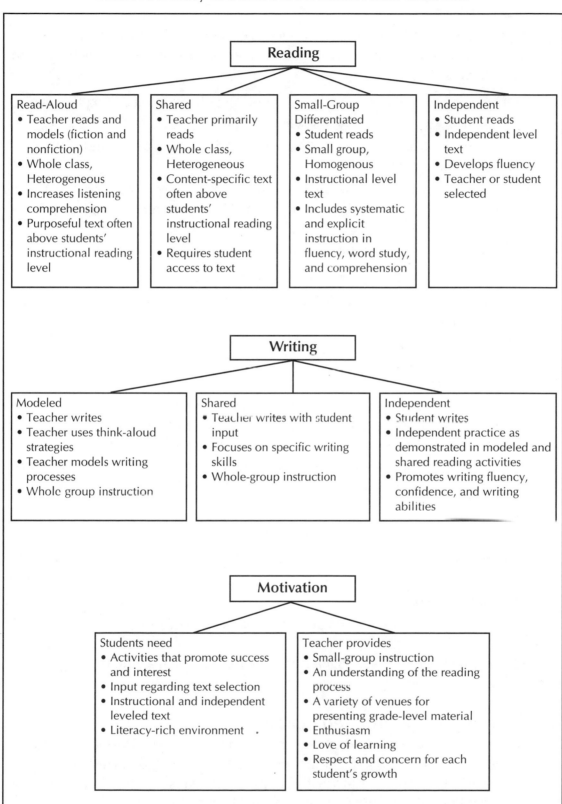

Reading

Read-Aloud
- Teacher reads and models (fiction and nonfiction)
- Whole class, Heterogeneous
- Increases listening comprehension
- Purposeful text often above students' instructional reading level

Shared
- Teacher primarily reads
- Whole class, Heterogeneous
- Content-specific text often above students' instructional reading level
- Requires student access to text

Small-Group Differentiated
- Student reads
- Small group, Homogenous
- Instructional level text
- Includes systematic and explicit instruction in fluency, word study, and comprehension

Independent
- Student reads
- Independent level text
- Develops fluency
- Teacher or student selected

Writing

Modeled
- Teacher writes
- Teacher uses think-aloud strategies
- Teacher models writing processes
- Whole group instruction

Shared
- Teacher writes with student input
- Focuses on specific writing skills
- Whole-group instruction

Independent
- Student writes
- Independent practice as demonstrated in modeled and shared reading activities
- Promotes writing fluency, confidence, and writing abilities

Motivation

Students need
- Activities that promote success and interest
- Input regarding text selection
- Instructional and independent leveled text
- Literacy-rich environment

Teacher provides
- Small-group instruction
- An understanding of the reading process
- A variety of venues for presenting grade-level material
- Enthusiasm
- Love of learning
- Respect and concern for each student's growth

Reading Components

Read-Aloud

The teacher reads aloud to provide a model and opportunity for students to engage in text that is most often above their instructional reading level. Read-alouds provide the following benefits:

- Offer whole groups of students an opportunity to experience text that is often above their instructional reading level
- Allow teachers to model proficient, fluent reading while also demonstrating effective think-aloud strategies
- Provide students with a model for comprehending a variety of texts and genres as well as for developing their listening vocabulary and listening comprehension

Read-alouds should be used in the following situations in intermediate classrooms:

- When working with heterogeneously grouped readers
- When sharing content-specific information related to grade-level standards in a whole group
- To motivate students through engaging genres in a whole-group setting

Shared Reading

Similar to a read-aloud, shared reading is an opportunity for the students to follow along with the text as the teacher reads aloud. The teacher is primarily responsible for reading the text, although students may read some short passages chorally. The most distinctive difference between shared reading and reading aloud is that during shared reading, students must be able to see the words and follow along as the teacher reads. Shared reading provides the following benefits:

- Allows students to share a common piece of text
- Allows students access to grade-level text that they cannot read independently
- Offers students exposure to content area information in accordance with prescribed standards
- Supports vocabulary and comprehension development

Shared reading should be used in intermediate classrooms in a whole group to share content-specific or grade-specific text.

Small-Group Differentiated Reading

This is the instructional time for homogenously grouped readers. During this time, the teacher carefully provides systematic instruction in the teaching of fluency, word study, and comprehension. Appropriate instructional level text is used during instruction. Small-group differentiated reading provides the following benefits:

- Maximizes optimal reading instructional time
- Affords the opportunity for all students to move forward in their reading abilities
- Allows the teacher to pinpoint students' difficulties and adjust instruction appropriately
- Supports reading comprehension

Small-group reading instruction should be used in an intermediate classroom during the literacy block time.

Independent Reading

This is an activity that promotes students reading at their independent levels. In other words, this is an opportunity for fluency practice. Independent reading provides the following benefits:

- Supports fluency development
- Provides students with many opportunities to practice reading on their own
- Motivates students because they are allowed to choose their own independent level reading material

Independent reading should be used in an intermediate classroom while the teacher is conducting small-group reading instruction.

Although more commonly associated with beginning readers, using leveled books with intermediate readers continues to be important to students' reading development. Leveled books for intermediate readers are books that vary in readability based on the structure of the text, content, vocabulary, theme, and grammatical structure. Using a leveled book approach allows teachers to differentiate reading instruction as students continue through upper elementary school and middle school. There are many leveling systems in place by a multitude of publishers and researchers. Throughout this book, we refer to two commonly used leveling systems: (1) Developmental Reading Assessment (DRA; Beaver, 1997) and (2) Fountas and Pinnell (1996). Each school should decide on a leveling system that is appropriate for the books available to them and that is expansive. Once this decision is made, all books should be leveled using one system.

Writing Components

Modeled Writing

This is an opportunity for students to observe the teacher as he or she models different types of writing (e.g., narrative, descriptive, expository, and persuasive) and different writing formats (e.g., poetry, letters, reports). Modeled writing provides the benefit of giving students the opportunity to observe a model for proficient writing. Modeled writing should be used in an intermediate classroom in a whole group when introducing a new type or format in writing.

Shared Writing

Similar to modeled writing, shared writing is an opportunity for the students to participate in the writing process directed by the teacher. The teacher is responsible for writing the text; however, students contribute as the text is composed. Shared writing provides the following benefits:

- Allows students to participate in a focused writing activity with teacher support
- Enables teachers to model a purpose-driven writing activity

Shared writing should be used in an intermediate classroom in a whole group when modeling a specific aspect of writing formats, types, and processes.

Independent Writing

This offers students time to practice focused writing skills that were previously taught through shared and modeled writing lessons. In addition, independent writing is an activity that promotes fluency and student choice in topic and format. Independent writing provides the following benefits:

- Offers students many opportunities to practice targeted writing skills
- Motivates students when they are allowed to write choosing their own topic, format, or both
- Helps develop confidence in student writing skills
- Allows the teacher to evaluate individual student writing and set realistic goals for improvement

Independent writing should be used in an intermediate classroom while the teacher is conducting small-group reading instruction.

Motivation

Motivation is essential if students are to become successful readers and writers. Further, it is perhaps the most difficult component to achieve in the intermediate grades. Often there is an assumption that all intermediate students can read on grade level. Students become frustrated when they are constantly forced to attempt to read material that is above their reading level. This, in turn, leads to teachers' frustration in having to teach content area standards when their students cannot read their textbooks. Unfortunately, some teachers lack the understanding of reading development and do not have the knowledge of differing venues to meet both the student needs and curriculum requirements.

In our experience, students become motivated when they are given text or activities they can successfully read and master. Additionally, teacher and student frustration is reduced when reading instruction is perceived as a doable task. Reading becomes a challenging yet achievable goal when students are presented with appropriate instructional level material.

It is difficult to imagine motivating students without a literacy-rich environment that includes a variety of leveled text types (novels, magazines, newspapers, content-specific books, poetry) for students to explore, read, and enjoy. It is impossible to motivate both teachers and students when they do not have the materials needed in order to succeed. Securing these materials must become a priority for the school and district-level administration. It is only with their support that teachers will feel empowered to teach and students will feel empowered to learn.

A Look Ahead

Chapter 2 takes an in-depth look at each of the lesson components: fluency, word study, and comprehension. Each component is defined and support research is cited as a rationale for including each component. Activities and routines that support each lesson component are thoroughly discussed, with an explanation for differentiation of these activities between stages.

Chapters 3–5 provide an in-depth look at each of the intermediate reader stages: evolving, maturing, and advanced. A lesson plan model for each stage is presented along with actual teacher–student dialogue centered around each lesson component. Appropriate text selections are also suggested for each reading stage.

Chapter 6 discusses pre-, post-, and ongoing assessments that support the Small-Group Differentiated Reading Model. These informal assessments include a review of informal reading inventories that can be used to assess word recognition and comprehension. Qualitative and quantitative fluency assessments will provide guidance in determining student progress. Spelling assessments are also included and will be used to guide word study instruction. These assessments provide valuable information for curriculum planning, flexible grouping, and individual assessment. Using the information gained through these assessments allows teachers to make informed decisions as they assign students to small groups based on individual literacy needs. These assessments are used routinely throughout the school year to track student progress in fluency, word study, and comprehension.

Finally, chapter 7 discusses the management of small-group differentiated instruction in the intermediate classroom. Classroom routines, organizational models, and sample schedules are included for successful small-group implementation. Quality independent reading and writing activities, as well as extension activities based on small-group instruction, are also provided.

Appendix A includes informal assessments for fluency, spelling, and comprehension as well as scoring guides for spelling assessments. Appendix B includes a word study glossary, word sort directions, word study scope and sequence information, word study lists, and dictated sentences—all of which support the evolving, maturing, and advanced reader stages. Appendix C includes reproducible support materials that will be useful for teachers as they implement the Small-Group Differentiated Reading Model in their classrooms.

Due to the extensive amount of materials in the appendixes, the word study cards that can be used by teachers and students during small-group reading instruction can be downloaded at the International Reading Association's website: www.reading.org.

Components of and Activities for the Small-Group Differentiated Reading Model

In developing the lesson plan models for small-group differentiated reading instruction, careful attention has been given to balancing the important research-based components, which include fluency, word study, and comprehension. These components have been identified as essential in the process of learning to read (Bear et al., 2004; Samuels, 1979; Sweet & Snow, 2002); therefore, the power of this reading model lies in the inclusion of each of these critical components into a manageable, cohesive plan.

This chapter provides the research base that validates the use of each component in the Small-Group Differentiated Reading Model. Further, we provide differentiated instruction and activities based on the developmental stage of the reader, which allows teachers to plan for and execute meaningful instruction for all of their students.

Fluency

Reading fluency is an important milestone in reading achievement. The foundation of fluency is in the ability to identify words quickly and accurately in context. Therefore, students' attention can be directed toward constructing meaning from the text rather than decoding text. The National Reading Panel Report (NICHD, 2000) describes fluency as the ability to read "with speed, accuracy, and proper expression" (p. 33-1). These three areas are further defined as follows:

1. *Speed*: Speed relates to the student's rate of reading and is usually determined in words per minute (WPM) or correct words per minute (CWPM).

2. *Accuracy*: Accuracy in reading is determined by the student's ability to recognize words correctly, without omissions, insertions, or substitutions.

3. *Expression*: Expression relates to the student's ability to read using correct phrasing, intonation, tone, and pitch so that the reading reflects the author's intended meaning. The word *prosody* is also used to describe these elements (Dowhower, 1991). Expression is subjective; therefore, it is more difficult to assess.

Research Base

For the past 20 years, fluency has been considered the "most neglected reading goal" (Allington, 1983, p. 556). The connection between decoding, fluency, and comprehension was often overlooked. However, thanks in part to the National Reading Panel Report and the subsequent publication *Put Reading First: The Research Building Blocks for Teaching Children to Read* (Armbruster, Lehr, & Osborn, 2001), fluency is currently one of the most widely discussed topics in reading. Research in fluency in the early 1970s (LaBerge & Samuels, 1974) focused on the relationship between automatic word recognition and reading achievement. This concept is now known as automaticity. Although automaticity is essential for proficient reading, there are students who have this skill yet lack the prosody that allows them to interpret the author's meaning of a given text. Obviously, without automaticity and prosody, a student cannot fully comprehend the text.

In 1992, the National Association for Educational Progress (NAEP) study (Pinnell et al., 1995) found that only 13% of all fourth graders could read with enough expression to interpret the author's meaning. The same study also found that the fourth-grade reading rates were linked with overall reading proficiency. Faster reading has long been associated with increased comprehension (Carver, 1990; Samuels, 1976). Clearly, we cannot ignore the implications of fluency as they relate to intermediate readers.

There are a limited number of activities that can be used to address both the word recognition and prosody issues as they relate to fluency. Arguably, the most effective and widely researched activity is repeated readings. Studies indicate repeated readings of a given text allow students the opportunity to practice reading fluency (Rasinski & Padak, 1998; Samuels, 1979; Samuels, Schermer, & Reinking, 1992). More recently, the National Reading Panel Report (2000) concluded that "repeated and monitored oral reading improves reading fluency and overall reading achievement" (as cited in Armbruster et al., 2001, p. 24). In order for this strategy to be effective, a student must reread independent or instructional level text. Although teacher read-alouds provide a model of a fluent reader, this activity will not necessarily increase a student's oral reading fluency.

Common sense tells us that if we want students to become more fluent readers, they need to have time each day to practice this skill. In our own observations, many fluency issues remain unresolved because students are not given ample time to read the appropriate levels of texts in a supported environment. We know from research and our own clinical observations that time spent in fluency practice results in dramatic increases in word recognition, speed, accuracy, and prosody (Samuels, 1979; Topping, 1987). It is similar to learning how to play a musical instrument. In order to play a Mozart piece, one has to sit down at the piano and start with "Old MacDonald." Both reading and musical skills must be practiced on a consistent basis.

More often than not, students in the intermediate grades are required to read silently and, therefore, do not practice their oral reading fluency. Although silent reading is faster and can increase comprehension, many intermediate students are still evolving readers. These readers struggle with automatic word recognition or they have passed the decoding phase but continue to read in a word-by-word fashion, disregarding punctuation and using little expression. For many evolving readers, fluency is an area in which they are lacking; therefore, the Small-Group Differentiated Reading Model includes this component. For the maturing and advanced readers, this component should still be practiced; however, it is done independently, outside of the small-group instructional time.

Activities That Support Fluency in the Small-Group Reading Model

Within a small-group setting, the following rereading activities are utilized with an evolving reader. Independent or instructional level text must be used for each of these activities.

Choral Reading—Using short selections, such as pieces of selected text or poems, the group reads and rereads the whole text or part of the text in unison. The teacher begins this activity by modeling the fluent reading of the text prior to the group's unison read. Choral reading cannot take the place of individual reading practice, but it can be used to provide support for students when necessary.

Partner Reading—Each student is paired with another student in the small group. The students take turns reading previously read text. One student reads while the other student gives assistance and feedback. Then, the process is reversed. The teacher monitors by listening in on the reading pairs, assisting when necessary. Partner reading also can be conducted outside the small group as students reread the text. This activity provides more practice for students as they reread text.

Whisper Reading—Students are asked to reread text that has been read by the group. Students read at their own pace in a whispering voice that allows the teacher to monitor and offer support when necessary.

Although there are other activities that promote fluency, such as Readers Theatre, we believe that these activities cannot take place within the designated small-group instructional time. There is just not enough time to complete these activities. However, teachers may decide to have the students complete these activities outside of the designated instructional time. Again, we want to stress the importance of using independent or instructional level text with any oral reading fluency activity.

Word Study

Word study is another term in education that is not only overused but also often misunderstood. As stated in chapter 1, we refer to word study as the systematic, developmental study of words (Bear et al., 2004; Ganske, 2000; Henderson, 1990). In considering the word study component for intermediate readers, we have included systematic phonics and vocabulary instruction. Although a "word study" or phonics component can be found in most published reading basal series, in our opinion, they lack a logical scope and sequence for instruction and fail to meet the developmental needs of all students. This scope and sequence is exactly what is most important when engaging students in the study of words at their developmental level. Invernizzi and Hayes (2004) attribute the lack of systematic classroom instruction in word study to be a combination of deficient teacher knowledge in this area as well as confusing information provided by both publishers and policymakers. We believe that by providing teachers with a logical scope and sequence for word study, they will be able to easily implement this component in their small-group instruction—which will ultimately allow for differentiated instruction that will better meet the needs of all their students.

Developing word study with intermediate readers is crucial to their continued success with reading and writing development. Typically in third or fourth grade, some students who have not previously struggled with reading and writing begin to have some difficulties. This could be due to a heavy focus on phonics and phonemic awareness and lack of focus on comprehension skills in the early grades. On the other hand, this may be caused by students relying on rote memorization for word identification. Thus, some students are unable to decode more difficult text. We believe that the difficulty some students experience is probably a combination of both factors. Beginning in third grade, there is a greater emphasis on expository text because content area instruction becomes integral to meeting state standards. Thus, as the text becomes more difficult, students need more explicit word analysis and vocabulary instruction in order to read to learn.

Research Base

Word study for beginning readers focuses on phonemic awareness and phonics (Armbruster et al., 2001). Phonemic awareness, typically taught in kindergarten and first grade, is defined as the student's ability to "hear, identify, and manipulate the individual sounds or phonemes in spoken words" (Armbruster et al., 2001, p. 4). Phonemic awareness development does not introduce letters as it relates to sounds; this is known as phonics. There is an important difference—phonemic awareness is an auditory skill, while phonics is the ability to make the connection between the sounds (phonemes) and the written letters (graphemes). Phonemic awareness is considered the precursor to phonics ability and is a powerful predictor of later reading success (Snow et al., 1998). Many students come to the intermediate classroom lacking these basic phonics skills. Therefore, phonics must be retaught in order for those students to progress in their reading development. The need for systematic phonics instruction delivered in small groups is well documented (Morris et al., 2000; NICHD, 2000; Santa & Hoien, 1999); therefore, we have included it in the Small-Group Differentiated Reading Model.

Much of what is currently known as word study grew out of developmental spelling research and theory (Invernizzi & Hayes, 2004). Research on developmental spelling is vast and has been done for decades (e.g., Bear, 1989; Bloodgood, 1991; Gill, 1992; Henderson & Templeton, 1986; Invernizzi, Abouzeid, & Gill, 1994; Nelson, 1989; Templeton & Morris, 1999). However, it has only been in the past 10 years that we have seen developmental spelling data driving classroom word study and reading instruction.

We believe this is due to a growing body of research that supports the connection between a student's ability in spelling and reading (Ellis & Cataldo, 1990). Invernizzi and Hayes (2004) found that spelling scores for almost 70,000 first graders correlated with both word recognition in isolation and oral reading accuracy. Word recognition in isolation is typically the best predictor of a student's reading level. If a student can read given words in isolation, it is likely that the student can read the words in context as well. Being able to accurately decode words allows the reader to focus on meaning rather than structure. The processes of spelling and reading are clearly related; in fact, they can be considered two sides of the same coin.

As readers mature, vocabulary development is widely considered to be the cornerstone of reading achievement (Blachowicz & Fisher, 2000; Hennings, 2000). As students transition from learning to read to reading to learn, vocabulary instruction becomes essential. This is increasingly important for maturing and advanced readers because they encounter much more content-specific vocabulary. Research shows that students who lack word knowledge or cannot access their word knowledge have difficulty understanding what they read (Chall, 1987; Daneman & Reingold, 1993). Thus, we have purposely embedded vocabulary development through both explicit word study and comprehension instruction.

Scope and Sequence

In order to fully understand the reading, writing, and spelling processes, teachers need a solid foundation in the structure of the English language (Moats, 2000). Henderson and Templeton (1986) refer to this structure as being divided into layers—alphabet, pattern, and meaning. When teachers become familiar with the aspects of each of these layers, they can use this information to assess students' developmental levels and then guide their classroom instruction in order to best meet the needs of the students.

Alphabet Layer

The alphabetic layer is taught in the beginning reader stages and consists of the basic letter–sound relationships in the left-to-right manner. For example, the word *big* is broken down into three sounds: /b/, /i/, and /g/. Each sound is directly represented by a letter. However, in the word *ship*, there are still three sounds even though there are four letters. *Sh* is a digraph that makes one sound. There are no silent or unsounded letters in this layer. Each sound is represented by one letter or sometimes by a pair of letters. (For more information on a word study scope and sequence for the beginning reader, see *Small-Group Reading Instruction: A Differentiated Teaching Model for Beginning and Struggling Readers* [Tyner, 2004].)

Pattern Layer

The pattern layer typically is taught in the beginning reader stages and continues into the evolving reader stage. The pattern layer includes studying words that have silent and unsounded letters and words with more than one syllable (i.e., syllabication). Initially, this layer includes a focus on vowel patterns in single-syllable words. In the word *time*, for example, we hear three sounds—/t/, /i/, and /m/—however, there are four letters and the *e* does not act with another letter. The focus in this layer progresses to examining more complex vowel patterns, such as the *air* in *chair*, and words having more than one syllable.

Meaning Layer

The meaning layer generally covers the end of the evolving reader stage and continues throughout the advanced reader stage. This layer primarily focuses on the morphology of words, that is, a group of letters directly associated with a particular meaning. For example, *spect* means "to look"; thus, we know that *inspector*, *spectator*, and *spectacle* are related in meaning and have something to do with "looking." This layer explores the Latin and Greek base words and root words. A base word can stand alone as a word (e.g., *train*). A root word cannot stand alone as a word, and its origin is in Latin or Greek (e.g., *spect*).

Curriculum Standards

In order to meet state standards, word study for students in grades 3–8 is a critical component of a language arts curriculum. For example, a benchmark for third graders in Kansas includes using "skills in alphabetics to construct meaning from text" (Kansas Department of Education, Standard 1, Benchmark 1). Likewise, fifth-grade students are required to use "a variety of word-recognition strategies (e.g., orthographic patterns, reading and writing text) to read fluently" and "determine meaning of words through knowledge of word structure (e.g., compound nouns, contractions, root words, prefixes, suffixes)" (Kansas Department of Education, Standard 1, Benchmarks 2 and 3). Seventh-grade students are supposed to be able to use a "variety of word-recognition strategies (e.g., orthographic patterns, reading and writing text) to read fluently" and "determine[s] meaning of words through structural analysis, using knowledge of Greek, Latin, and Anglo-Saxon roots, *prefixes*, and *suffixes* to understand complex words, including words in science, mathematics, and social studies" (Kansas Department of Education, Standard 1, Benchmarks 2 and 3). Without a doubt, the importance of a word study component in the small-group reading model cannot be overlooked as it relates to intermediate readers.

The scope and sequence we have created for word study (see Appendix B) is based both on the aforementioned layers and curriculum standards that dictate what students will encounter in state testing. Both of these factors must be considered in structuring an effective word study sequence. Each word study feature (i.e., a specific word pattern) is studied for at least one week. For example, in the evolving reader stage, students study long-vowel patterns, which is a feature. We suggest one week is an appropriate amount of time to ensure students understand the feature.

Activities That Support Word Study in the Small-Group Reading Model

In the small-group setting, the following activities are utilized during the word study component of the lesson. However, for purposes of differentiated instruction, we have noted which activities are appropriate for each stage of reader. Some of the activities in this section have corresponding reproducibles in Appendix C; this information is noted after each activity.

As previously noted, features typically are studied for one week. During this time, students work with the same group of words. Every week, each student is given a copy of the words (again, the word study cards are available at www.reading.org). Students cut out the word study cards prior to small-group instruction. These word study cards can be used for small-group and independent word study activities. (Teachers can provide students with envelopes or plastic bags to store their cards.)

Many activities here and throughout the book can be completed in word study notebooks. Word study notebooks can be an important resource for intermediate students. Students use them to keep track of the word features they have studied. In addition, the word study notebook can serve as a resource to students as they work independently. For example, if students are editing written work and they have misspelled words with features they already studied, the teacher can direct them to the appropriate section in their word study notebooks so they can correct the words.

Word Sorting and Spelling Sorting—Sorting is fundamental to word study. Through this activity, students compare and contrast word features (e.g., pattern, meaning). Students categorize words based on the features being studied. Students can sort words into an "oddball" category for those words that do not follow a specific generalization. After students have sorted their words (see Figure 2), the teacher should lead a discussion about the categories the students used and what they discovered about the words through the activity. In addition, the teacher should lead a discussion about the meaning of the words.

There are two different types of word sorts: (1) closed and (2) open. In a closed sort, the teacher gives the students explicit instructions regarding the word study features and can provide header cards showing these features. (Teachers can create the

FIGURE 2
Completed Word Sort

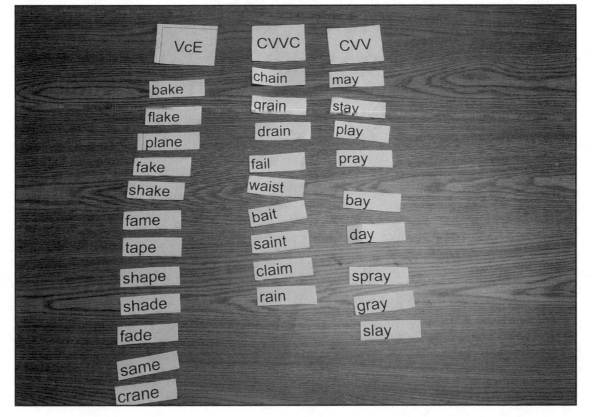

header cards by using the header words on the word study lists in Appendix B and the blank word study card form available at www.reading.org. The header card information we have provided includes words and patterns, and teachers can determine how they would like to present specific sorts. For example, in the evolving reader stage, cycle 1, week 9, teachers can choose to use the header words [e.g., *green, deal, he*] or header patterns [e.g., *ee, ea, e*].) Students then sort the word study cards based on these features. An open sort gives students the opportunity to sort the word study cards without explicit teacher directions regarding the word features; this process allows students to use critical thinking skills to discover patterns in words.

A second type of sorting activity is a spelling sort. This type of sort is critical in solidifying students' abilities to recognize and reproduce the patterns being studied. In this activity, the teacher calls out words for students to sort visually and then spell. This activity can be completed with evolving, maturing, and advanced readers when more than one feature is being studied. (See Spelling Sort sheet in Appendix C.)

Dictated Sentences or Student-Generated Sentences—Dictated sentences are used to ensure that students can make the transition from sorting the word patterns to spelling the word patterns in context, which also allows the students to solidify word meanings. This activity is appropriate for evolving and maturing readers. Advanced readers are required to create their own sentences to demonstrate their understanding of the words being studied. (See Appendix B for dictated sentences for evolving and maturing readers.)

Word Hunts—The word hunt activity is an optional activity that can be completed independently outside of the small-group time. Students are asked to find words in independent or instructional level text that have the same features they are currently focusing on in their small-group time. They can write these words in their word study notebooks. This activity allows students to make the connection between studying words in isolation and recognizing generalizations in context; it is appropriate for evolving, maturing, and advanced readers.

Root Tree—This activity is appropriate for maturing and advanced readers who are studying Latin or Greek root words. Students write the words with the same roots on the leaves of the tree and then discuss how all the words are related in meaning. (See Root Tree in Appendix C.)

Name That Word—This activity is appropriate for maturing or advanced readers who are studying Latin or Greek root words. The teacher reads the definition of a given word and the students write the word in their word study notebooks. This activity allows the teacher to check students' abilities to spell and comprehend given words.

Again, word study in the intermediate grades is essential because students at this level need to understand more difficult text.

Comprehension

Improving comprehension is the major goal of intermediate school teachers. The students' abilities to comprehend text affects every aspect of their educational endeavors.

While beginning readers are "cracking the alphabetic code" and developing automaticity, intermediate readers continue to develop important word study knowledge because the focus at this stage shifts to comprehending the text's message. Although comprehension seems to develop as a process similar to osmosis (i.e., it would naturally occur after students mastered basic decoding skills) for some students, this is not true for all students. As previously noted, comprehension must be taught through systematic instruction across content areas.

Comprehension instruction should be a part of beginning reading instruction, and it should begin in preschool. Just as phonemic awareness is a precursor to phonics, listening comprehension is a precursor to reading comprehension. For example, those strategies associated with story structure, sequence, or summarizing that a kindergarten teacher directs after a read-aloud of "The Three Little Pigs" are essentially the same strategies that an intermediate student will engage in as he reads the text on his own. Comprehension for intermediate readers is focused on the student's reading and using and refining these strategies.

Although there is an abundance of research on developing reading comprehension, our focus will be on comprehension instruction as it relates to the Small-Group Differentiated Reading Model. This instruction includes the following strategies:

- Previewing the text, which includes predicting, and accessing prior knowledge (making connections)
- Identifying the text structure and previewing specialized vocabulary
- Generating questions by the teacher and the students (i.e., literal, inferential, and application questions)
- Summarizing, which includes identifying the main idea and supporting details and the sequence of events, the ability to compare and contrast and examine cause-and-effect relationships, and identifying major story elements

We did not include specific metacognitive strategies because we believe teachers should teach these monitoring techniques as a part of every lesson. When comprehension breaks down, the teacher should continually talk about and demonstrate how to repair meaning. This may include rereading passages, discussing other's perceptions of the text, recognizing how to utilize word structure and syntax knowledge, or simply reminding students to make a conscious effort to think about the text they are reading and connect it to their own knowledge base. Our intent is to give teachers an explicit lesson plan model that structures the teaching of comprehension strategies that not only are supported by research but that we also have observed to be most effective and closely matched to the reader's developmental needs.

As readers progress through the developmental stages of reading, comprehension becomes more important; therefore, we adjusted the lesson plan to support more advanced comprehension skills. That is, we have scaffolded the strategies to best meet the needs of readers at any given stage because the comprehension skills build upon one another from simple to complex. In addition, teacher support should decrease as students become more competent in their abilities to fully understand the text.

Research Base

The amount of research that supports systematic comprehension instruction is vast. Based on the findings of the National Reading Panel Report (NICHD, 2000), Armbruster and colleagues (2001) identified strategies including story structure, questioning, and summarizing as "appear[ing] to have a firm scientific basis for improving text comprehension" (p. 49). Furthermore, strategies related to previewing and predicting text also have shown to be effective for improving comprehension (Guthrie, 2005). In fact, research also verifies that these strategies can and should be systematically taught (Dowhower, 1999; Menke & Pressley, 1994; Pearson, 1993; Pressley & Afflerbach, 1995). Furthermore, there is an evidence base that supports students using these strategies in independent reading situations when they have been explicitly taught (Griffin, Malone, & Kameenui, 1995; Pressley, Symmons, Snyder, & Cariglia-Bull, 1989).

Predicting and Previewing

Previewing the text includes making predictions about the text based on title and illustrations (for narrative text), activating background knowledge (for expository text), making connections related to background knowledge, and discussing possible unknown vocabulary. All of these techniques are used to support comprehension prior to the reading of the text. Research supports the notion of actively engaging students before reading a text (Guthrie, 2005; Stevens, 1982; Tierney & Pearson, 1985). Previewing is similar to reading the jacket of a book before reading the entire book. The quick blurb whets a reader's appetite for the book and gives the reader a glimpse of what is to come.

Identifying Text Structure

Identifying text structure enables students to identify critical elements, which allows them to differentiate between narrative and expository text. This, in turn, aids in their understanding of the purpose and content of the text. In narrative text, this structure typically includes characters, setting, plot, events, and conflict and resolution. In expository text, there are many different structures. The most common expository text structures include descriptive, sequence, cause and effect, comparison and contrast, and problem and solution. Special features (e.g., graphs, diagrams) are also included in expository text structure. Following are descriptions of each of the most common expository text structures.

Descriptive Text Structure

- Provides information about a topic, concept, event, object, person, idea, and so forth
- Describes facts, characteristics, traits, and features, usually qualifying the listing by criteria, such as size or importance
- Connects ideas through description by listing the important characteristics or attributes of the topic

Sequence Text Structure

- Puts facts, events, or concepts in order
- Traces the development of the topic or gives the steps in the process

- Makes references to time that are explicit or implicit, but a sequence is evident in the pattern

Cause-and-Effect Text Structure

- Shows how facts, events, or concepts (i.e., effects) happen or come into being because of other facts, events, or concepts (i.e., causes)

Comparison-and-Contrast Text Structure

- Points out similarities or differences among facts, people, events, concepts, and so forth

Problem-and-Solution Text Structure

- Shows the development of a problem and one or more solutions to the problem

Currently, identifying text structure often is found on state-mandated assessments for intermediate readers (Armbruster, Anderson, & Ostertag, 1989; Cudd & Roberts, 1987; Fowler, 1982). Because the purpose of narrative and expository text is different, students need to be able to adapt their knowledge of comprehension strategies to meet the demands of the text. When students are able to identify how a text is organized, they are better equipped to extract its meaning.

Questioning

There are two types of questioning that occur in a classroom: (1) questioning that the teacher generates and (2) questioning that the students generate. Both are important and are steeped in supportive research (Cohen, 1983; Wixon, 1983). Teacher questioning in oral or written form is probably the oldest and most commonly used comprehension strategy. Questioning helps clarify the teacher's knowledge of the students' understanding. Do students really understand? Did they catch the important parts? Can they make inferences from the text?

By asking questions during small-group time, the teacher is able to ask more questions and there is more time for individual student responses. This question–answer scenario allows teachers to assess their students' comprehension levels. The ultimate goal of questioning is to develop advanced readers who intuitively question their own reading; thus, demonstrating self-questioning is a strategy that must be modeled and taught (Pearson & Fielding, 1991; Wong, 1985). Many students view questioning as a form of interrogation, a way for a teacher to find out what they know and what they don't know. On the contrary, when used appropriately, questioning is meant to extend students' understanding of the text's message.

Another aspect of questioning that has received much attention as it relates to reading comprehension is the type of questions that both a student and a teacher ask (Bloom, 1956; Wixon, 1983). Simply asking recall questions—which is typical in many classrooms—leaves many aspects of comprehension unaddressed. Rather, questions should be varied to ensure that all levels of thinking are addressed.

Effective questioning requires careful planning and appropriate feedback to student responses. It is just as important to ask appropriate questions as it is to give appropriate feedback to student responses. Key points to remember to increase comprehension include

- Providing immediate feedback to all question responses whether correct, incorrect, or partially correct
- Offering information with regard to why an answer was correct
- Probing to solicit a correct response before asking another student to answer the question

For the purpose of the lesson plan model, questions are categorized as literal, inferential, and application.

- Literal questions require basic recall of facts from the text—that is, the answer is directly stated in the text. Although these questions require little reflection by the reader, basic recall is an important aspect of the foundation for comprehension.
- Inferential questions require students to synthesize information found in more than one place in the text or to surmise information to form an answer. Although the answers to these types of questions may be provided in the reading, the students must look in several places to find them. However, students also may have to rely on their own background knowledge to "read between the lines."
- Application questions require students to draw on their own prior knowledge and experiences to interact with the text. This type of question requires students to formulate and justify an opinion. In other words, students must go beyond the printed word and think deeply about the text in order to respond appropriately.

Summarizing

We believe summarizing is the most necessary comprehension component because it requires students to provide a general analysis and synthesis of key text components, whether using a narrative or expository text selection (Pearson & Dole, 1987; Pressley, 1990). Summarizing in narrative text involves synthesizing major story elements. Summarizing as it relates to expository text engages the reader in activities that allow him or her to extrapolate the main ideas and supporting details, explore relationships, sequence important information, and evaluate causal relationships. With each type of text, students must select certain features and omit others, in effect differentiating essential from nonessential details (Rinehart, Stahl, & Erikson, 1986). Again, this is a skill that must be modeled and taught explicitly.

Teacher Tools That Support Comprehension in the Small-Group Reading Model

As you may have noticed, we have revised the wording of this section from *activities* to *teacher tools* because we firmly believe that comprehension involves much more than handing out blackline masters. We cannot stress enough the importance of meaningful teacher-led discussions and questioning that needs to happen during small-group instruction. In most cases, small-group time is the only time during the school day that students have the opportunity to engage in meaningful, instructional conversations related to their reading. Thus, we feel it is important to provide a few activities to supplement these conversations as needed. Teachers need to be mindful of the time involved in using these supplemental activities and balance this with the aforementioned discussions. For example, a teacher may feel that students need some way to keep track of events that have occurred while reading a chapter book. Rather than giving each student a graphic organizer (web) to fill out during small-group time, the teacher may act as the scribe, while the students each contribute orally to completing the visual aid. There is no substitute for the insight that both students and teachers bring to the reading table. The following are intended to be collaboratively completed activities with the teacher acting as a scribe. Some of the activities in this section have corresponding reproducibles in Appendix C; this information is noted after each activity.

Before Reading

Predicting and Previewing

Directed Reading–Thinking Activity (DR–TA)—This activity (adapted from Vacca et al., 2003) includes having students make predictions about what they think will be the first thing that happens in the story before reading it. The teacher writes down a prediction from one student. After reading a few pages, the teacher stops and asks the students to revisit the prediction. The teacher then asks the remaining students what their predictions were and what actually happened. The teacher writes down a prediction from another student. The teacher continues this process of predicting and revisiting until the entire book is read. (See Directed Reading–Thinking Activity Sheet in Appendix C.)

Text Walk—Due to the nature of previewing, this activity is done orally. After distributing the books, the teacher leads the students in examining the text by pointing out features such as pictures, photographs, maps, charts, headings, and subheadings. In addition, to help students navigate expository text, the teacher should be sure to point out the table of contents and appendixes.

Vocabulary

Very Important Predictions (VIP)—For this activity, the teacher preselects important words from the story that relate to the characters, setting, problem, action, or solution. Each student contributes to the VIP Map (see VIP Map in Appendix C and Figure 3) by predicting which words will correspond to which story elements before reading the story. Then, students check their predictions while reading the story or after reading the story. Teachers also can ask students to justify their responses.

Select, Teach, Activate, Review, and Revisit (STARR)—Adapted from Blachowicz (1987), this activity is actually a prompt for teachers to use as they identify important words in a given text for students to study. These words should be written on notecards and revisited routinely in small-group instruction. In addition to previewing vocabulary words,

FIGURE 3
Completed VIP Map

these words can be used after the reading to summarize the selection. (See STARR Vocabulary Development in Appendix C.)

Activating Background Knowledge

ABC Brainstorm—This activity (adapted from www.readingquest.org) can be used either to activate prior knowledge or summarize what has been learned. This strategy also helps students brainstorm and summarize the key ideas associated with a given concept by thinking of words or phrases associated with that concept; each concept begins with a letter of the alphabet. (See ABC Brainstorm in Appendix C and Figure 4.)

K-W-L (Ogle, 1986)—As mentioned in chapter 1, this activity is useful for assessing student knowledge as it relates to the subject matter. When beginning to discuss a new concept, the teacher leads the discussion of what the students Know about the topic. The teacher then asks the students what they Want to learn about the topic. After the topic has been learned, the teacher then asks the students what they Learned about the topic. Identifying what students learned is often overlooked; however, it is critical to the intended learning process. (See K-W-L form in Appendix C.)

FIGURE 4
Completed ABC Brainstorm

Making Connections—With this oral activity, students are encouraged to make personal connections to the text based on their experiences. These connections can be to their own lives, to other texts, or to the outside world.

During Reading

Questioning

Question Maker—This activity encourages critical thinking skills. Students work with a partner and take turns questioning each other at strategic points in the text previously determined by the teacher. Students are encouraged to create challenging questions that might stump their partners. (See Question Maker in Appendix C.)

Questioning Guides—These guides can be a catalyst for in-depth questioning by the teacher. Questions are geared specifically to increase comprehension in both narrative and expository text. (See Questioning Guides in Appendix C.)

5 Ws?????—This is another type of questioning activity that promotes identifying the main idea from a text; it can be done before, during, or after reading a text. Each student draws a card on which is written one of five question words (who, what, where, when, and why). Students are asked to use their words as a stem for a question they generate as they read the next section of the text. Then, students pose their questions to the group to generate discussion about the reading.

Summarizing

Stop and Go!—This activity can be used either during reading or after reading. If used during the reading, the teacher stops at strategic points to ask students (who should be called on randomly) to summarize what has happened in the text thus far. As the student summarizes the text, the teacher stops the student abruptly and asks another student to take over the summarizing. This process continues until all the events or details have been discussed.

After Reading

Text Structure

Story Map—This graphic organizer (adapted from Beck, McKeown, McCaslin, & Burket, 1979) is a visual aid that represents the elements of narrative text. (See Story Map in Appendix C.)

Cause and Effect—This graphic organizer helps students collaborate and discuss examples of cause and effect in narrative and expository text. (See Cause and Effect form in Appendix C.)

Compare and Contrast—This graphic organizer, or Venn diagram, is used by students to compare and contrast characteristics of given topics. (See Venn Diagram in Appendix C.)

Sequencing—This graphic organizer helps students recall important events and place the events in the order in which they occurred in the story. (See Sequencing form in Appendix C.)

Summarizing

Sum It Up—This strategy (adapted from www.readingquest.org) helps students write more concise summaries, so they focus on the main idea of a text. As a group, students have to imagine they are placing a classified ad or sending a telegram, and every word costs them a certain amount of money. (This activity is also great for teaching math.) The teacher determines how much each word will cost and how much students can spend. For example, a teacher might determine that students have $5.00 to spend and that each word costs $.10. Then, students have to write a summary using 50 words or less. This may seem like a large number of words, but teachers can adjust the number and cost based on the text students are summarizing. Teachers also can have students write multiple summaries from their first summary in which case they are given successively less money to spend. For example, after students write their 50-word summaries, the teacher can reduce their spending money to $3.00, so students have to cut out 20 words. (See Sum It Up form in Appendix C.)

What's the Big Idea?—This activity can be used during or after reading as students summarize key points from the text. Students use this strategy to identify the main ideas and supporting ideas in expository text. (See What's the Big Idea? form in Appendix C.)

Bio-Poem—This activity can be used after reading a narrative text or a biography. Students contribute pertinent attributes about a character in the form of poetry. The poem follows an established, free verse pattern. (See Bio-Poem form in Appendix C and Figure 5.)

FIGURE 5
Completed Bio-Poem

Line 1:	First Name:	Jess
Line 2:	Four traits that describe # 1:	Imaginative, caring, patient, talented.
Line 3:	Related to:	May Belle
Line 4:	Cares about:	Leslie
Line 5:	Who feels:	Sad that Leslie is dead.
Line 6:	Who needs:	Courage
Line 7:	Who gives:	Understanding
Line 8:	Who fears:	Being without Leslie
Line 9:	Who would like to see:	the bridge to Terabithia rebuilt.
Line 10:	Resident of:	Terabithia
Line 11:	Last name:	Aarons

Comprehension instruction should not be limited to reproducibles or blackline masters. Rather, teachers need to engage students in a balance of authentic, meaningful activities that include discussion, visual aids, and writing opportunities. Small-group instructional time is an ideal venue to allow students to understand how they, as individuals, make meaning from text.

Conclusion

Because there is conflicting information in the theoretical base of reading instruction, at times it can be difficult to understand the research. However, even more challenging is the ability to apply the research to practical classroom instruction. Until we apply current research to the classroom level, it remains an untapped resource. In extracting what we feel are the most important research-based components and strategies, we hope to make this transition for teachers more effective and efficient. In our experience, teachers are overwhelmed with training and information about "research-based" strategies without a model for practical classroom application. Thus, in this chapter we have attempted to provide this important research base along with ideas for classroom use that will be beneficial for teachers and students.

CHAPTER 3

The Evolving Reader Stage

Evolving readers are best described as readers who have made the transition or are in the process of making the transition from learning to read to reading to learn. Instruction for this type of reader must be geared toward continuing to develop fluency that will transform the reader from a basic decoder to a comprehender of text. At this time, evolving readers also are learning about patterns in words, which is the basis for their journey into the spelling–meaning connection. Students are typically in the evolving reader stage for about two years—mostly during grades 3 and 4. This is a critical stage for students because, in effect, it sets the stage for their reading abilities as adults.

Characteristics of Evolving Readers in Reading, Writing, and Spelling

Reading

Evolving readers need time to build fluency. That is, they need time to develop automatic word recognition. Evolving readers can decode fairly accurately in appropriate text; however, they are refining their automaticity or ability to decode words automatically. These readers use a variety of word-recognition strategies when decoding unknown words. Further, they use their knowledge of syntax such as question marks, exclamation points, commas, apostrophes, and hyphens to read fluently. As students' automaticity increases, so does their oral reading fluency. This occurs as a result of being able to focus on the meaning of words rather than on the decoding of words. Thus, when students can focus on the author's meaning, expression naturally follows.

As the focus of instruction shifts to comprehension, evolving readers determine the meaning of unknown words or phrases using context clues (e.g., definitions, restatements, examples, descriptions, illustrations). They also are learning to identify and use synonyms, antonyms, homographs, and homophones to determine the meaning of words.

Evolving readers also are exploring new genres in the classroom and in their personal reading. As mentioned previously, in the typical third- or fourth-grade setting there is a greater focus on content area curriculum. Thus, evolving readers are becoming increasingly familiar with expository text (including persuasive and technical text) in order to meet the demands of the curriculum. They are learning how to differentiate between expository and narrative text structure, and they are beginning to develop comprehension strategies for each text type.

Texts for Evolving Readers

The evolving reader begins this stage by reading popular book series, such as Henry and Mudge (Rylant), Frog and Toad (Lobel), Frances (Hoban), and Little Bear (Minarik). These types of books offer predictable story lines, familiar characters, and other aspects typical of series—all of which offer the support the evolving reader needs in order to be successful. Evolving readers can and should read a variety of other leveled texts offered by publishers such as Rigby, Sundance, Newbridge, and Modern Curriculum Press. These readers need to balance their reading of narrative text by including expository text, which is critical to preparing evolving readers for future curriculum demands. Examples of expository text that supports an evolving reader include Beginning Biographies (Modern Curriculum Press), Rigby Focus (Rigby), and Steck-Vaughn Shutterbug books. In addition, the publications *National Geographic Explorers* and *Time for Kids* are great resources for providing experiences with expository text. As students progress through this stage, the text should become more difficult.

At this stage, evolving readers are still reliant on carefully leveled texts. It is important to remember, though, that a variety of genres should be chosen from the leveled texts. Evolving readers are now responsible for the reading of varied text types across the content areas. In addition, other text types such as poetry, newspaper articles, and other nonfiction selections should be considered.

For teachers using leveled texts as a resource to support small-group differentiated reading instruction, the following book levels are appropriate for evolving readers:

Leveling System	Book Levels
Fountas and Pinnell	K–R
DRA	20–40

Writing

At the same time that evolving readers are developing their reading abilities, they also are developing their writing abilities. As they begin to read different genres, they also begin to experiment with writing for different purposes, and thus, the writing process. Evolving readers need teacher support to study the various components of the writing process in depth, and then they need time to practice these components independently. Evolving readers are able to write a cohesive paragraph with details and create their own stories, which begin to include character development. In this stage, we often find that students' writing mimics that of their favorite authors. The more proficient they become as readers, the more they develop as writers.

Writer's workshop, a process-centered approach to writing, is commonly included in the evolving reader's classroom. This approach allows students to work at their own levels and write about topics that interest them. The philosophy guiding this approach is to allow students time and choice: time to practice and choice of format. However, this approach should not be students' only writing instruction; it should be balanced with explicit instruction in the areas of the writing process, types of writing, and grammar.

Spelling

As mentioned in chapter 2, spelling involves multiple layers. Evolving readers are typically in the pattern layer of spelling and are moving into the meaning layer of spelling development. These readers have their phonology in place; they can represent every sound they hear in words. For example, they recognize that the word *rain* is not spelled *ran*. They realize that the word needs another vowel in order to make the long *a* sound. Evolving readers should be able to spell almost all short-vowel, one-syllable words correctly.

As students study the pattern layer of the English language, they are building a foundation for the study of syllable patterns and morphology. This early knowledge of vowel patterns is essential as they progress through the maturing and advanced stages of reading and study morphemic units. We often find that many older students lack the knowledge of vowel patterns necessary to develop automaticity. Students in the evolving reader stage are experimenting with and learning about these spelling features. The features studied during the evolving reader stage are outlined in Table 4.

A weekly word study scope and sequence has been provided in Appendix B. Please note that the scope and sequence is provided only as a guideline. It is crucial for teachers to use assessments to guide their instruction. If students have not mastered a specific list, they should not move on to study new features. Rather, teachers should reteach and review the features with which students are having difficulty.

Differentiating the Lesson Plans

Due to the differing nature of narrative and expository text, we developed different lesson plans for each type of text, and we provide dialogue to guide readers through each lesson plan. We also provide completed lesson plans at the end of each section. The narrative and expository lesson plans follow two different groups of students. The students in the narrative lesson are in the beginning of the evolving reader stage, and the students in the expository lesson are in the middle of the evolving reader stage.

Instructional Components of the Evolving Reader Lesson Plan: Narrative Text

The evolving reader lesson plan has three distinct components: (1) fluency, (2) word study, and (3) comprehension (see Figure 6). The fluency component calls for students to reread the text or part of the text. The word study component identifies the word study features and corresponding activities. Word study begins either with a word sort or a spelling sort and concludes with a dictated sentence incorporating words with the features being studied. The comprehension component focuses on the strategies that will be used before, during, and after reading. Before-reading strategies include predicting, making connections, and previewing story vocabulary. During-reading strategies focus on teacher- and student-generated questions. The after-reading focus includes summarizing

TABLE 4
Word Study Features for the Evolving Reader

Common Long-Vowel Patterns	• Long *a*—*a_e* (gave), *ai* (train), *ay* (say) • Long *e*—*ee* (green), *ea* (leaf), *e* (be) • Long *i*—*i_e* (hive), *igh* (might), *y* (by), *iCC* (mind, child) • Long *o*—*o_e* (hope), *oa* (boat), *ow* (know), *oCC* (cold, ghost) • Long *u*—*u_e* (cute), *oo* (root), *ew* (flew)
Less Common Long-Vowel Patterns	• Long *a*—*ei* (weigh), *ey* (hey) • Long *e*—*ie* (chief) • Long *o*—*oe* (doe), *o* (so) • Long *u*—*ue* (blue), *ui* (fruit)
R-Controlled Vowel Patterns	• *A* patterns—*ar* (car), *are* (dare), *air* (hair) • *E* patterns—*er* (term), *ear* (earth, fear), *eer* (cheer) • *I* patterns—*ir* (sir), *ire* (hire) • *O* patterns—*or* (born), *ore* (pore), *oar* (roar) • *U* patterns—*ur* (burn), *ure* (cure, lure)
Ambiguous Vowel Patterns	• *oo*—moon, book • *oy*/*oi*—joy, coin • *ow*/*ou*—brown, cloud • *aw*/*au*/*al*—claw, fault, bald • *wa*—swan, war
Complex Consonants—Beginning and Ending	• Hard and soft *c* and *g*—car/cent, game/germ • Triple-letter blends—**str**ipe, **spl**ash, **scr**ape, **squ**irt, **spr**ing, **shr**ink, **thr**ee • Final *k* sound—black, bake, week • Final *ch*/*tch* and *ge*/*dge*—coach/catch, page/large/edge • Silent consonants—*kn*/*wr*—know/wrench
Contractions	• are (they're) • had/would (he'd) • have (I've) • is/has (here's) • not (can't) • will (I'll) • am (I'm) • us (let's)
Compound Words	• Base words combined to form one new word (aircraft, snowball)
Homophones	• Words that sound the same but are spelled differently (mail, male)
Easy Suffixes—Inflected Endings (examples)	• Sounds of *ed*—(/ed/ folded, /t/ trapped, /d/ boiled) • *ing*—folding, trapping, boiling • Plurals and possessives—*s*, *es*, *'s*, and *s'* (kids, wishes, kid's, kids')
Easy Prefixes	• *un*—not (untie) • *re*—again (rebuild) • *pre*—before (precook) • *mis*—not (misuse) • *dis*—not (disappear) • *in*—not (incorrect)

Components/Activities	Comments
FLUENCY (REREADING) Text _____ pp. _____ ☐ Choral ☐ Partner ☐ Whisper	
WORD STUDY Patterns_____ Cycle _____ Week _____ ☐ Word Sort or ☐ Spelling Sort and ☐ Dictated Sentence_____ Outside of Group Activity (optional) ☐ Word Hunt ☐ Other vocabulary activity Specify _____	
COMPREHENSION Text _____ pp. _____ Before Reading ☐ Predicting ☐ Making Connections ☐ Previewing Vocabulary List _____ _____	
During Reading Teacher-Generated Questions (during or after) ☐ Literal _____ _____ ☐ Inferential _____ _____ ☐ Application _____ _____ ☐ Student-Generated Questions (during or after)	
After Reading Summarizing Text Structure ☐ Characters ☐ Setting ☐ Events (sequencing) ☐ Conflicts/Resolution (cause/effect) Activity for Above ☐ Oral discussion ☐ Graphic organizer Specify _____ ☐ Independent Written Response (optional) Specify _____ _____	

specific story elements. The final part of the lesson plan includes an optional writing activity to support comprehension development. It allows teachers to specify an independent written response that supports the comprehension focus.

Fluency (Rereading)

Generally, evolving readers lack the fluency necessary to comprehend the text and, therefore, need to practice this important skill. Thus, rereading the text or part of the text is the first activity in the lesson plan for evolving readers. The teacher may determine if the entire text or portions of the text should be reread to improve fluency. This reread can be accomplished in several ways: partner reading, choral reading, or whisper reading. (We recommend choral reading be used when the text is a short poem.) Teachers also should take turns with the rereading of the text to provide a model for fluency for these evolving readers. In the following example, students are rereading *The Horse and the Bell* (Randell, 2001), which is a level 22 book or K designation. The teacher begins with a short review of the major story elements, then provides an oral reading model of the first page, and finally has the students reread the rest of the book with a partner.

Teacher: Yesterday, we finished reading *The Horse and the Bell*. Let's review the story for a few minutes. Who were the main characters in the story?

Jack: I think that the main character was the horse. The soldier was in the story, but I don't think he was the main character.

Teacher: Why don't you think that the soldier is a main character?

Jack: Well, he isn't even given a name in the story.

Leslie: I think that the horse and the soldier were both main characters. If there wasn't a soldier in the story, the whole thing couldn't have taken place.

Teacher: Sometimes we can have our own opinions about the main characters, and I think you are both right.

Teacher: Where did the story take place?

Susan: Most of the story took place in the castle, but some of it took place outside the castle walls.

Teacher: Today, we are going to reread this book with a partner. Remember, if you are the listening partner, you must follow along and assist your partner if necessary. Please use your "6-inch" or whisper-reading voices so that I can hear you, but you won't disturb others in the group. Remember to give your partners "wait time" if they come to a word that they don't know, so that they have a chance to figure it out on their own. I will be listening in so that if you both need help, just raise your hand and I will help you. I will read the first page to get us started. I am going to read the page and try to make it sound like a real conversation. I will try to use the proper expression and pause at punctuation marks, when necessary. Everyone turn to page 3, and I will begin reading. Use your reading markers to follow along as I read.

(The teacher reads page 3 as the students follow along.)

Teacher: Turn to page 4. Now you will read the rest of the book with your partner. Try to read the story with expression so that the story will be interesting for someone else to listen to. You may begin.

(The students begin partner reading the book while the teacher monitors.)

Word Study

As previously mentioned, the word study component of the small-group model was designed for students to study the same word features for one week. Therefore, teachers would use the first day of the week to introduce and explain the word sort, which typically takes 8–10 minutes. The complete lesson is designed to be implemented in approximately 30 minutes. (See chapter 7 for more details on managing small-group instruction.) However, because of time constraints, it may not be possible to complete the dictated sentence activity on the first day. During the remaining four days, students may complete some word study activities, such as word sorts and word hunts, outside of small-group time, which typically takes 8–10 minutes each day. As previously mentioned, students should have their word study cards ready before coming to the small group to save valuable instructional time.

In the following dialogue, the students are starting a new word sort. Because it is a closed sort, the teacher provides the header words. In addition, students consider the word *have* an oddball word when they sort by sound and pattern. Oddball words are those words that do not follow a generalization. (These words are indicated by an asterisk in the word study lists in Appendix B.) Although *have* follows the V C E (vowel-consonant-final *e*) pattern, it has a short-vowel sound—unlike the other V-C-E words that contain a long-vowel sound.

Teacher: We're going to look at a different pattern for long *a* today. Take a look at these headers, and tell me what you notice.

Benjamin: Well, we have *sail*, *gave*, and *say*. *Sail* is the new one.

Teacher: You're right; *sail* is the new header. What is the pattern for *sail*?

Susan: The *ai* pattern.

Teacher: Yes, those are the letters of the pattern, but how would we label the pattern?

Jack: We would mark it CVVC, because there are two vowels in the middle of the word.

Teacher: That's right, this is a consonant, vowel-vowel, consonant pattern. This is another vowel combination that makes the long *a* sound. Let's review the other patterns for long *a* we have learned so far, and then we'll start the sort together. What is the first pattern for long *a* that we learned?

Susan: We learned the V-C-E pattern.

Teacher: Good. Can you give me an example of a word that follows that pattern?

Benjamin: The header *gave* follows that pattern.

Teacher: Good. What is the other pattern we learned?

Leslie: The V-V pattern.

Teacher: Yes. What is an example of a word that has that pattern?

Jennifer: *Say*? Would that be an example of that pattern?

Teacher: Good. OK, now let's sort our new words. Where would this word (teacher shows *train* on a card) go in our sort?

(The teacher shows the word card as the students read the words and figure out where to sort them.)

Leslie: *Train* would go under *sail*.

Teacher: Why, Leslie?

Leslie: Because it has the *ai* pattern.

Teacher: Good! How about this word *make*; where would this word go?

(The teacher shows *make* on a card.)

Benjamin: That would go under *gave*, because it has the vowel-consonant-e [V-C-E] pattern.

Teacher: You're right again!

(Students continue to sort the words.)

Teacher: Where would this word go?

(The teacher shows *have* on a card.)

Jack: Are we sorting by sound or by pattern?

Teacher: What do the rest of you think?

Leslie: We're sorting by pattern, because we've been looking at the headers and sorting the words according to the pattern they follow.

Teacher: Yes, we have been sorting by pattern. So what do we do with *have*?

Jack: If we sort by pattern, it has to go with the V-C-E words.

Susan: But, we say *hăv*, not *hāv*.

Teacher: You have a good point, Susan. What do you think, Leslie?

Leslie: I think if we are sorting by pattern, then we should put it with the V-C-E words.

Teacher: Jennifer, what do you think?

Jennifer: Why don't we sort by pattern and the way it sounds?

Teacher: So you want to sort by sound and pattern?

Benjamin: Yes, that way, *have* can be an oddball.

Teacher: What do you (looking at entire group) think of Benjamin's idea?

Leslie: That makes sense, because then we have to think about the way we say the word as well as the way we spell the word.

| Teacher: | It's a good idea to think through those ideas when you have words that follow the same pattern but have different sounds than the rest of the words in the sort. Another idea is to sort first by sound, then by pattern, and then by both sound and pattern. |

(The teacher continues to give words for the students to sort by both sound and pattern.)

Teacher:	OK, now that the words are all sorted, let's go back and reread them to make sure they are in the right category. Jack, how about if you read the first list, the V-C-E words?
Jack:	(reads) *Ape, chase, grave, quake, trace, whale, place, stage.*
Teacher:	Do all of those words have the long *a* pattern and sound we are looking for?
Jennifer:	Yes, but I have a question about the word *quake*; does this mean like an *earthquake*, where everything shakes?
Teacher:	Who can help Jennifer understand the word *quake*?
Susan:	That is kind of what *quake* means; quake is part of *earthquake*. But it doesn't always have to be an earthquake; it can also just mean something is shaking.
Teacher:	You're right, Susan; *quake* can simply mean something is shaking, but we typically think of quake when we think of an earthquake. Do you know what kind of word *earthquake* is?
Susan:	Like when we put two words together and come up with a new one?
Teacher:	Yes, when we take two words that can stand alone, like *earth* and *quake*, and put them together to get *earthquake*.
Benjamin:	I think we call that a compound word.
Teacher:	Yes, we're going to learn about more compound words later this year. But when you're reading and you come across a compound word, looking at the two words separately can help you understand the meaning of the word. OK, now we need to get back to the sort. Who wants to read the next list?
Leslie:	I will: (reads) *chain, hail, saint, stain, waist, plain, train, paint, paid, braid.*
Teacher:	Good. Did anyone notice a word that didn't fit the sound and pattern we are looking for?
Students:	No.
Teacher:	Jack, how about if you read the last list for us?
Jack:	(reads) *Bay, day, play, stay, tray, way, pray, may, slay.*

See Figure 7 for a completed word sort for this lesson.

Dictated Sentence

| Teacher: | Today's sentence is *A whale was swimming in the bay*. |
| Teacher: | Let me say that again. |

FIGURE 7
Completed Word Sort

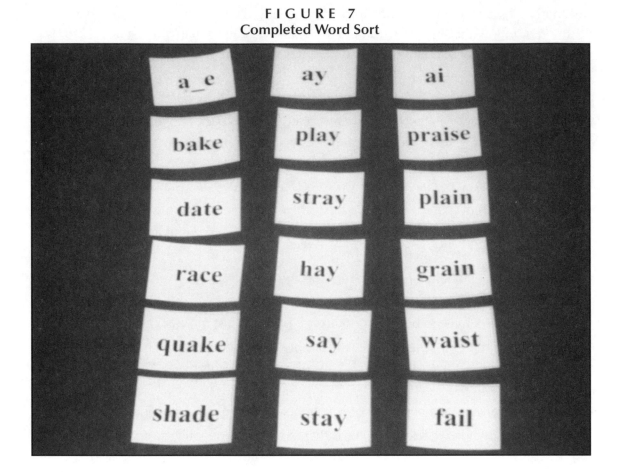

a_e	ay	ai
bake	play	praise
date	stray	plain
race	hay	grain
quake	say	waist
shade	stay	fail

(Teacher repeats sentence.)

Teacher: Now I want you to say the sentence with me.

(Students repeat sentence together.)

Teacher: Think about the vowel sounds and patterns you hear as you are writing the sentence.

(Teacher monitors as students write.)

Teacher: Now circle all of the long *a* pattern words that you see in the sentence.

(Teacher checks for correct responses.)

Comprehension

In the following dialogue, the reading group is beginning to read a new book. The teacher introduces the book and encourages the students to make connections to the book and some predictions. In addition, the teacher introduces important story vocabulary. The teacher preselected vocabulary words that she felt would be important for the students to know before they read the story. The teacher also wrote the words on notecards so that they could be used in a review after the story is read.

Before Reading

Predicting and Making Connections

Teacher: We are going to begin a new book today called *Pandas in the Mountains* [Randell, 1999]. It is in the realistic fiction genre. This means that it is a story that could actually happen, but it is not real. Let's take a look at the front cover. We see two panda bears climbing on a tree. What do you know about panda bears? (With this question, the teacher leads students to make connections about what they already know about pandas.)

Susan: Well, I have seen them on TV on *Animal Planet*, and they were in a zoo. I think that there aren't many panda bears left.

Teacher: That's right. Panda bears were almost extinct a few years ago. That means that there were only a few left. Now, people are being more careful with the pandas to make sure that they will survive. What else do you know about pandas?

Leslie: I know that pandas like to eat bamboo. I saw on TV that bamboo is like candy to the pandas and people give it to them as a treat.

Previewing Story Vocabulary

Teacher: I want to show you a few words in the story that might be tricky. The first one is the name of the mother panda, *Ping Ping*. Ping Ping is a Chinese name because most pandas live in China. We will also see another Chinese name in the book, *Lin Lin*. Does anyone want to guess who Lin Lin will be in the story?

Jennifer: I think that will be Ping Ping's friend because there are two pandas on the cover.

Teacher: Let's write a few of our predictions on this Directed Reading–Thinking Activity Sheet [see Appendix C] so we can look at them as we read the story to see if they are correct, and then we can make new ones as we go along, or we can change our predictions.

(Teacher writes *Lin Lin is a friend of Ping Ping* on the DR–TA Sheet.)

Teacher: There is only one more word that I want to show you. Does anyone know this word?

Jack: *Bamboo*. That's the stuff that the pandas like to eat.

Teacher: Let's take a look at the first couple of pages to see what the book might be about. On page 2, we see the mother panda coming up the hill. She's looking at that old hollow tree. Now turn to page 4. What do you suppose the mother panda is holding?

Jennifer: It looks like a baby pig or something. I wonder why she would be holding a baby pig?

Teacher: Why don't we write down that prediction: *The panda is holding a pig*. Let's look at the next page and see if it gives us any clues.

Teacher: On page 7, it looks like the panda is chasing the wildcat? Why do you think she would be doing that?

Jack: Maybe the panda is trying to catch the wildcat to eat for food.

Teacher: That's a good guess. Let's write that down as our final prediction before we read the story. Let's turn back to the beginning of the book and read the story to find out if our predictions were right.

(By writing down the student predictions on the DR–TA Sheet, the students have a starting point for discussion as the story unfolds. The chart also serves the important purpose of demonstrating that predicting benefits students as they read.)

During Reading

Teacher-Generated Questions

Teacher: I'll take a turn first and read page 2. You follow along with your markers while I read.

(The teacher takes the first turn to provide a fluent model for the students to emulate, and the students use a marker to show that they are following along.)

Teacher: We found out on this page that Ping Ping is about to give birth to her cub. What did she need to find before she gave birth? (The teacher asks a literal question.)

Benjamin: She needed to find a safe place for him to be born.

Teacher: Why would she need a safe place?

(The teacher asks an inferential question. Although the answer cannot be found in the text, the students are asked to make inferences about why this is important.)

Jennifer: Maybe the mother will feel sick after she has the baby and she needs to be in a safe place.

Teacher: That makes sense. Let's turn to page 3 and read this page together. Remember to read smoothly, and watch the punctuation marks so that we can read it with the correct meaning.

(Teacher and students read chorally. This allows teachers to "pull students through" difficult phrasing, and it provides necessary support for expressive reading.)

Teacher: So what has happened so far in the story?

(The teacher asks the students to summarize the story frequently while they are working on comprehension.)

Susan: Not much. The mother bear is going to have a cub, and she made a den in a hollow tree.

Teacher: That was a very good summary of what has taken place so far. Now let's all turn to page 4. I want everyone to whisper read this page, and I will listen in. If you need help with a word, just raise your hand. Remember to read loud enough so I can hear you but not loud enough to disturb the others.

(The students whisper read the page while the teacher monitors.)

Teacher: So was it a pig the mother panda was holding? (literal question)

Benjamin: No, it was the baby panda. I can't believe it is so small when it is born.

Leslie: Our prediction was wrong.

Teacher: OK. Give me a good sentence that tells what really happened, and I will write it on our DR-TA Sheet.

(By asking students to express themselves in complete sentences, teachers can help students improve their sentence construction, which they will need to write independently. The students continue reading the text by alternating oral reading strategies, including choral reading, partner reading, and whisper reading. The teacher also continues asking a variety of questions to increase story comprehension.)

Teacher: What do you think the mother panda was thinking as the door of the trap slammed shut? (inferential question)

Jennifer: I think she was afraid that she might never see her baby again.

Teacher: I think you are probably right.

Teacher: Do you think it is OK to catch wild pandas and scare them like that? Why or why not? (application question)

Susan: I don't like it, but it is the best thing to keep the pandas alive.

After Reading

Summarizing

After reading the story, the teacher begins to summarize the story by asking students to review the new story vocabulary and create a sentence using each word that tells about important events in the story. Then, the group reviews the DR–TA Sheet (see Figure 8) as a way to further summarize the story.

Teacher: In looking at our predictions before we read, we were really wrong about what we thought would happen. We can't always tell by the title or a few pictures what the real story is going to be. The important thing to remember is that we had all of our questions answered when we finished the story.

Teacher: Let's take another look at the vocabulary words and think about how they were used in the story. What about this word?

FIGURE 8
Completed DR–TA

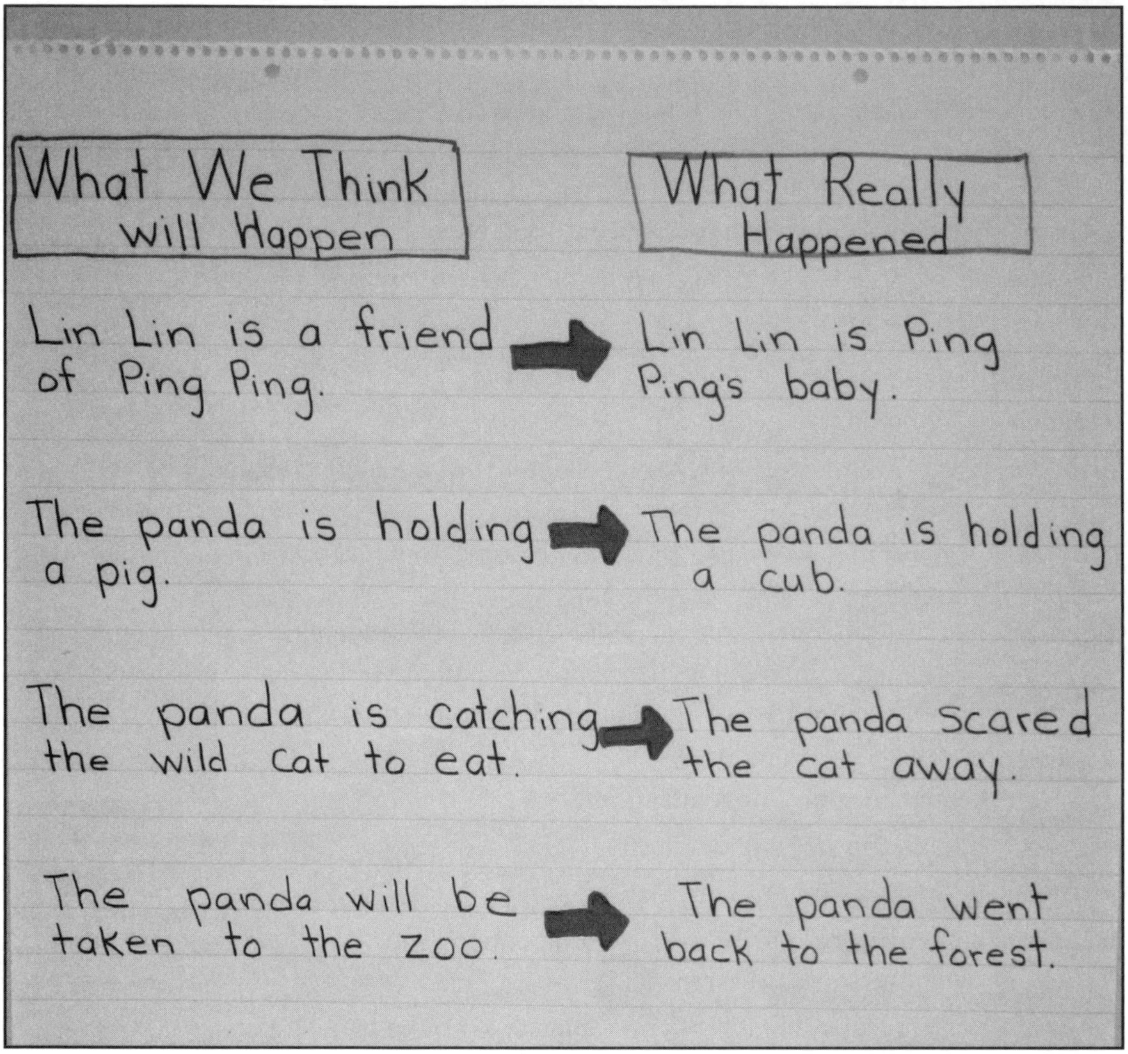

What We Think will Happen	What Really Happened
Lin Lin is a friend of Ping Ping.	Lin Lin is Ping Ping's baby.
The panda is holding a pig.	The panda is holding a cub.
The panda is catching the wild cat to eat.	The panda scared the cat away.
The panda will be taken to the zoo.	The panda went back to the forest.

(The teacher holds up card with *bamboo* on it.)

Jack: The bad men used bamboo in the trap to catch the panda.

Teacher: Yes, and that was a real problem for the panda.

(The teacher continues the process of reviewing the vocabulary to summarize the story.)

See Figure 9 for a completed lesson plan for narrative text. Again, this lesson plan addresses the comprehension strategies that are most appropriate for this genre. Note that this and subsequent lesson plans include a column for teacher comments where the teacher can indicate strengths and weaknesses of the lesson and student performance. Teachers can use this valuable information to plan future instruction.

Components/Activities	Comments
FLUENCY (REREADING) Text _Reread The Horse and the Bell_ pp. _all_ ☑ Choral ☑ Partner ☑ Whisper	Jack struggling with rereads, may need to move down. Whole group needs to use more expression
WORD STUDY Patterns _a_e/ai/ay_ Cycle _1_ Week _8_ ☑ Word Sort or ☐ Spelling Sort and ☑ Dictated Sentence _A whale was swimming in the bay_ Outside of Group Activity (optional) ☐ Word Hunt ☐ Other vocabulary activity Specify _____	Sort was good, need more practice with transfer to writing. (Benjamin and Susan confused whale with wail)
COMPREHENSION Text _Pandas in the Mountains_ pp. _all_ Before Reading ☑ Predicting ☑ Making Connections ☑ Previewing Vocabulary List _Ping Ping, Lin Lin, bamboo_	Good predictions
During Reading Teacher-Generated Questions (during or after) ☑ Literal _What did she need to find before she gave birth?_ ☑ Inferential _Why would she need a safe place?_ ☑ Application _Do you think it is OK to catch wild pandas and scare them like that? Why or why not?_ ☐ Student-Generated Questions (during or after)	Better with literal than inferential— surface level understanding Next time have them come up with inferential to help with this type of question.
After Reading Summarizing Text Structure ☐ Characters ☐ Setting ☐ Events (sequencing) ☐ Conflicts/Resolution (cause/effect) Activity for Above ☐ Oral discussion ☐ Graphic organizer Specify _DRTA_ ☐ Independent Written Response (optional) Specify _____	Good job summarizing DR–TA

Instructional Components of the Evolving Reader Lesson Plan: Expository Text

The lesson plan used for reading a nonfiction book is similar to the lesson plan for the narrative text with differences that reflect the individual genre in the area of comprehension (see Figure 10). Students continue to work on fluency by rereading text. The word study component is the same and is incorporated into the lesson plan as before—through word sorting, spelling sorting, and dictated sentences. The strategies used before, during, and after reading specifically address expository text and support the strategies needed to successfully understand the book. These strategies include summarizing, identifying the main idea and supporting details, sequencing, and comparing and contrasting.

Fluency (Rereading)

The group begins by rereading the part of the book that was read as a new read the day before. Although these students are evolving readers, they are still working on fluency issues that can only be developed through rereading independent or instructional level text.

Teacher: Today, you are going to reread a part of the book you read yesterday with your reading partner. Remember, when we reread, we are practicing to make our reading sound like a real conversation. Turn to page 3. I will read this page first, and then we will read it together. After that, you will reread to page 13 with your partner. Be sure to alternate reading with your partner. I will be listening in if you need help.

(The students take turns with their partners and finish reading the text while the teacher monitors.)

By rereading texts at their independent or instructional levels, students will be able to increase their oral reading fluency.

Word Study

In the following dialogue, the students are beginning a new sort. It is an open sort, thus, the students must decide on categories in which to place the words they are studying. Then, the teacher asks the students to write dictated sentences using words with the features being studied. Students will need a full week to study new features.

Teacher: This week, we will be looking at contractions. Does anyone know or remember what a contraction is?

Brian: A contraction is like a compound word; you put two words together and come up with a new word.

The Evolving Reader Lesson Plan: Expository Text

Components/Activities	Comments
FLUENCY (REREADING) Text _____ pp. _____ Rereading ☐ Choral ☐ Partner ☐ Whisper	
WORD STUDY Patterns_____ Cycle _____ Week _____ ☐ Word Sort or ☐ Spelling Sort and ☐ Dictated Sentence_____ Outside of Group Activity (optional) ☐ Word Hunt ☐ Other vocabulary activity Specify _____	
COMPREHENSION Text _____ pp. _____ Before Reading ☐ Activating Background Knowledge ☐ Previewing Text Structure ☐ Previewing Vocabulary List _____ _____ _____	
During Reading Teacher-Generated Questions (during or after) ☐ Literal _____ _____ ☐ Inferential _____ _____ ☐ Application _____ _____ ☐ Student-Generated Questions	
After Reading Summarizing Text Structure ☐ Main Ideas/Supporting Details ☐ Sequencing ☐ Compare/Contrast ☐ Cause/Effect Activity for Above ☐ Oral discussion ☐ Graphic organizer Specify_____ ☐ Independent Written Response (optional) Specify _____	

Teacher: It is kind of like a compound word; however, it is different in one distinctive way. Does anyone know what that is?

Suellen: In a contraction, you have to take out a letter and put an apostrophe in its place.

Teacher: Right, we use apostrophes as a placeholder. Let's look at our words. Can you think of a couple of categories?

David: Well, we could use *have*, *not*, and *will*.

Teacher: How did you come up with those categories, David?

David: Because this way all the words that mean something to do with *have* can go in the same category.

Teacher: OK, let's try David's way. I'll pass out the words, and you can take turns reading them and decide which category to put them in.

(Teacher passes out the cards.)

Teacher: Who would like to start?

Katie: I'll start. I have the word *they've*. I think it goes in the *have* category.

Teacher: Why do you think that Katie?

Katie: Because *they've* is made up of *they* and *have*.

Teacher: Right, Katie. What word do you have, Clint?

Clint: I have *couldn't*. It goes in the *not* category because it means *could not*.

Teacher: Good, Clint!

(Students continue to sort based on the identified categories and come up with three oddball words.)

have	not	will
they've	couldn't	we'll
would've	won't	that'll
you've	doesn't	she'll
should've	haven't	you'll
we've	isn't	it'll
could've	wouldn't	that'll

Teacher: What do you notice about the words in the *not* category?

David: The apostrophe takes the place of only one letter.

Teacher: What do you mean, David?

David: Well, in the word *couldn't*, the apostrophe takes the place of the *o*. But, in the *have* category, the apostrophe takes the place of two letters: the *h* and the *a*.

Teacher: David is right, and he brings up a good point. Does anyone notice anything else about the words in the *not* category? Think about what you know about parts of speech.

Suellen: All the words are verbs.

Mary: *Could* is not a verb, neither is *would*.

Suellen: Yes it is. We *could* go to the zoo if we want to see the elephants.

Teacher: Let's look it up and see what we find.

(Students look up *could* in the dictionary.)

Teacher: What did we find out?

Brian: The definition reads "past tense of can."

Teacher: So Suellen was right. All of the *not* words are verbs. How about the words in the *have* category—what type of words are those?

(Teacher continues to discuss the parts of speech for the categorized words.)

Teacher: OK, when you get back to your seats, you are going to do a spelling sort with your partner in your word study notebook. For this sort, you have to write the contraction and the two words that make up the contraction next to it.

Dictated Sentence

Teacher: Our dictated sentence for the day is *It'll be a great day for a picnic if it doesn't rain*. Remember to think about contractions as you write this sentence.

(The teacher monitors the students as they write their sentences.)

Comprehension

The focus of the lesson is completing the book *Deserts* (Anderson, 2001), which the students began reading during the previous lesson, and then summarizing and comparing and contrasting different regions. The students recently studied the rainforest; therefore, this region is used as the basis for comparison in the lesson on deserts. Before reading, the teacher has the students examine the text structure of the remainder of the book and look for similarities and differences from the first part of the book. The teacher also introduces story vocabulary with which students are not familiar—specifically how the words relate to the content area. During reading, the teacher uses a variety of types of questions, including literal, inferential, and application. Students also generate their own questions to improve critical thinking skills. After reading, students summarize the information they learned by comparing and contrasting desert and rainforest regions on a graphic organizer.

FIGURE 11
Completed What's the Big Idea? Activity

Before Reading

Activating Background Knowledge and Previewing Text Structure

The teacher begins the lesson by asking the students to review—or summarize—the information that was learned the previous day.

Teacher: Yesterday, we started reading a book called *Deserts*. Let's all turn to the table of contents to review what we read. We actually read the first five chapters. After the introduction, we read about how deserts are formed. Let's take a look at the What's the Big Idea? graphic organizer we completed yesterday [see Appendix C and Figure 11]. Who would like to summarize that information based on yesterday's read?

Katie: Well, deserts are very hot and dry places that form when there is no rain or a whole lot of wind.

Teacher: Why is the wind a problem?

Clint:	If the wind blows really hard, it can blow everything away, including the trees, and then there isn't any shade. That causes the land to become a desert.
Teacher:	We also read about the types of deserts. Again, let's take a look at our graphic organizer to summarize that information. Do you remember the most famous sandy desert?
Mary:	I think it is called the Sahara Desert. It is made of all sand and then there are deserts that are made of small stones and others with big rocks.
Teacher:	Yes. You remembered a lot about that. How do people in the desert get water?
Suellen:	They can only get water when it rains, or they might be able to dig a deep hole like a well and get some water.
Teacher:	What do we call the people who live in deserts in tents that they move around as they travel?
David:	Those people are called nomads. I really don't understand why they would want to stay in the desert.

(Before reading, the teacher spends some time previewing the text format and introducing story vocabulary.)

Teacher:	Today we will learn about the homes, foods, plants, and animals that are found in the desert. Let's flip through the rest of the story. Do you notice anything different about these pages as opposed to the first part of the book?
Mary:	No. It looks the same to me. It even has the same colored boxes at the end of each chapter called "Do you know?"
Teacher:	Usually, the format stays the same throughout the book. That is helpful to the reader so we know what to expect. Let me introduce a few words that we will be seeing in our reading that have to do with deserts.

Previewing Vocabulary

The teacher introduces the words written on notecards: *nomads, oasis, cactus, dew,* and *sprout.* The teacher, students, or both define each word and discuss them. Students also make predictions about how the words will be used in the text.

During Reading

Teacher-Generated Questions

Teacher:	Everyone turn to page 14 in your books. Our first chapter today tells about homes in the desert. I am going to read first while you follow along. Listen to find out where people in the desert build their homes and why they build them there. (By reading orally, the teacher is providing a fluent model of the reading while the students follow along. The students are also listening for important information that will enhance their comprehension.)

Teacher: So where do people in the desert choose to build their homes? (literal question)

David: They try to build them near an oasis or even under the ground or in caves. They have to stay cool during the day and stay warm at night. They also have to protect themselves from sandstorms.

Teacher: What kinds of homes do they build? (literal question)

Mary: They have tents made of goatskin or caves.

Katie: Some of them have real houses but they have to be near an oasis.

Student-Generated Questions

Teacher: Now, I want you to whisper read pages 16 and 17 to find out what kind of food is available to eat in the desert. While you are reading, think of a question to ask the group when you finish.

(Teacher monitors as students read the text.)

Teacher: Mary, do you have a question for the group?

Mary: Yes. What kinds of trees grow near the oases?

Clint: Date trees. The people eat dates from these trees.

Teacher: So what other kinds of foods do they eat in the desert?

David: They eat goat meat and kangaroo meat.

Teacher: Anything else?

Brian: Yes. It's gross. They eat grubs. That's like eating bugs.

Teacher: Why do you think they eat grubs? (inferential question)

Clint: They don't have many choices of meats to eat.

Teacher: That's true. They are also a good source of protein and have lots of vitamins.

Teacher: Do you think it would be hard to make a living if you lived on a desert? Why or why not? (application question)

Mary: Yes. If you didn't have much food or water, it would be hard to work. It would also be hard to get people to move to the desert to work.

Teacher: Good, Mary. Although it didn't tell us that in the book, we could "read between the lines" and figure that out on our own.

(Students complete the story by alternating partner reading, teacher read-aloud, and whisper reading.)

After Reading

Summarizing: Compare and Contrast

Teacher: We certainly have learned a lot about deserts. Let's discuss what we have learned.

(Teacher and students discuss key points about desert life.)

FIGURE 12
Completed Venn Diagram

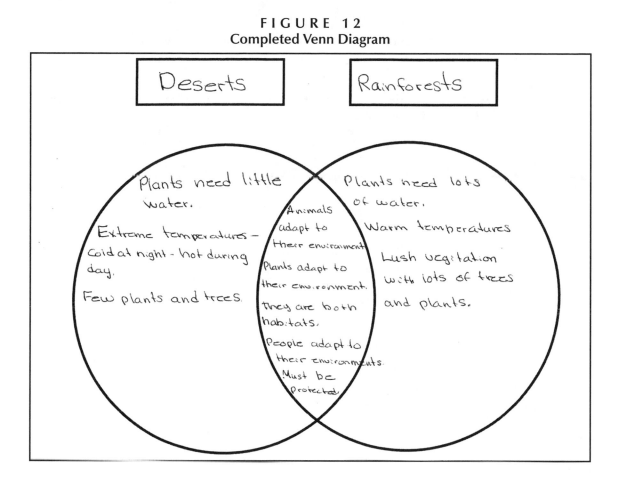

Deserts

Rainforests

Plants need little water.

Extreme temperatures – Cold at night - hot during day.

Few plants and trees.

Animals adapt to their environment. Plants adapt to their environment. They are both habitats. People adapt to their environments. Must be protected.

Plants need lots of water.

Warm temperatures

Lush vegetation with lots of trees and plants.

Teacher: How do you think the desert is different from the rainforest, based on what you learned about the rainforest?

Suellen: The rainforest is really wet, and the desert is really dry!

Teacher: Are they alike at all?

Mary: Well, they both have animals that live in them.

Teacher: Let's see how many things we can list that are similar and different about these regions. We can put the information on our graphic organizer called a Venn Diagram [see Appendix C].

(Teacher and students complete Venn Diagram [see Figure 12].)

See Figure 13 for a completed lesson plan for expository text. Again, the expository lesson plan focuses on comprehension instruction with strategies that support this genre, which allows students to develop a thorough understanding of the text while learning strategies that can be applied to their independent reading, especially in the content areas. Because the curricular demands for the evolving reader become more focused on expository text, developing strategies students can use to comprehend this type of text becomes more important.

FIGURE 13
Completed Evolving Reader Lesson Plan: Expository Text

Components/Activities	Comments
FLUENCY (REREADING) Text _Deserts_ pp. _4-12_ Rereading ☐ Choral ☑ Partner ☐ Whisper	Partners: Clint & Katie, Suellen & David, Brian & Mary All did well!
✓ **WORD STUDY** Patterns _contractions-have, not, will_ Cycle _2_ Week _5_ ☐ Word Sort or ☐ Spelling Sort and ☐ Dictated Sentence _It'll be a great day for a picnic if it doesn't rain._ Outside of Group Activity (optional) ☐ Word Hunt ☐ Other vocabulary activity Specify _____	Began with open sort – Caught on really quickly to contractions
COMPREHENSION Text _Finish up Deserts_ pp. _complete_ Before Reading ☑ Activating Background Knowledge ☑ Previewing Text Structure ☐ Previewing Vocabulary List _nomads, oasis, cactus, dew, sprout_ During Reading Teacher-Generated Questions (during or after) ☐ Literal _Where do people in the desert choose to build their homes? What kind of food is available to eat in the desert?_ ☐ Inferential _Why do you think they eat grubs?_ ☐ Application _Do you think it would be hard to make a living in the desert? Why or why not?_ ☑ Student-Generated Questions After Reading Summarizing Text Structure ☐ Main Ideas/Supporting Details ☐ Sequencing ☑ Compare/Contrast ☐ Cause/Effect Activity for Above ☐ Oral discussion ☑ Graphic organizer Specify _Venn diagram_ ☐ Independent Written Response (optional) Specify _____	Began by summarizing what was read yesterday (review What's the Big Idea) Good understanding of vocab. so far – they used vocab. appropriately in summarizing info so far. Need to work more on inferential questions, answers were a bit surface level. Ex. – Because it's dry? Had a hard time going further. All were able to contribute to the Venn Diagram.

Conclusion

Evolving readers continue to need both teacher and text support in order to achieve success. We began the chapter by describing each component of the lesson plan as it relates to the evolving reader. In addition, we have provided teacher–student dialogue to guide the reader through actual lesson plans. As evidenced throughout the dialogue, evolving readers require the appropriate amount of teacher scaffolding as they move through the stage, which allows them to develop independent strategies as they focus on gaining information from text rather than decoding it.

CHAPTER 4

The Maturing Reader Stage

M aturing readers are fully able to read to learn. Both in their classrooms and in everyday life, they are immersed in different types of text, which may include novels, content area textbooks, reference material, and a variety of magazines and newspapers. Exposure to these texts challenges maturing readers to fine-tune their thinking about and comprehension of a given text. Thus, maturing readers must learn to adapt their thinking to promote understanding.

Characteristics of Maturing Readers in Reading, Writing, and Spelling

Reading

Maturing readers have well-developed oral reading fluency. They can read expressively with appropriate pace, phrasing, intonation, and rhythm of speech. However, as research indicates, oral reading fluency directly affects a student's ability to comprehend text. Therefore, fluency is a skill that needs to be continually practiced. Although fluency is not part of the maturing reader's small-group lesson plans, we have provided examples of appropriate independent activities to promote fluency in chapter 7.

Maturing readers also understand the differences between the characteristics of narrative and expository text (including technical and persuasive). Further, they understand the purposes of text features such as graphs, charts, maps, tables of contents, pictures and illustrations, headings and subheadings, glossaries, and indexes. Maturing readers use these features to locate information in the text and to gain meaning from them.

While reading, maturing readers are learning to generate and respond to literal, inferential, and application questions before, during, and after reading. Thus, they begin to use this information to make inferences and draw conclusions about a given text. They compare and contrast varying elements of text, including topics, character traits, and themes, and identify problems and solutions and cause-and-effect relationships. Maturing readers are able to retell main ideas or events as well as provide supporting details about both narrative and expository text.

In the classroom, there is an emphasis on content area knowledge. As a result, maturing readers are expected to know and be able to use technical vocabulary associated with each specific content area. Consequently, they use their knowledge of word structure, such as syllable patterns, contractions, root words, prefixes, and suffixes, when faced with an unknown word.

Maturing readers also are beginning to learn about the meaning and elements of figurative language, such as similes, metaphors, analogies, personification, and symbolism. In addition, these readers are learning about the relationship between an author's use of literary devices in a text (e.g., foreshadowing, flashback, irony) and his or her purpose for writing the text.

Finally, maturing readers are developing their abilities to make inferences, synthesize, and evaluate information; therefore, comprehension is the main focus of instruction for maturing readers. These higher level thinking skills will continue to be fine-tuned well into adulthood.

Texts for Maturing Readers

Maturing readers should read silently from a variety of genres; however, they need explicit comprehension instruction in order to fully understand the author's meaning. Text selections for maturing readers should consist of novels, magazines, poetry, newspaper articles, and expository pieces that support content area standards. Traditionally, chapter books have been the genre of choice for maturing readers; however, we believe instruction should not be limited to chapter books. Although teachers often feel constrained by their resources, they should attempt to share additional available materials, such as newspaper articles and information on the Internet, with students.

Some examples of appropriate chapter books for maturing readers include *Bridge to Terabithia* (Paterson, 1987), *A Wrinkle in Time* (L'Engle, 1973), *Holes* (Sachar, 1998), and *Maniac Magee* (Spinelli, 1999). Although some of the novels read during this stage may not be challenging with regard to word recognition, the content is meant for mature audiences who can conceptualize more difficult topics such as death, racism, time travel, and freedom.

For those using leveled texts as a resource to support small-group differentiated reading instruction, the following book levels are appropriate for maturing readers:

Leveling System	Book Levels
Fountas and Pinnell	S–W
DRA	40–44+

Writing

At the same time that maturing readers are fine-tuning their reading abilities, they are also fine-tuning their writing abilities. They often know the steps of the writing process and can use them independently. However, many students still may need additional instruction in a specific area in order to achieve proficiency.

Maturing readers also are able to express themselves in their writing—which they no longer view as a laborious process because of their word knowledge. They are not limited by the number of words they can spell automatically; therefore, they have more mental energy to expend on their ideas.

The link between reading and writing is essential at this stage. Maturing readers should be encouraged to respond to what they have read in a variety of formats. For example, when reading narrative text, students can be encouraged to write from a character's perspective, create a new ending for a story, or write a letter to the author. When reading expository text, students can be encouraged to research and write a report on a given topic.

Spelling

Maturing readers are typically in the meaning layer of spelling development and should be able to spell all one-syllable words correctly. They are continuing to learn about the spelling–meaning connection, particularly with regard to content-specific vocabulary.

As students study the meaning layer of the English language, they are able to make spelling–meaning connections. Although students have been reading and writing poly-syllabic words for some time, it is in the maturing reader stage that the study of these words moves to the forefront.

A weekly spelling scope and sequence for maturing readers is provided in Appendix B. Again, please note that the scope and sequence is provided only as a guide-line. It is crucial for teachers to use assessment to guide their instruction. If students have not mastered particular features, do not move on. Rather, reteach and review the fea-tures students are confusing. The features studied during the maturing reader stage are outlined in Table 5.

Differentiating the Lesson Plans

Again, we present two different lesson plans to support narrative and expository text. Please note that, for consistency, the word study sequence for the maturing reader re-mains the same regardless of the lesson plan used. We provide classroom dialogue to guide readers through each lesson plan. We also provide completed lesson plans at the end of each section. The lesson plans follow two different groups of students. The group of students completing the narrative lesson plan is in the beginning of the maturing reader stage. The group of students completing the expository lesson plan is nearing the middle of the maturing reader stage.

Instructional Components of the Maturing Reader Lesson Plan: Narrative Text

The are two components for the narrative lesson plan for maturing readers (see Figure 14). For the first component, word study, the teacher records the current word study fea-ture on the lesson plan and determines whether the students will be completing a word sort or a spelling sort. Then, through the dictated sentence activity, students practice using the word study features. In addition, students can complete a word hunt or other word study activity outside of small-group time. For the second component, compre-hension, students focus on more challenging aspects of narrative text. The teacher and the students participate in extensive questioning during reading and after reading. Although the strategies used before reading and during reading are the same as in the evolving reader stage, they are appropriate for the maturing reader stage, too. However,

Word Study Features for the Maturing Reader

Review Suffixes: Plurals and Past Tense	• Doubling (*ed*, *ing*) • Plurals
Syllable Patterns	• Open syllables end with long-vowel sound—**open**; **to**day • Closed syllables end with short-vowel sound—**think**er; **sip**ping • VCCV (vowel-consonant-consonant-vowel—regular/doublet)—thu**nd**er/fo**ll**ow • VCV (vowel-consonant-vowel—open/closed)—ch**osen**/**R**obert • VV (vowel-vowel—riot, liar)
Vowel Patterns in Stressed Syllables (examples)	• Sensitizing to stress—al**low**/**com**fort • Vowel patterns in the stressed syllable—embr**oi**der
Vowel Patterns in Unstressed Syllables (examples)	• Spelling patterns at end of words—pencil/able/label; motor/baker/dollar
Syllable Stress (examples)	• Homophones and homographs—bridle/bridal; pre'sent/present'
Ending Suffixes (examples)	• Final *K* sound • *ful, ly, er, est, ing*
Prefixes (examples)	• *anti*—against; *super*—higher, greater; *trans*—over, across
Compound Words	• Three plus syllables—underlying, overhead
Number-Related Prefixes and Roots (examples)	• *cent, centi*—hundred • *pent, penta*—five • *poly*—many • *quad, quadric*—four
Latin and Greek Roots (examples)	• *ant/ent*—defiant, patient • *ible/able*—edible, breakable
Contractions	• Review all
Vowel Alternations	• Long to short—cave/cavity • Silent versus sounded—sign/signal

the strategies used after reading focus on summarizing as it relates to plot, conflict resolution, comparing and contrasting, and sequencing. Teachers should identify on the lesson plan the particular elements they are studying; for example, teachers can choose to complete the oral discussion using a graphic organizer or independent written response. This should be noted on the lesson plan.

FIGURE 14
The Maturing Reader Lesson Plan: Narrative Text

Components/Activities	Comments
WORD STUDY	
Features_____ Cycle _____ Week _____	
☐ Word Sort or ☐ Spelling Sort and	
☐ Dictated Sentence_____	
Outside of Group Activity (optional) ☐ Word Hunt ☐ Other vocabulary activity Specify _____	
COMPREHENSION	
Text_____ pp. _____	
Before Reading ☐ Predicting ☐ Making Connections ☐ Previewing Vocabulary List _____ _____	
During Reading Teacher-Generated Questions (during or after) ☐ Literal _____ _____ ☐ Inferential _____ _____ ☐ Application _____ _____ ☐ Student-Generated Questions (during and after)	
After Reading Summarizing Text Structure ☐ Plot ☐ Compare/Contrast ☐ Sequencing (events) ☐ Conflicts/Resolution Activity for Above ☐ Oral discussion ☐ Graphic organizer Specify _____ _____ ☐ Independent Written Response (optional) Specify _____ _____	

Word Study

In the following dialogue, the students are starting a new sort. When teachers introduce a new sort, it typically takes about 10 minutes. On subsequent days, however, the time allocated for word study will be less. (This lesson can be broken into two lessons if there is a time constraint.) This will be an open sort; thus, the teacher does not provide the header words or tell the students the pattern they are studying.

The lengthy dialogue that occurs between the teacher and the students is essential in order for students to be able to analyze words using higher level thinking skills.

Teacher: Today we are going to start a new sort.

(The teacher lays the words out on cards in front of the group.)

Teacher: Can anyone tell me what you notice about the words?

Carla: All the words have *ing* at the end of them.

Teacher: Yes, they do. What do we call *ing*? Try to recall when we learned about *ing* and *ed*.

Janette: Those are called suffixes.

Teacher: OK. Now I think we are ready to start sorting. Who wants to start?

Melody: I'll start. I'm going to put *melting* in a column with words that have a short-vowel sound.

Carla: I'm going to put *snowing* in a column with words that have a long-vowel sound.

Janette: What about *spoiling*? That has an ambiguous vowel sound so it doesn't fit with the long or the short sounds. Can I make a new column?

Teacher: Yes, you can if you want. What does the rest of the group think?

Harrison: Well, because *spoiling* doesn't have a long or short sound, you have to put it in a different category.

Janette: OK, but what about *scarring*? *Scarring* has an *r*-controlled pattern. Do we make another category for those?

Teacher: What does the group think?

Melody: We can for now, or we can make this the oddball column and put in words that don't have the long or short sound.

Donita: Let's do that, because otherwise we may have a lot of columns!

(Students continue sorting words in the three categories they have determined. See the following completed sort.)

Short Vowel	Long Vowel	Oddball
puffing	snowing	spoiling
tugging	loading	scarring
sprinting	blaming	chewing
melting	placing	shouting
popping	screaming	stirring
quitting	speeding	blurring
sobbing	shaping	
dragging	driving	

Teacher: OK, how else could we sort these?

Harrison: We could sort them by vowel pattern.

Teacher: Let's do that and see what we notice. Let's also write the base words that go along with the words with suffixes on my dry erase board.

Carla: Where would we put *scarring*? If we look at the pattern of the base word, it's a C-V-C pattern. But we know that *ar* is an *r*-controlled pattern.

Teacher: What does the group want to do with *scarring*?

Janette: Let's put it in an oddball category for now and then we can always change it later on.

(Students continue sorting the pairs of words. They decide to put additional words in the oddball category as well.)

C-V-C		C-V-C-C		C-V-V-C/C-V-V		C-V-Ce		Oddballs	
tugging	tug	puffing	puff	snowing	snow	blaming	blame	scarring	scar
popping	pop	sprinting	sprint	spoiling	spoil	placing	place	stirring	stir
quitting	quit	melting	melt	loading	load	shaping	shape	blurring	blur
dragging	drag			shouting	shout	driving	drive		
				screaming	scream				
				speeding	speed				
				chewing	chew				

(Note: Teachers can end the lesson here, if necessary, and continue the lesson the next time the group meets.)

Teacher: What else do you notice about these words other than they all have *ing*?

Donita: Sometimes you have to add another consonant, but other times you don't.

Melody: And sometimes you have to drop the *e* in order to add the *ing*.

| | Teacher: | Good! You're both right; sometimes we have to double the consonant before we add a suffix, sometimes we have to drop the final *e* before we add the suffix, and other times we don't have to do anything. |

Teacher: Good! You're both right; sometimes we have to double the consonant before we add a suffix, sometimes we have to drop the final *e* before we add the suffix, and other times we don't have to do anything.

Harrison: So we just have to remember that rule?

Teacher: Well, Harrison, we don't just memorize rules when we are learning to spell. What happens to rules?

Group: They get broken!

Teacher: Yes, rules are sometimes broken. This is why we look at patterns and make generalizations, and then when we come across words like this in our reading and writing, we'll know how to read and spell them.

Janette: So how do we remember when to double the consonant and when not to?

Teacher: Let's look at our words and see if there is another way to sort them.

Carla: Why don't we sort them by what we have to do with them before we add the *ing*.

Teacher: Let's try that and see what happens.

(Students sort the words. See completed sort below.)

Double	Nothing	Drop
tugging	puffing	blaming
popping	sprinting	placing
quitting	melting	shaping
dragging	snowing	driving
scarring	spoiling	
stirring	loading	
blurring	shouting	
	screaming	
	speeding	
	chewing	

Teacher: What do you notice?

Donita: Well, all the words in the Drop category are C-V-Ce [consonant-vowel-consonant-silent *e*] pattern words.

Teacher: Yes, what else do you notice?

Carla: The words that we have to double are all short or *r*-controlled vowel words, but when they are *r*-controlled, they are simple *r*-controlled—not like the more complex *r* patterns; take *eer* in *cheer*, for example.

Teacher: Good observation. How about the words we don't have to do anything to?

Harrison: Well, they are a combination of long- and short-vowel words. But the short-vowel words all have two consonants after the vowel. See, like *melt*. It has the *lt* after the *e*, but the other words that we have to double the consonant don't, like *tug* for example.

Teacher: Good! The reason we have to double the consonant for the words in the first column is to protect the short-vowel sound. If we don't double the consonant, then we would have *pō/ping* rather than *pop/ping*. This aspect of protecting the short-vowel sound will become more important as we keep learning about different types of syllables. The *r*-controlled words are a bit less common, but I wanted to include them so you could analyze them as well. What about the long-vowel words; what do you notice with these words?

Melody: Well, with the words that have the C-V-Ce pattern, you have to drop the *e* before you add *ing*, but the words with the C-V-V-C or C-V-V pattern, you don't have to drop anything.

Teacher: You're right! This is because the words that have the C-V-V-C pattern already have another vowel there to protect the long-vowel sound. But the words that have the C-V-Ce pattern don't need the *e* because the *i* in *ing* acts as another vowel for the word. If we didn't drop the *e*, we would be adding another vowel pattern between the juncture of the base word and the suffix, and they are different parts of the word. Look at this in *driveing*. This is why we have to drop the *e*.

Teacher: Here's a way for you to decide if you have to double the consonant. Ask yourselves the 1-1-1 check [Ganske, 2000]. Remember, this is only a generalization.

Does the word have one syllable?
Does the word have one vowel?
Does the word end with one consonant?

Teacher: During your independent work time, I want you to do a word hunt and look for the words that have the features we are studying. Look through the chapters we have read in *Bridge to Terabithia* [Paterson, 1987] to do your word hunt. Next week, we are going to look at these words again when we talk about open and closed syllables.

(The dictated sentence was omitted for the purpose of time in this lesson.)

Comprehension

In the following dialogue, the discussion focuses on the chapter from *Bridge to Terabithia* (Paterson, 1987), which was assigned for homework the previous night. Following the discussion, the teacher leads the students in predicting, making connections, and previewing story vocabulary.

Before Reading

Predicting

Teacher: The end of the chapter brought the shocking news that the character Leslie had died while Jess was away in Washington. We haven't found out yet how she died. How do you think Jess will feel knowing that he was away when Leslie died and that he didn't invite her to go with them to Washington?

Harrison: I think that Jess will be feeling a lot of guilt. It doesn't really matter how she died; the fact is that Jess wasn't with her and he was off having a great time.

Melody: Yeah, besides that, Jess really loved Leslie as his best friend and his girlfriend.

Teacher: So how do you think that Jess will handle the tragic news of Leslie's death?

Carla: I think that his reaction will depend on how she died. Maybe she committed suicide after she found out that Jess went to Washington with his teacher. Maybe he will feel that he betrayed Leslie.

Making Connections

Teacher: Have you ever had a friend or relative that you were really close to die? What were your first reactions?

Janette: Well, it wasn't a person who died—it was my cat. I really loved her, and I slept with her every night, and when I found out she died, I started crying and throwing things.

Melody: When my grandmother died last year, I was really angry because I wanted things to stay like they always did, like having Thanksgiving at her house.

Teacher: So do you think it is logical to predict that Jess might react in the same way?

Donita: I don't know. Losing a close friend that was your own age would be different, I think. I think it would be a lot worse.

Previewing Vocabulary

Teacher: Let's look at a couple of words that we will read in the next chapter. The first one is *relentlessly*. Does anyone know what this word means?

(After some wait time and no response from the students, the teacher discusses the meaning with the students.)

Teacher: Let's break the word into chunks. The base word *relent* means to not be so hard on someone, for example, "I hope my dad will relent and let me stay up to watch the late movie." Now, let's add *less* to the word. *Less* means "not," so *relentless* means "not letting up," for example, "My dad was relentless and refused to let me stay up late to watch the movie." By adding the *ly* to the word, it becomes an adverb that will describe a verb or another adverb.

(The teacher also introduces the words *uncertainty*, *lopsided*, *curtainless*, and *threateningly* and uses student responses and supports when necessary.)

Teacher: Let's all turn to chapter 11 titled "No!" I'll begin reading while you follow along.

(The teacher reads the first two pages of the chapter and then poses the first question to the group.)

During Reading

Teacher-Generated Questions

Teacher: So how did Leslie die? (literal)

Donita: She was swinging on the rope, and it broke. When she fell, she hit her head and died.

Teacher: Did Jess's father respond to the situation in a way that you would have expected based on his previous treatment of the boy? (inferential)

Carla: No. I was really shocked. The book never really let us see another side of his father other than being cold and mean. The part where his dad chases him down and carries him back to the truck shows that he really loved Jess.

Student-Generated Questions

The teacher then asks students to come up with their own questions.

Teacher: Harrison, have you thought of a question for the group?

Harrison: Yes, I have. Why do you think Jess thought that running away would keep Leslie from dying?

Teacher: Before you answer, let's decide which type of question Harrison is asking. Remember, knowing the type of question will help you decide where you have to go in the text to find the answer.

Carla: I think it is an inferential question because he asked, "Why do *you* think...."

Teacher: Good. Now, who wants to answer the question?

Melody: He knew it really wasn't going to make her not be dead. He was really running away from reality.

Janette: On page 104 it says that he ran west, away from Washington and Laura's house. He was probably blaming himself for her death because he went to Washington and didn't invite her.

(The teacher and students take turns reading and continue to discuss and question the text.)

After Reading

Summarizing

The teacher uses questioning to summarize the plot.

FIGURE 15
Completed Story Map

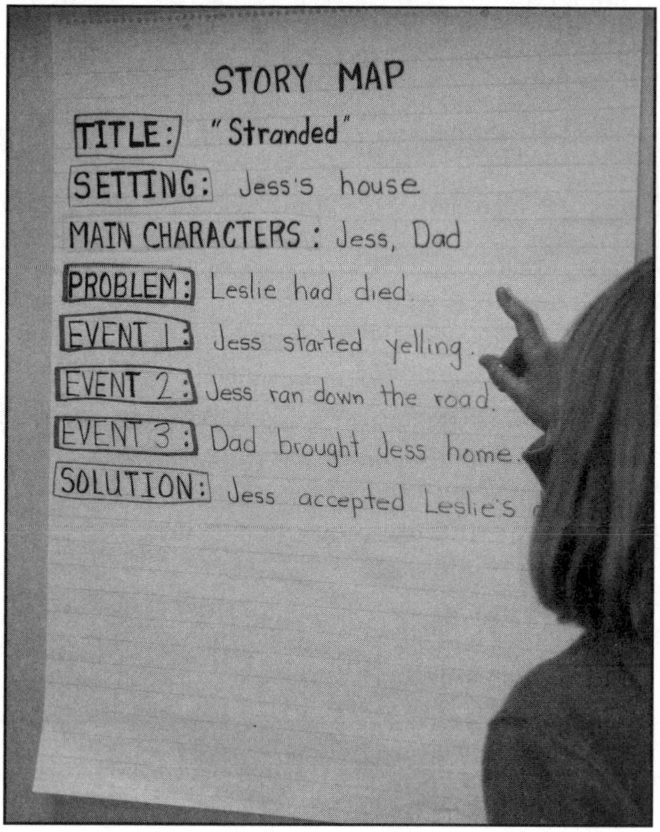

STORY MAP
TITLE: "Stranded"
SETTING: Jess's house
MAIN CHARACTERS: Jess, Dad
PROBLEM: Leslie had died.
EVENT 1: Jess started yelling.
EVENT 2: Jess ran down the road.
EVENT 3: Dad brought Jess home.
SOLUTION: Jess accepted Leslie's

Teacher: Let's summarize this chapter together using this story map (see Figure 15). Who were the main characters in this chapter?

Melody: There were only two main characters, Jess and his dad.

Teacher: Does everyone agree with that?

Students: Yes.

Teacher: OK, I'll write that under main characters. Where did most of this chapter take place?

Carla: Most of the story took place either in Jess's house or around his house.

Teacher: Does everyone agree with that?

Students: Yes.

Teacher: So that brings us to the problem, which is pretty obvious—Leslie is dead.

(Teacher writes the information on the graphic organizer.)

Teacher: What were the actions taken as a result of the problem?

Harrison: Actually, there were several. First, Jess started yelling. Next, he took off running down the road, and, finally, his dad brought him home and he went to bed.

(Teacher records responses on the organizer.)

Teacher: Do you think that the problem has been solved or will there be a solution?

Donita: Well, Leslie isn't going to return from the dead. I guess the problem really is that Jess doesn't know how to deal with her death.

Teacher: Maybe we should leave this part blank until we read the rest of the story.

Independent Written Response

Teacher: For homework tonight, I want you to read chapter 12 titled "Stranded." After you read the chapter, I want you to write a paragraph explaining why you believe the author used this title for the chapter (see Figure 16).

Independent writing activities may take more than one day to complete, depending on the assignment. These written responses provide an opportunity to extend students' comprehension. Students also can share their work in the next small-group meeting. Teachers can create a writing rubric to score students' work, if desired.

FIGURE 16
Student Writing Sample Based on "Stranded"

"Stranded"

I think that "Stranded" is a very appropriate title for this chapter. Jess felt stranded because Leslie deserted him. Jess was thrown into a very uncomfortable situation trying to deal with Leslie's death. He didn't know what to say, and he didn't know what to do. Jess felt stranded without Leslie to talk to.

See Figure 17 for a completed lesson plan for narrative text. The narrative lesson plan for the maturing reader requires careful teacher planning in order to ensure that students are being challenged at an appropriate level. As students engage in reading and discussing more complex story lines, teachers need to scaffold instruction to enhance students' critical thinking, a skill that is necessary throughout the maturing reader stage.

Instructional Components of the Maturing Reader Lesson Plan: Expository Text

There are two components to the expository text lesson plan (see Figure 18). The first component, word study, is the same as the narrative text lesson plan. The second component, comprehension, focuses on teacher and student questioning because this strategy enables students to develop critical thinking skills with content area material. Additional strategies include extrapolating the main idea and supporting details, sequencing, comparing and contrasting, and identifying cause-and-effect relationships. All of these strategies help students summarize information from the text. Finally, by completing an independent written response, students are able to summarize information from the text while experimenting with different types of writing formats for expository text.

Word Study

The following dialogue focuses on students who are continuing to learn about the connections between stress, meaning, and parts of speech. This exchange takes place on the second day of the sort as students study two-syllable homographs.

Teacher: Today, we are going to do a spelling sort. I am going to say the homographs we learned yesterday in a sentence, and I want you to place each word in one of two columns, depending on whether the stress is on the first or second syllable.

(After the students complete the spelling sort, the teacher leads the discussion.)

Teacher: OK, let's take a look at the first word, *REcord*. What syllable is stressed?

Jerry: I have it in the first syllable column.

Teacher: How about *conDUCT*?

Maury: That word is stressed in the second syllable.

(Students continue to go through the words and discuss each word as the stress changes from first to second syllable.)

Teacher: OK, let's review our homographs and their parts of speech.

Ginny: When the stress is on the first syllable, the word is a verb.

Kathy: And when the stress is on the second syllable, the word is a noun.

FIGURE 17
Completed Maturing Reader Lesson Plan: Narrative Text

Components/Activities	Comments
WORD STUDY Features _Drop, Double, or Nothing with ing_ Cycle __3__ Week __2__ ☑ Word Sort or ☐ Spelling Sort and ☐ Dictated Sentence _____ Outside of Group Activity (optional) ☐ Word Hunt ☑ Other vocabulary activity Specify _____	They were talking through the process of adding the ing and seemed to be getting the pattern. Will have to emphasize the idea of "protecting the short vowel sound" as we continue. Omitted dictated sentence b/c this was the first lesson.
COMPREHENSION Text _Bridge to Terabithia_ _____ pp. _chapter 11_ ____ Before Reading ☐ Predicting _from reading last night Chapter 10_ _____ ☑ Making Connections ☑ Previewing Vocabulary ☑ st _relentlessly, uncertainty, lopsided, curtainless, threateningly_ _____ During Reading Teacher-Generated Questions (during or after) ☑ Literal _How did Leslie die? Where did most of the story take place?_ ☐ Inferential _Did Jess's father respond to the situation in a way that you would have expected based on his previous treatment of the boy?_ ☑ Application _(see written response activity)_ _____ ☑ Student-Generated Questions (during and after) After Reading Summarizing Text Structure ☑ Plot ☐ Compare/Contrast ☐ Sequencing (events) ☐ Conflicts/Resolution Activity for Above ☐ Oral discussion ☑ Graphic organizer Specify _story map_ ☑ Independent Written Response (optional) Specify _Why do you think the author used the title "Stranded" for this chapter?_	Students seem to really like the story and are doing the reading – they were able to ask and answer questions. Vocab. was challenging – needed to review Students were insightful about Jess's father – they made a personal connection with Jess!

The Maturing Reader Lesson Plan: Expository Text

Components/Activities	Comments
WORD STUDY Features _____ Cycle _____ Week _____ ☐ Word sort or ☐ Spelling sort and ☐ Dictated Sentence _____ Outside of Group Activity (optional) ☐ Word Hunt ☐ Other vocabulary activity Specify _____	
COMPREHENSION Text _____ pp. _____ Before Reading ☐ Activating Background Knowledge ☐ Previewing Text Structure ☐ Previewing Vocabulary List _____ _____	
During Reading Teacher-Generated Questions (during or after) ☐ Literal _____ _____ ☐ Inferential _____ _____ ☐ Application _____ _____ ☐ Student-Generated Questions (during and after)	
After Reading Summarizing Text Structure ☐ Main Ideas/Supporting Details ☐ Sequencing (events) ☐ Compare/Contrast ☐ Cause/Effect Activity for Above ☐ Oral discussion ☐ Graphic organizer Specify _____ _____ ☐ Independent Written Response (optional) Specify _____ _____	

Dictated Sentence

Teacher: Now it's time for our dictated sentence. Today, I'd like you to use an apostrophe to show where the words are stressed: *I am going to record your conduct on your report card.*

Teacher: I'll say it again and then you can say it.

(The teacher repeats sentence and then students say sentence chorally. The teacher then monitors while students complete their sentence.)

Comprehension

The text used for the lesson is an article from *Time for Kids*. This special supplement discusses the United Nations International Children's Emergency Fund (UNICEF) and the implications for this organization as they relate to children around the world.

Before Reading

Activating Background Knowledge

Teacher: Yesterday, we began reading about the world help organization called UNICEF. Who remembers what UNICEF is and what it does?

(Students recall factual information about UNICEF from the previous lesson.)

Teacher: Today, we are going to read about how UNICEF is helping with supplying clean water to many people around the world. Turn to page 4 and take a look at the one-page article.

Previewing Text Structure

Teacher: In looking at this one-page article, what do you notice about the way the article is laid out?

Kathy: It looks like a newspaper article, and it also has a graph.

Jerry: There is also a separate box at the bottom of the page with a large question mark. I guess this will be a question for us to answer after we read the article.

Maury: I also notice that there is a subheading under the main title.

Previewing Vocabulary

Teacher: Let's look at some words that will be important to understand as we read this article. The first word is *sanitation*. Does anyone know what that word means?

Ginny: I think is has something to do with garbage collection.

Teacher: Yes, that is a part of sanitation. It means to keep the environment clean. Sanitation also includes keeping the water and air clean so that we can prevent disease. Another word that you may not have heard before is *latrine*.

A latrine is an outside toilet. Many places in the world still do not have toilets inside their houses, which can create health problems.

Teacher: I think we are ready to being reading the article. Read the first two paragraphs to yourself and then we'll talk about it.

(The students read the first two paragraphs of the article.)

During Reading

Teacher-Generated Questions

Teacher: Name two reasons that it is difficult to get clean water in some parts of the world? (literal)

Gian: For one thing, some people have to walk for an hour to get to a river or a water pump.

Jerry: Even if they get to the water, much of it is dirty and dangerous to drink.

Teacher: What are the major problems in drinking dirty water? (literal)

Maury: Many children become sick when they drink dirty water. In one city, 55 children die each day from drinking dirty water.

Teacher: The next part of the article is titled "Making a Difference." The heading can give us a good idea about what the next section will be about. What do you think the article will be talking about in this section?

Ginny: Well, this whole magazine is about UNICEF, so I think it will tell us how UNICEF is helping with the dirty water problem.

Teacher: I want you to partner read the rest of the article. You read the first two paragraphs, and your partner will read the last two paragraphs. Read to find out how UNICEF is helping these poor communities get clean water.

(The teacher monitors as the partners complete reading the article.)

Teacher: How did the money collected by the children help with the dirty water problems in Mozambique? (literal)

Kathy: The money they collected was used to build latrines in schools.

Gian: The money was also used for clubs that help spread the news about good health practices.

Teacher: Do you think that adults listen to the children when they tell them what they need to do to keep the water supply clean? (inferential)

Maury: They must listen some because the article said that 800 million people are drinking cleaner water.

(The teacher and students end the lesson by reviewing the data found in the chart concerning daily water consumption in selected cities.)

After Reading

Summarizing: Cause-and-Effect Relationships

Teacher: There are several cause-and-effect relationships that we can review in the article that we read today. Let's look back in the article to find four important cause-and-effect relationships to include in our graphic organizer. (See Figure 19 and Cause and Effect form in Appendix C.)

Independent Written Response

Teacher: I would like you to write a short paragraph explaining why clean water is a valuable resource. You can work on your paragraph during independent work time, or you can complete it for homework. Bring your paragraphs to our next group meeting so you can share them with the group.

See Figure 20 for a completed lesson plan for expository text. The expository lesson plan for maturing readers focuses on summarizing information so students are able to identify essential details and differentiate between essential and nonessential details of content area material. Again, teacher preparation is key to students' success because as students navigate difficult text, teachers provide them with the supportive environment necessary to guide their understanding.

FIGURE 19
Completed Cause and Effect Organizer

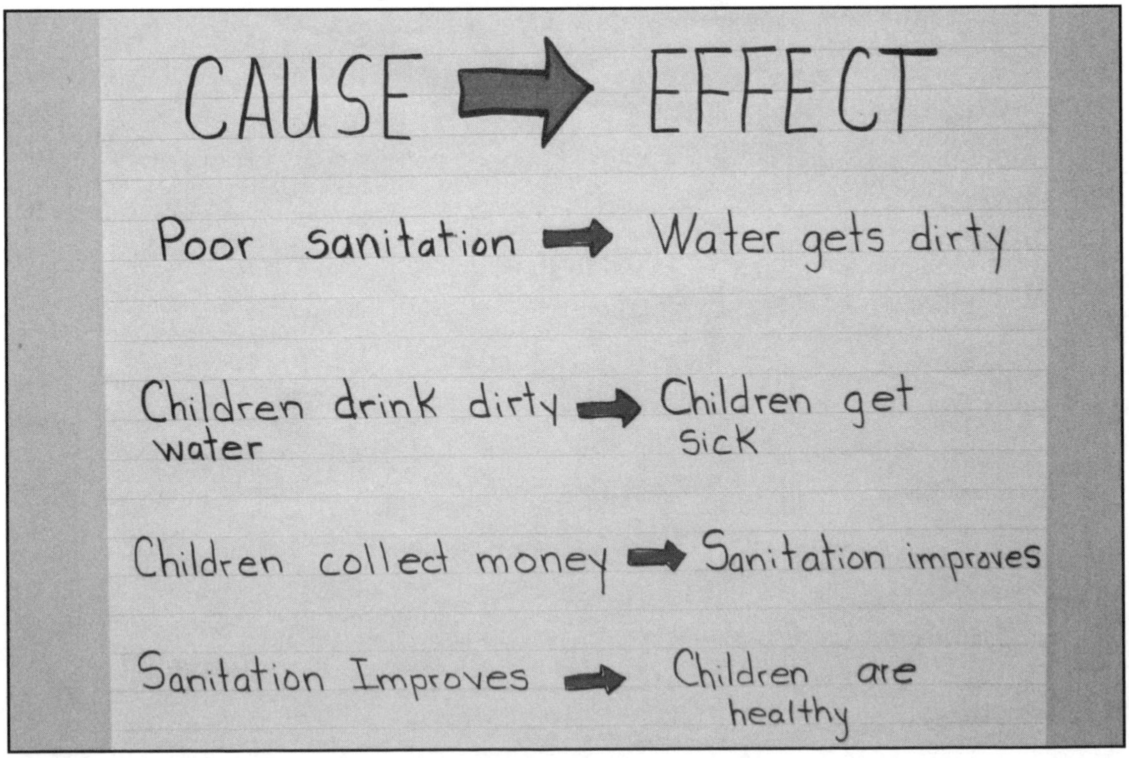

CAUSE ➡ EFFECT

Poor sanitation ➡ Water gets dirty

Children drink dirty water ➡ Children get sick

Children collect money ➡ Sanitation improves

Sanitation Improves ➡ Children are healthy

FIGURE 20
Completed Maturing Reader Lesson Plan: Expository Text

Components/Activities	Comments
WORD STUDY Features _Homographs–syllable stress_ Cycle __3__ Week __5__ ☐ Word sort or ☑ Spelling sort and ☑ Dictated Sentence _I am going to record your conduct on your_ _report card._ Outside of Group Activity (optional) ☑ Word Hunt ☐ Other vocabulary activity Specify _____	They didn't quite get it at first. We practiced stress with their own names and then they had an easier time. Part of speech took some time! Will need to do this again.
COMPREHENSION Text _UNICEF article from Time for Kids (cont.)_ pp. __4__ Before Reading ☑ Activating Background Knowledge ☑ Previewing Text Structure ☑ Previewing Vocabulary List _sanitation, latrine_	Students had a hard time relating to this — they've never been out of water or have had to purify water before they drank it.
During Reading Teacher-Generated Questions (during or after) ☑ Literal _Name two reasons why it is difficult to get clean water in_ _some parts of the world._ ☑ Inferential _Do you think that adults listen to the children when_ _they tell them what they need to do to keep the water supply clean?_ ☑ Application _See Written response_ ☐ Student-Generated Questions (during and after)	
After Reading Summarizing Text Structure ☐ Main Ideas/Supporting Details ☐ Sequencing (events) ☐ Compare/Contrast ☑ Cause/Effect Activity for Above ☐ Oral discussion ☑ Graphic organizer Specify _What's the Big Idea?_ ☑ Independent Written Response (optional) Specify _Explain why clean water is a valuable resource._	 Share written responses to tomorrow's group.

Conclusion

Maturing readers are developing their skills as critical readers and writers. Although they do the majority of their reading silently and independently, the teacher needs to provide explicit instruction, particularly in the area of comprehension. This scaffolding of instruction is essential for maturing readers as they move toward the advanced reader stage.

CHAPTER 5

The Advanced Reader Stage

Advanced readers can independently read and understand text on a literal level. However, they still require teacher assistance as they continue to develop their higher level thinking skills, which include evaluating and critiquing texts. The goal for advanced readers is to be able to read and understand text independently as well as be able to form an opinion about the information presented to them.

The main difference between maturing readers and advanced readers is that advanced readers read the majority of their texts independently, outside of small-group instruction. Therefore, the lesson plan for advanced readers does not include a "During Reading" section. However, to accommodate these readers, we have moved the "Before Reading" section to the end of the lesson plan to help prepare students for independent reading. During their independent reading, students can formulate different types of questions or complete an independent written response. The teacher's role with advanced readers is to guide their higher level thinking about text rather than their actual reading of text.

Characteristics of Advanced Readers in Reading, Writing, and Spelling

Reading

Most students in the advanced reading stage are fervent readers. They are mastering their metacognitive skills as they monitor, regulate, and repair their learning. Advanced readers are learning how to critically evaluate text and combine their learning from multiple sources in order to make an informed conclusion or opinion. They can take what they have learned and apply this knowledge to new situations.

Advanced readers continue to learn about the meaning and elements of figurative language including analogies, hyperbole, idioms, and imagery. Advanced readers are also learning about the relationship between an author's use of literary devices in a text (e.g., irony, symbolism, tone, and mood) and his or her purpose for writing the text.

These students are taught how to identify an author's position in persuasive text and describe techniques the author uses to support that position. These techniques may include testimonials, statistics, and other methods that appeal to reason or emotion. In addition, students can distinguish between fact and opinion and recognize propaganda (e.g., advertising, media, politics, warfare), bias, and stereotypes in various types of texts.

Advanced readers form and revise questions for investigations, including questions arising from readings, assignments, and units of study in order to create a hypothesis statement. Students also create literal, inferential, and application questions as they read to clarify the text's message. They can locate appropriate print and nonprint information using texts and technical resources, including databases. Finally, they are learning to distinguish between accurate and inaccurate or misleading information.

Texts for Advanced Readers

Advanced readers need a variety of challenging material to further advance their critical reading skills. They continue to read from a variety of genres as they automatically incorporate a wide variety of comprehension strategies. Appropriate texts are rich in vocabulary and provide a variety of the aforementioned language elements. Poetry, magazine articles, and documents, as well as award-winning and classic literary pieces, should all be a part of advanced readers' reading experience. Comprehension instruction focuses on crucial thinking skills as students become more responsible for reading text independently.

For teachers who continue to use leveled books as a part of their literacy program, the following book levels are appropriate for advanced readers:

Leveling System	Book Levels
Fountas and Pinnell	U–Z+

Writing

In addition to being avid readers, students in the advanced stage of reading are avid writers. They write in a variety of forms, including descriptive, narrative, expository, persuasive, and technical. Advanced readers are fine-tuning their abilities to express themselves in a clear, concise manner.

Students in the advanced reader stage continue to learn how to use specialized vocabulary in their writing. They attempt to choose words and phrases appropriate for specific purposes and various audiences. In addition, they use more precise words such as powerful verbs, specific nouns, and vivid adjectives and adverbs to help create images in the reader's mind. They also use these words to convey mood and develop characters. Students in the advanced reader stage continue to develop the use of voice appropriate to the purpose of the piece.

Advanced readers also are able to use the writing process effectively to publish final copies of various writing formats. Finally, they are learning to use the previously mentioned elements of figurative language in their writing.

Spelling

Advanced readers hold a solid placement in the meaning layer of spelling development. These students have mastered basic issues related to syllable patterns. They are continuing to learn about the spelling–meaning connection, particularly with regard to content-specific vocabulary. Students in this stage are becoming proficient with structural analysis—that is, they recognize meaningful word parts such as base words, root words, prefixes, and suffixes.

In order for students to understand the spelling–meaning connection, words in the meaning layer are often presented in *derivationally related* pairs—for example, pre-*scribe* and pre*scrip*tion. Students are able to detect the relationship between these two words based on the Latin root *scrib*, meaning "to write." Because of the significant number of Latin and Greek roots in the English language and their relation to the spelling–meaning connection, students should continue studying them throughout the advanced reader stage.

It is best to begin word study at this stage with words that have obvious connections, such as those with Greek roots or the most common pairs that students encounter. Once students have established a foundation of these common derivationally related words, then they will be ready to study the less frequent pairs and morphemes. Students typically study one root word per week when studying Latin or Greek root words; therefore, a word sort or spelling sort is not an appropriate word study activity. During the word study component of the lesson plan, students should be actively engaged in a discussion of the meaning of the root word and the meaning connection to the list of words. For example, students can use a dictionary to find out if the root has a Latin or Greek origin. Further, students can complete other vocabulary activities, such as the Vocabulary Word Map (see Appendix C), Root Tree (see Appendix C), or Name That Word (see chapter 2), so students can focus on the spelling and the meaning of the words.

A weekly scope and sequence has been provided in Appendix B to assist teachers as they plan for and teach the word study component of the lesson. It has been adapted and modified from *Words Their Way: Word Study for Phonics, Vocabulary and Spelling Instruction* (Bear et al., 2004) and *Word Journeys: Assessment-Guided Phonics, Spelling, and Vocabulary Instruction* (Ganske, 2000). Please note that the scope and sequence is provided only as a guideline. It is crucial for teachers to use assessment to guide their instruction. If students have not mastered a given list, do not move on to study new features. Rather, reteach and review the features students are confusing. The features studied during the advanced reader stage are shown in Table 6.

Differentiating the Lesson Plans

Advanced readers can successfully navigate through most narrative and expository pieces with ease. Again, we present two lesson plans: narrative and expository. We also include classroom dialogue to guide readers through each section of the lesson. A completed lesson plan can be found at the end of each lesson.

Instructional Components of the Advanced Reader Lesson Plan: Narrative Text

The narrative text lesson plan for advanced readers (see Figure 21) begins with the word study component. Although the word sort and spelling sort remain the same as the

Consonant Alternations (examples)	• Adding /SHəN/ with *ation* (pronunciation changes—import/importation, plant/plantation) • Adding /SHəN/—*ss* + *ion* (pronunciation changes—aggress/aggression, obsess/obsession) • Adding /SHəN/—*c* + *ian* (pronunciation changes—music/musician, politic/politician) • Adding /SHəN/—*e*-drop + *ion* (pronunciation and spelling changes—calculate/calculation, educate/education) • Adding /SHəN/—*e*-drop + *ion* (pronunciation and spelling changes—immerse/immersion, revise/revision) • Adding /SHəN/—*de*-drop + *sion* (pronunciation and spelling changes—collide/collision, expand/expansion, provide/provision) • Adding /SHəN/—other predictable changes (pronunciation and spelling changes—admit/admission, describe/description, convert/conversion) • Other consonant alternations with pronunciation changes (authentic/authenticity, confident/confidential) • Other consonant alternations with pronunciation and spelling changes (face/facial, influence/influential, space/spacious)
Vowel Alternations (examples)	• Long to short (nation/national, dream/dreamt, divide/division, telescope/telescopic, induce/induction) • Long to schwa (major/majority, gene/genetic, invite/invitation, compose/composition) • Short to schwa (emphatic/emphasis, celebrate/celebrity, critic/criticize, chronic/chronology)
Latin Suffixes (examples)	*ary/ery/ory* (primary/discovery/history) *ity* with base words, *e*-drop, and *ble* (minor/minority, active/activity, able/ability)
Doubling With Polysyllabic Base Words	• Inflected endings—*ed, ing*—Doubling with polysyllabic base words (expel/expelled, submit/submitted) • Inflected endings—*ed, ing*—No doubling with polysyllabic base words (appear/appeared, attend/attended) • Other suffixes—Doubling and no change with polysyllabic base words (regret/regrettable/regretful)
Polysyllabic Homographs	• Pronunciation and part of speech—verb, noun, adjective (graduate/graduate, separate/separate)
Polysyllabic Plurals	• Spelling changes in plurals (analysis/analyses, vertebra/vertebrae, memorandum/memoranda, syllabus/syllabi)
Assimilated Prefixes (examples)	• *ad* • *com* • *dis* • *ex* • *in* • *ob* • *sub*
Other Latin and Greek Roots (examples)	• *aud*—to hear • *sope*—to see • *ped*—foot, child • *spir*—to breath • *phon*—sound • *aud*—to hear

Components/Activities	Comments
WORD STUDY Features_____ Cycle _____ Week _____ ☐ Word Sort or ☐ Spelling Sort or ☐ Word meaning discussion Outside of Group Activity (optional) ☐ Word Hunt ☐ Student sentences ☐ Other vocabulary activity Specify _____	
COMPREHENSION After Reading Summarizing Text Structure ☐ Plot ☐ Compare/Contrast ☐ Sequencing (events)_____ ☐ Conflicts/Resolution Activity for Above ☐ Oral discussion ☐ Graphic organizer Specify _____ Teacher-Generated Questions ☐ Literal _____ _____ ☐ Inferential _____ _____ ☐ Application _____ _____ ☐ Student-Generated Questions (during or after)	
Before Reading ☐ Predicting ☐ Making Connections ☐ Previewing Vocabulary List _____ Independent Reading Assignment (during or after) Text _____ pp. _____ Independent Written Response (during or after) Specify _____ _____ _____	

previous lesson plans, the dictated sentence is no longer completed because students compose their own sentences to demonstrate that they understand the words they are studying. These sentences, along with word hunts and other vocabulary-building activities, are completed outside of small-group time. The comprehension component is the focus of this lesson plan as students refine their critical reading skills. The "Before Reading" and "After Reading" sections have been transposed on this lesson plan to accommodate the reading that students do independently. Therefore, the comprehension component begins with after-reading activities, including summarizing and teacher and student questioning. The lesson concludes with before-reading activities, including predicting, making connections, and previewing vocabulary, so that the teacher can prepare students for their independent reading assignment.

Word Study

The students in this lesson are learning the spelling–meaning connection as they explore number-related root words. During this week, the students are sorting three different root words: *quad*, *pent*, and *uni*. In this exchange, the students are starting a new sort. It is an open sort; therefore, the teacher will not provide students with the header words or show the students the pattern they are studying. Teachers should allow students a full week to study the new features. Again, students should prepare their individual word study cards before coming to the small group to save valuable instructional time.

Teacher: Today we are going to start a new sort. (The teacher lays the words cards in front of the group.)

Teacher: OK, what do you notice about the words in this week's sort?

Michael: Well, they have similar beginnings.

Teacher: What do you mean?

Michael: Well, the words all begin with *penta*, *quadr*, or *uni*.

Teacher: Does anyone remember what we call a group of letters that has direct meaning?

Meghan: It's either a prefix or a root word.

Teacher: Right, Meghan. It's one of those. Can anyone help her out?

Kevin: It's a root word. A prefix can be added onto a root word or base word, but they both have specific meanings and cannot stand alone as a real word.

Teacher: Good. You remembered a lot about root words and prefixes. Let's start sorting them and see what we come up with.

(The teacher guides sort, and then students discuss the words *square* and *reunion* because the students are not sure why they might be included in this sort or where they go.)

pentadactyl	quadrangle	unicycle
pentagon	quadrant	unicorn
pentameter	quadriceps	uniform
pentathlon	quadrilateral	unify
pentatonic	quadruple	unilateral
	quadruplets	unison
	squad	unity
	square	universal
		universe
		unique
		reunion

Teacher: Who thinks they know what the root words mean? Let's get the dictionary and see what we come up with for meaning for our three root words.

Meghan: These are easy. *Uni* means one—I know that because a unicycle only has one wheel and a unicorn has that one horn on the top of its head.

Teacher: Good. Who else wants to try?

Michael: I think *penta* means six; I think I remember seeing something about the Pentagon building in Washington, DC, having six sides. I'm not sure of the other words though.

Kevin: Well, I think that *quad* means four because we put square in that category, and a square has four sides.

(Using the dictionary, students discover the correct spelling of the root words and the correct meaning of each word. Then, students discuss each word and how it is related in meaning to other words and the root word.)

Teacher: When you go back to your seats, I'd like you to work with a partner and choose three words from each category to use in sentences. Remember to write sentences that show you understand what the words mean. Write your sentences in your word study notebooks, and we will share them during our small-group meeting tomorrow.

Comprehension

The basis for this lesson is a poem titled "The Piano" (Lawrence, 1998). During the previous lesson, the teacher completed the before-reading activities with students, including making connections, predicting, and previewing story vocabulary. The students then were responsible for reading the poem independently.

Before Reading (Previous Lesson)

Making Connections and Predicting

Teacher: Today we are going to look at a poem that falls in the category of a lyric. What do you think of when I say the word *lyric*?

Meghan: When I hear the word *lyric* it makes me think of words in songs.

Teacher: When we talk about lyrics in poetry we are talking about a type of short poem that expresses thoughts or feelings much like those in the lyrics of some songs. The poem we are going to read today is "The Piano." What kind of experiences have you had related to a piano?

Maggie: My experiences with the piano are that my mom makes me practice every day and I don't like to.

Kevin: Pianos remind me of church because that is about the only place I hear it played.

Previewing Vocabulary

Teacher: There is one word that I want you to look at before you read the poem. The word is *insidious*. What does this word mean?

Michael: I'm not sure, but I think it has something to do with evil.

Teacher: In a way you are right. The word *insidious* means harmful or enticing. For example, taking illegal drugs can be an insidious habit.

The teacher ends the lesson by asking students to read the poem for homework. In addition, the teacher asks the students to come up with three questions—one literal, one inferential, and one application—as they read the poem. These questions will be shared with the group the next day.

After Reading (Next Lesson)

Teacher: Because the poem is short, I'm going to read it again to refresh your memories.

(Teacher reads poem as students follow along.)

Teacher: Why don't we share some of the questions you came up with when you read this poem yesterday. Who would like to start?

Student-Generated Questions

Michael: What is the setting of the poem?

Maggie: It takes place in a parlor, on a Sunday evening long ago.

Katie: Who is playing the piano?

Kevin: The child's mother.

Teacher: So far, we've only heard literal questions. Who has an inferential or application question they would like to ask?

Meghan: I do. How do you know that the author is writing about something that happened in the past?

Michael: The poem talks about "taking me back" and "flood of remembrance."

(Students continue to share their questions.)

Teacher-Generated Questions

Teacher: What do you think is the subject of Lawrence's poem? (inferential)

Katie: I think it is loneliness or regret. The author seems really sad.

Teacher: How does Lawrence use the word *insidious* in the poem? (literal)

Meghan: I think it has something to do with hearing the music over and over again that makes him remember things that are sad or troubling.

(The teacher leads students further in a discussion of this word and the poem.)

Independent Written Response

Teacher: For homework tonight, I want you to paraphrase this poem to show what the speaker says is happening at the present time and also what he finds himself remembering. This assignment requires you to both summarize and analyze the poem.

The narrative text lesson plan has been adapted to meet the needs of the advanced reader within the context of narrative material. (See Figure 22 for a completed lesson plan for narrative text.) Specifically, the lesson plan addresses the need for advanced readers to begin reading independently, which allows for more small-group instructional time to discuss, analyze, and share ideas students have about the text.

Instructional Components of the Advanced Reader Lesson Plan: Expository Text

The expository lesson plan (see Figure 23) for the advanced reader follows the same sequence as the narrative lesson plan—that is, the lesson plan concludes with the before-reading activities that prepare students for independent reading. The lesson plan begins with the word study component followed by the after-reading activities. The before-reading section also includes an optional independent written response that teachers can assign to students.

Word Study

The following group of students is beginning to study a new Greek root, *hydr*. The teacher introduces the new root and then asks the students to define new words based on their common feature. Because students are only studying one root this week, the focus is vocabulary building; therefore, word sorting and spelling sorting are not

FIGURE 22
Completed Advanced Reader Lesson Plan: Narrative Text

Components/Activities	Comments
WORD STUDY Features _Greek roots_ Cycle _2_ Week _4_ ☑ Word Sort or ☐ Spelling Sort or ☐ Word meaning discussion Outside of Group Activity (optional) ☐ Word Hunt ☑ Student sentences ☐ Other vocabulary activity Specify _Discuss word meanings with a partner; write three sentences from each category._	Able to make the connection with en as a suffix. Good!
COMPREHENSION After Reading Summarizing Text Structure ☑ Plot ☐ Compare/Contrast ☐ Sequencing (events)_____ ☑ Conflicts/Resolution Activity for Above ☐ Oral discussion ☐ Graphic organizer Specify _____ Teacher-Generated Questions ☑ Literal _How does the poet use the word insidious in the poem?_ ☑ Inferential _What do you think is the subject of Lawrence's poem?_ ☐ Application ☑ Student-Generated Questions (during or after)	Michael didn't do the independent reading assignment. Note: Need to do more with poetry – they had a difficult time with this genre.
Before Reading ☑ Predicting ☑ Making Connections ☑ Previewing Vocabulary List _insidious_____ Independent Reading Assignment (during or after) Text _"The Piano"_____ pp. _poem_____ Independent Written Response (during or after) Specify _Summarize and analyze by paraphrasing the poem to show what the speaker says is happening at the present time and what he finds himself remembering_	Challenging vocab. at first – needed to put words into context of poem for better understanding.

FIGURE 23
The Advanced Reader Lesson Plan: Expository Text

Components/Activities	Comments
WORD STUDY Features _____ Cycle _____ Week _____ ☐ Word Sort or ☐ Spelling Sort or ☐ Word meaning discussion Outside of Group Activity (optional) ☐ Word Hunt ☐ Student sentences ☐ Other vocabulary activity Specify _____	
COMPREHENSION After Reading Summarizing Text Structure ☐ Main Idea/Supporting Details ☐ Compare/Contrast ☐ Sequencing (events)_____ ☐ Cause/Effect Activity for Above ☐ Oral discussion ☐ Graphic organizer Specify _____ Teacher-Generated Questions ☐ Literal _____ _____ ☐ Inferential _____ _____ ☐ Application _____ _____ ☐ Student-Generated Questions (during or after)	
Before Reading ☐ Activating Background Knowledge ☐ Previewing Text Structure ☐ Previewing Vocabulary List _____ _____ ☐ Independent Reading Assignment (during or after) Text _____ pp. _____ ☐ Independent Written Response (during or after) Specify _____	

appropriate activities. Rather, the teacher should involve the students in alternating vocabulary activities to enhance their learning about this new word feature.

Teacher: Today we are going to continue our study of Latin and Greek root words. Let's take a look at our words for this week.

(Teacher lays out word cards.)

hydr
hydroplane
hydrate
hydrophobia
hydrology
hydrangea
hydrant
hydrant
hydraulic
hydroelectric
hydroponics

Tom: Well, they all begin with the letters *h, y, d, r.*

Teacher: Are you familiar with any of these words?

Thelma: Well, the only ones I recognize are *hydrant* and *hyroplane.*

Teacher: What do these two words mean?

Bernice: I know that you get water from a hydrant, and when your car hydroplanes, it slides on water.

Teacher: So we know that both words have something to do with water. What about some of these other words?

Paul: I know that a hydrangea is a kind of flower, but I don't know what that would have to do with water except that it needs water to survive—but all flowers need water.

Teacher: I want you to work with your partner today to create a vocabulary root tree for the Greek root *hydr.* You need to find these and other words in the dictionary if you don't know what they mean and then add them to your Root Tree. After you complete your Root Tree, choose five of the words with which to write sentences in your word study notebooks. The next time you come to your small group, I will expect you to tell the rest of the group your words on the Root Tree and what each word means—in your own words. (See Appendix C for a blank Root Tree and Figure 24 for a completed root tree.)

FIGURE 24
Completed Root Tree

Comprehension

This lesson is based on a newspaper article, more specifically a commentary written by Leonard Pitts, Jr., from the *Chattanooga Times Free Press* (2004). The author attempts to persuade the audience that soldiers who are hurt during battle also should be considered as casualties of war. Both the authentic format and content of this piece make this selection an appropriate choice for advanced readers because it exemplifies persuasive text.

Before Reading (Previous Lesson)

Previewing Text Structure

Teacher: The article that you are going to read today is a commentary from the local newspaper written by Leonard Pitts, Jr. In this article, Pitts presents the argument that war casualties should include the injured as well as the dead.

(The teacher continues to discuss with students the purpose of a commentary.)

Activating Prior Knowledge

Teacher: Have you ever known anyone who was injured or who died in a war?

Paul: Yes. My grandfather lost a leg in the Vietnam War.

Abigail: I never knew my uncle, but he died in a war before I was born.

Teacher: As we look at the title, we can tell what the author's viewpoint is going to be. The article is titled "The Wounded Must Be Counted as Casualties of War, Any War." Let's discuss some ideas about what arguments the author might make based on the title.

(The teacher leads the students in a discussion about their ideas.)

Previewing Vocabulary

The teacher did not identify any vocabulary that needed to be introduced.

Independent Written Response

Teacher: As you read this article, list the arguments the author uses to persuade his audience.

After Reading (Next Lesson)

Summarizing (Main Ideas and Supporting Details)

Teacher: Let's take a look at the arguments that you listed.

(Students share their arguments, and the teacher leads the discussion.)

Teacher-Generated Questions

Teacher: Is the author saying that most Americans don't really care about the soldiers who are wounded in the war? (inferential)

Paul: No. I think that he clearly says that it isn't a matter of they don't care, but probably that they just don't understand the implications. I think that most people don't even want to think about it because it is so sad.

Bernice: I guess if you had a friend or relative that was killed in a war, being wounded just doesn't seem that bad. At least they survived.

Teacher: What role do you think the United States government should take in supporting the soldiers that have been wounded in Iraq? (application)

Tom: I think that the government should take full responsibility for supporting them and their families. They have given up so much to protect our country and we should be grateful. Anyone who is wounded in the war should continue to get paid and his or her family should be taken care of. I thought we already did that for the soldiers.

(The discussion continues and is led by both the teacher and the students.)

Independent Written Response

Teacher: Take a look at the last statement in the article: "There's no such thing as 'only wounded.'" Do you agree or disagree with this statement? I want you to write a response to this question; I want you to state your opinion and give at least three supporting details. Bring your assignment back tomorrow to share with the rest of the group. (See Figure 25 for a sample written response to this assignment.)

FIGURE 25
Sample Independent Written Response

> There's No Such Thing As Only Wounded
>
> Suppose that you volunteered to serve your country by joining the army. You leave your family and go to a far away land giving up the finer things in life. Unfortunately, you were a victim of a road side bomb and both your legs are blown off.
>
> You return home for several months in the hospital. You can't afford a car with special gears so you can't get to work. Did I say work? What if you can no longer work? Don't worry, you are only wounded and certainly not a casualty of war.

FIGURE 26
Completed Advanced Reader Lesson Plan: Expository Text

Components/Activities	Comments
WORD STUDY	Students did well with the root words and were coming up with their own words.
Features <u>Hydr (root words)</u> Cycle <u>4</u> Week <u>5</u>	
☐ Word Sort or ☐ Spelling Sort or ☑ Word meaning discussion	
Outside of Group Activity (optional)	
☐ Word Hunt	
☑ Student sentences	
☑ Other vocabulary activity	
Specify <u>Root tree</u>	
COMPREHENSION	
After Reading	
Summarizing Text Structure	
☐ Main Idea/Supporting Details ☐ Compare/Contrast	
☐ Sequencing (events)_____ ☐ Cause/Effect	Arguments were surface level; they are unable to identify the less obvious arguments – lack of personal connection, background knowledge.
Activity for Above	
☑ Oral discussion ☐ Graphic organizer	
Specify <u>Arguments/Supporting points from students</u>	
Teacher-Generated Questions	*Have students also talk about this with their parents as well.
☐ Literal _____	
☑ Inferential <u>Do you think that the author is saying that most Americans don't really care about the soldiers who are wounded in the war?</u>	
☑ Application <u>What role do you think the U.S. gov't should take in supporting the soldiers that have been wounded in Iraq?</u>	
☐ Student-Generated Questions (during or after)	
Before Reading	
☑ Activating Background Knowledge	
☐ Previewing Text Structure	
☐ Previewing Vocabulary	
List <u>None</u>	
_____	Students were able to identify people who had been in a war, but not in their lifetime.
☐ Independent Reading Assignment (during or after)	
Text <u>Newspaper article "Wounded Must Be Counted as Casualties of War, Any War"</u> pp. _____	
☐ Independent Written Response (during or after)	
Specify <u>List arguments made by author as he tries to persuade his audience</u>	

Small-Group Reading Instruction: A Differentiated Teaching Model for Intermediate Readers, Grades 3–8 by Beverly Tyner and Sharon E. Green © 2005. Newark, DE: International Reading Association. May be copied for classroom use.

The expository lesson plan for the advanced reader focuses both on meaning as it relates to the study of words and meaning as it relates to comprehending text. (See Figure 26 for a completed lesson plan for expository text.) As with the narrative lesson plan, the expository lesson plan allows for independent student reading, which is essential for advanced readers who are required to do extensive reading.

Conclusion

Advanced readers are able to draw from experience and knowledge while comprehending the text that they read. They start assuming more responsibility for their learning; however, they still require teacher direction as they critically evaluate text. Advanced readers have reached a level of literacy learning that allows them to access and apply their own knowledge and relate it to the text. They are developing an understanding of the structure of the English language and can apply this understanding when faced with challenging texts. The journey of reading and learning is never ending, but advanced readers are well equipped for their future reading endeavors.

Assessing Student Performance in the Small-Group Differentiated Reading Model

Assessing student performance is critical for many reasons, including tracking student progress, assigning students to flexible groups based on individual need, and assisting in planning appropriate instruction. Assessing student performance in the Small-Group Differentiated Reading Model consists of several informal measures. Although we recognize the importance of formal, standardized, state-level assessments, we do not believe they provide the quality of information necessary to guide a teacher's daily instruction. In many instances, the standardized assessment results are not available until the following school year after the students have matriculated to the next grade. Therefore, teachers cannot use the information to guide their instruction on a daily basis.

There are two types of assessments that will be used in the Small-Group Differentiated Reading Model: (1) pre- and postassessment and (2) ongoing, or formative, assessment. Pre- and postassessment data give the teacher information about overall reading progress and provide instructional reading levels. The pre- and postassessments for fluency should be completed every nine weeks or at the end of each quarter. The pre- and postassessment for word study and comprehension should be completed at the beginning and at the end of the year. (See Table 7 for a brief description of these assessments and timelines for administering them.) Ongoing, or formative, assessments give teachers data to make sound, instructional decisions as they relate to fluency, word study, and comprehension and are, therefore, completed on a continual basis. Teachers should use this formative assessment information to create flexible groups that are the most cohesive at any given time. In other words, if a student is performing above or below that of the others in his or her small group, the teacher can identify another small group in the class that will be a better instructional fit.

Prior to beginning small-group differentiated reading instruction, it is essential to assess the literacy knowledge of each student as it relates to fluency, word study, and comprehension. Using the assessment data, flexible small groups are established based on student needs in these areas. Flexible grouping refers to the teacher's ability to move students in and out of groups as needed based on these aforementioned informal assessments. Assessment should be ongoing to ensure students' instructional needs continue to be met. In our experience, the most powerful assessment data for intermediate readers come from daily teacher observation and interaction with the students within the small-group setting.

This chapter provides assessment information for both fluency and word study. We also examine a variety of informal assessments that measure a student's instructional

T A B L E 7
Pre- and Postassessments vs. Ongoing Assessments for Intermediate Readers

	Fluency	Word Study	Comprehension
Pre/Post	• 4 x 4 Oral Reading Fluency Rating Scale • Every 9 weeks	• Cumulative spelling assessment • Beginning/end of year	• Informal reading inventory with narrative and expository passages (student reads orally/silently) • Assess ability to summarize (retell) and answer different question types (literal, inferential, and application) • At least two times per year (beginning and end)
Ongoing	• Teacher observation • Weekly	• Weekly • Cycles (8–9 weeks)	• Teacher observation • Oral summary in narrative text • Expository Comprehension Assessment • Oral Questioning Response Checklist

reading level and specific aspects of reading comprehension. These aspects include a student's ability to summarize information and answer different types of reading comprehension questions. Note, however, that there are no clearly delineated scores that teachers can use to move students from group to group. Rather, a teacher needs to analyze all available assessment data, including day-to-day observations in small-group instruction. These day-to-day observation data are critical when evaluating the placement of students in flexible groups.

Fluency

Fluency assessment is a critical component of any successful reading program. This is especially important for the evolving reader. Informal measures that are both quantitative (i.e., providing numeric results) and qualitative (i.e., providing information about student behaviors) are helpful in assessing fluency. We discuss fluency assessment in the area of fluency rate (words per minute), as well as attention to phrasing, punctuation, smoothness, and expression. Fluency is an important aspect of a student's overall reading development and, as such, will be documented using pre- and postassessments as well as ongoing assessments. Although fluency is not a part of the maturing reader or advanced reader lesson plans, it should be assessed using the pre- and postassessment to monitor student progress because it continues to play an important role in reading comprehension. However, the ongoing assessments for fluency are only applicable for the evolving reader.

Pre- and Postassessment

Although reading fluency relates to both oral and silent reading, only oral reading fluency is assessed as it relates to this small-group model. Silent reading fluency becomes more important as students matriculate through the grades and is best assessed as it relates to comprehension discussed later in this chapter. A student's reading rate is assessed by determining the number of correct words read per minute (CWPM). It is used as the pre- and postassessment to gauge fluency progress.

Reading rate is reported most often in words per minute (WPM). The following steps are necessary to accurately determine a student's reading rate.

1. Count the actual number of words in the text selection (no less than 150 words).
2. Multiply the number of words by 60.
3. Ask the student to read the appropriate instructional level passage.
4. Time the student's reading of the passage in seconds (e.g., 120 seconds).
5. Divide the words read per minute by the number of seconds to get the words per minute.

WPM Example

Number of words in passage: 250

Multiply by 60 (250 x 60 = 15,000)

Number of seconds to read passage: 100

Divide 15,000 by 100

The total WPM = 150 words per minute

To determine the correct words per minute (CWPM), simply subtract the number of errors from the number of words read.

CWPM Example

Number of words in passage: 250

Student errors: 10

Number of words read correctly: 240 (250 - 10)

Multiply by 60 (240 x 60 = 14,400)

Number of seconds to read passage: 100

Divide 14,400 by 100

The total CWPM = 144 words per minute

The next step is to determine what oral reading rates are acceptable for various grade levels. Although there are a number of studies that have established norms, Table 8 is based on large-scale norms for students in grades 3 through 5. Hasbrouck and Tindal (1992) normed over 7,000 students reading correct words per minute at three points (fall, winter, and spring) during the school year. (Note that correct words per minute will vary slightly from words per minute in that the rates will be lower.) This table also gives percentile information that will be helpful in tracking student progress. These norms were established regardless of a student's instructional reading level so that these norms can only gauge a student's ability to read at a particular grade level.

TABLE 8
Median Oral Reading Rates for Students in Grades 3–5

Grade	Percentile	Fall CWPM*	Winter CWPM*	Spring CWPM*
	75	107	123	142
3	50	79	93	114
	25	65	70	87
	75	125	133	143
4	50	99	112	118
	25	72	89	92
	75	126	143	151
5	50	105	118	128
	25	77	93	100

* Reported in Correct Words Per Minute (CWPM)

TABLE 9
Median Oral Reading Rates for Students in Grades 6–8

Grade	Percentile	Fall CWPM*	Winter CWPM*	Spring CWPM*
	90	171	185	201
	75	143	160	172
6	50	115	132	145
	25	91	106	117
	10	73	81	90
	90	200	207	213
	75	175	183	193
7	50	147	158	167
	25	126	134	146
	10	106	116	124
	90	208	217	221
	75	183	196	198
8	50	156	167	171
	25	126	144	145
	10	100	113	115

* Reported in Correct Words Per Minute (CWPM)

Oral reading rates for students in grades 6 through 8 are found in Table 9. These norms were established for more than 3,500 students in a study conducted by Howe and Shinn (2001). Again, these norms were established using correct words per minute and provide percentiles for three points during the school year (fall, winter, and spring.) These norms can be used to monitor student progress in fluency development or can be compared to standard measures established by the school district.

In addition to quantitative data, a 4 x 4 Oral Reading Fluency Rating Scale (see Appendix A) can be used to assess qualitative skills in oral reading fluency. These skills include appropriate phrasing, attention to punctuation, general rate and smoothness, and expression. This instrument can be used as a pre- and postassessment as students read an instructional level passage individually. The teacher marks the rating scale in each of the four areas as he or she listens to the student read. The 4 x 4 Oral Reading Fluency Rating Scale is structured so that quarterly data can be recorded on the same sheet.

Ongoing Assessment

Ongoing assessment in the area of reading fluency can be assessed easily in daily small-group instruction. Ongoing assessment data is collected on a weekly basis by making informal anecdotal notes during small-group reading instruction.

While listening to students read orally, the teacher makes notes concerning the qualitative fluency skills such as those listed on the 4 x 4 Oral Reading fluency Rating Scale. This gives the teacher a "snapshot" of the student's progress in fluency to supplement the pre- and postassessment data.

Tracking Progress

Teachers can use the Oral Reading Fluency Class Profiles (see Appendix A) to record and track student fluency at established points during the school year. First- and fourth-quarter results can serve as the pre- and postassessment, along with midyear or quarterly assessments that can be completed during small-group instruction. Oral reading fluency class profiles specific to each grade level provide median scores at three points during the school year so that the teacher can easily identify students who might need extra fluency practice and support.

Figure 27 displays the Oral Reading Fluency Class Profile for Mrs. Harmon's fifth-grade class. Mrs. Harmon plans to assess fluency in her classroom three times during the school year. Thus far, she has completed the fluency assessments for fall and winter. Notice that the median fluency rate is shown on each of the three scales. In the fall, nine of the students in the classroom scored below the median fluency rate of 105, although four of these students were close to the median and scored in the 90s range. Using this information, Mrs. Harmon supported students with repeated readings of independently leveled text and additional oral reading practice with feedback. Notice that the scores for the winter assessment show three additional students reaching grade-level scores on oral reading fluency.

Word Study

Word study is assessed easily by giving and analyzing an informal spelling inventory. Spelling inventories can be done as both pre- and postassessments and ongoing assessments. Pre- and postassessments should be given at the beginning and end of the year. Ongoing assessments should be administered weekly and at the end of each cycle. Again, cycles typically last eight weeks. Each of the eight weeks contains different features for study and corresponding word lists. If students are not able to achieve at

FIGURE 27
Oral Reading Fluency Class Profile
Grade 5 Teacher: Mrs. Harmon

Fall		Winter		Spring	
-180-	Laura (178)	-180-	Laura & Paul (180+)	-180-	
	Paul (175)				
-170-		-170-	Pedro (172)	-170-	
			ShaDerrika (161)		
-160-	Pedro (160)	-160-	Jenae (160)	-160-	
	Jenae (154)				
-150-	ShaDerrika (150)	-150-		-150-	
-140-	Mark (140)	-140-		-140-	
	Adrien (138)				
-130-	Leuel (128)	-130-	Rodney (129)	-130-	
	Andre (120)		Anna (125)		←——→ (125)
			Andre (125)		
-120-	Rodney (119)	-120-	Jennifer (120)	-120-	
			Mason (120)		
		←——————→	Bill (119)		
	Bill (114)		John (118)		
-110-	Lee (107)	-110-	Lee (115)	-110-	
←——————→	Mason (105)				
-100-	Jennifer (100)	-100-	Michael (100)	-100-	
	John (96)		Meredith (95)		
-90-	Anna (95)	-90-		-90	
	Michael (90)				
-80-	Meredith (83)	-80-	Spencer (82)	-80-	
	Spencer (78)		Clyde (75)		
-70-		-70	Dedrick (70)	-70-	
	Clyde (67)				
-60-	Dedrick (60)	-60-	Pat (61)	-60-	
-50-	Pat (50)	-50-		-50-	
-40-		-40-		-40-	
-30-		-30-		-30-	
-20-		-20-		-20-	

Date _____   Date _____   Date _____

Passage _____   Passage _____   Passage _____

_____   _____   _____

_____   _____   _____

Comments _____   Comments _____   Comments _____

_____   _____   _____

_____   _____   _____

least 90% on their weekly spelling assessment and 85% on their cycle assessment, teachers should spend more time teaching a given feature(s). Mastery is critical because the scope and sequence for word study is organized in such a way that the identified features build on one another.

Pre- and Postassessment

Teachers first should administer one of the reader stage pretests in order to find out the specific strengths and areas of need for each student in the class. (See Appendix A for the word study pre-and postassessments.) For students in grades 3 and 4, administer the evolving reader pretest. For students in grades 5 and 6, administer the maturing reader pretest. For students in grades 7 and 8, administer the advanced reader pretest.

When administering the assessment, have the students first number their papers from 1 to 30—similar to a weekly spelling test. Read each word on the pre- and posttest list in the following manner: Read the word, use the word in a sentence, and then read the word again. For example: *Chain*. The *chain* on his bicycle was broken. *Chain*.

To score the pre- and postassessments, determine the score for each cycle area. To determine the cycle score, add the number of incorrect words within a given cycle. Then, use this score to determine a starting point of cycle instruction. A student is allowed one error per cycle. When a student makes two or more errors in a given cycle, this becomes the starting place for instruction. For example, in Figure 28, during the Evolving Reader Year 2 Preassessment, the student made one error in Cycle 1, two errors in Cycle 2, four errors in Cycle 3, and three errors in Cycle 4. As such, the starting point for instruction would be in Cycle 2. Based on the student's errors, instruction should begin in week 1 of Cycle 2. If a student has less than two errors per cycle on any given pretest, the teacher should administer the assessment for the next stage. For example, if a student spells all the words on the Evolving Reader Year 2 Preassessment correctly, give the student the Maturing Reader Year 1 Preassessment.

Ongoing Assessment

There are different types of ongoing assessments. The first is a weekly assessment develped by the teacher. Using this weekly spelling assessment, a teacher will be able to identify whether the students have mastered the features studied on a given week and are ready to move forward. The second ongoing assessment is the nine-week cycle assessment (see Appendix A). This assessment is given at the end of each cycle and will provide data that will allow a teacher to determine if students have internalized previous features studied. Administration for both ongoing assessments is the same as the pre- and postassessment instructions: Read the word, read the sentence provided, and then read the word again.

To score the ongoing assessments, determine the score based on a percentage. To determine this percentage, add the total number of correct words and divide by the number of test items. In the example in Figure 29, the student scored 88% correct. This score shows that the student is ready to move on; however, a further analysis of his errors shows he would benefit from some additional work with the digraphs *ph* and *qu*.

Sample Spelling Preassessment: Evolving Reader: Year 2

Name: _____

Date: _August 20, 2004_____

Stage: _Evolving_____

Year (circle one)   1   (2)

(Pre)   Post   (circle one)

	Word	Student Spelling	Number of Errors Per Cycle
1	charm	charm	
2	your	your	
3	dear	deer	X
4	hurt	hurt	
5	gym	gym	
6	stretch	stretch	
7	judge	judge	
8	screw	screw	
	Cycle 1		**1**
9	squint	scint	X
10	you'd	you'd	
11	heck	heck	
12	gnat	nat	X
13	sprung	sprung	
14	unkind	unkind	
15	headstone	headstone	
16	overview	overview	
	Cycle 2		**2**
17	how's	how's	
18	they're	their	X
19	whizzed	whizzed	
20	dotted	doted	X
21	riding	rideing	X
22	know	know	
23	bravest	bravest	
24	lawful	lawfull	X
	Cycle 3		**4**
25	speechless	speechless	
26	humid	humid	
27	napkin	napkin	
28	mammal	mamal	X
29	migrate	migrait	X
30	construct	costruct	X
	Cycle 4		**3**
Total Number of Errors			**10**

FIGURE 29
Sample Ongoing Spelling Cycle Assessment for an Evolving Reader

Name: _____

Date: _November 2, 2003_____

Stage: _Evolving_____

Year (circle one) (1) 2

Cycle (circle one) (1) 2 3 4

	Word	Student Spelling	Number of Errors
1	camp	camp	
2	crude	crude	
3	fast	fast	
4	grade	grade	
6	graph	graf	X
5	mule	mule	
7	phone	phone	
8	plump	plump	
9	quaint	kwaint	X
10	quake	quake	
11	skunk	skunk	
12	speck	speck	
13	steam	steam	
14	stray	stray	
15	swell	swell	
16	teeth	teeth	
17	theft	theft	
18	tilt	tilt	
19	waist	waist	
20	white	white	
21	teeth	teeth	
22	street	street	
23	deal	deal	
24	quote	quote	
25	spruce	spruse	X

Score
(% correct)   88%

Therefore, the teacher should be sure to include a discussion of these features as he or she continues the word study sequence.

Comprehension

We believe comprehension is the most challenging aspect of reading to assess; yet, it is the also the most important. If students are experiencing difficulty comprehending a given text, the teacher needs an understanding of where their comprehension is breaking down in order to tailor instruction to best meet their needs. We have included information on both pre- and posttesting and ongoing comprehension assessments, which are all necessary to make effective instructional decisions.

Pre- and Postassessment

An informal reading inventory is, by far, the most effective tool available to gauge a student's instructional reading level. This individualized assessment is not only used to determine reading level but also to provide quality information about how a student comprehends a given text. Informal reading inventories comprise a series of leveled passages that typically begin with a preprimer level and progressively become more difficult. Each inventory that we review in this section contains assessment for word recognition in isolation, word recognition in context, and comprehension questions. We feel these are essential components for determining a student's reading level. This reading level takes into account not only word recognition accuracy but also understanding of a given passage.

The information gleaned from an informal reading inventory can be used to monitor progress over time. Specifically, the information provides the teacher with critical baseline and ending year data to show gains in reading ability. In this current age of teacher accountability, teachers need accurate, usable information. They need to be able to show where the students began and ended the year in reading. In other words, they need to show what impact the teacher's instruction had on the students' gain.

In the Small-Group Differentiated Reading Model, we use an informal reading inventory to make initial placements in reading groups and to monitor yearly progress. In our experience, any informal reading inventory is quite lengthy, some taking several hours to administer. Therefore, we recommend the following specific components be used to gauge an instructional reading level and provide in-depth comprehension data:

- Word recognition in isolation
- Word recognition in context
- Retelling
- Comprehension questions (literal, inferential, and application)

There are many commercial informal reading inventories available. The results from any given inventory are *fairly* comparable. However, we do believe in consistency. Teachers need to give the same assessment in the beginning of the year, middle of the year (if applicable), and at the end of the year. If an entire district is tracking their students' progress through an informal reading inventory, the entire district needs to administer the same assessment.

The following informal reading inventories are widely used and are respected in the reading community:

Analytical Reading Inventory (ARI) 7th Ed. (Woods & Moe, 2003)
Key features include

- Independent, instructional, and frustration level for narrative and expository passages (preprimer to grade 9);
- Word recognition in isolation;
- Word recognition in context ability (miscue analysis);
- Assessment of different question types (literal to application);
- Fluency rating scale;
- Student predictions, prior knowledge, and retelling abilities;
- Emotional status report;
- Interest inventory/reading survey;
- Silent and listening comprehension assessment; and
- Practice CD.

The key features needed for small-group assessment include

- Narrative and expository passages with accuracy rates and comprehension questions;
- Word recognition in isolation (best indicator of a student's reading level);
- Retelling ability in instructional passages (summarizing); and
- Assessment of different question types (literal to application).

Qualitative Reading Inventory (QRI) 3rd Ed. (Leslie & Caldwell, 2001)

Key features include

- Independent, instructional, and frustration level for narrative and expository passages (preprimer to high school);
- Word recognition in isolation;
- Word recognition in context ability (miscue analysis);
- Assessment of different question types (explicit and implicit);
- Student predictions, prior knowledge, and retelling abilities; and
- Silent and listening comprehension assessment

The key features needed for small-group assessment include

- Narrative and expository passages with accuracy rates and comprehension questions,
- Word recognition in isolation,
- Retelling ability in instructional passages (summarizing), and
- Assessment of different question types (explicit and implicit).

Informal Reading Inventory (IRI) 6th Ed. (Burns & Roe, 2002)

Key features include

- Independent, instructional, and frustration level for narrative and expository passages (preprimer to grade 12);

- Word recognition in isolation;

- Word recognition in context ability (miscue analysis);

- Assessment of different question types (main idea, detail, inference, sequence, cause and effect, vocabulary); and

- Silent and listening comprehension assessment.

Key features needed for small-group assessment include

- Narrative and expository passages with accuracy rates and comprehension questions;

- Word recognition in isolation; and

- Assessment of different question types (main idea, detail, inference, sequence, cause and effect, vocabulary).

Ongoing Assessment

Ongoing assessments are those given by the teacher in response to the text selections read in the small group. Teacher observation is invaluable when students are seen in small groups on a regular basis. This provides the teacher with current information regarding the authentic ability of a student to process and understand text. This information is helpful particularly when determining student report card grades. We provide samples of what these data collection tools might look like. Whatever the teacher decides to use to monitor student achievement, it must be easy to implement and easy to manage. Most important, the tool must provide useful data. These tools also can be used to monitor students' oral responses.

Oral Questioning Response Checklist—This simple checklist allows the teacher to track the types of questions he or she is asking as well as whether students are able to answer the question correctly (see Appendix A).

Narrative Text Comprehension: Classroom Profile Sheet for Oral Summary—This easy-to-implement tool tracks student understanding of narrative text structure. After reading a given text, students are asked to orally summarize what they have read. During this oral response, the teacher notes which elements of narrative text the student has included. The teacher also can track whether the student needed prompting in order to respond successfully (see Appendix A).

The following tools can be used by teachers to monitor students' written responses.

Written Questioning Response Sheet—This sheet (which teachers can create by reserving the top portion of a sheet of paper for their questions and the bottom portion for student response) can be used in conjunction with any text as an assessment of a student's level of understanding. Following the reading of a text, the teacher creates a question at each level (literal, inferential, application) and asks for a written response from each student in the small group. Students also are responsible for identifying the question type.

Expository Comprehension Assessments—These assessments (see Appendix A) monitor a student's ability to identify the major elements of expository text. After the students complete one of the element assessments (e.g., main idea and supporting details, cause and effect, sequencing, compare and contrast), the teacher uses the rubric on the bottom of the assessment to evaluate the student's ability. The student's scores can be tracked on the Expository Text Comprehension: Classroom Profile Sheet for Written Summary (see Appendix A).

Using this classroom profile sheet allows teachers to quickly identify students' strengths and areas of need. Using this information, teachers can plan small-group instruction more effectively. And, as mentioned previously, this information helps teachers make decisions about students' placement in flexible groups.

Conclusion

The importance of assessment cannot be overlooked in the Small-Group Differentiated Reading Model. Both pre- and postassessments and ongoing assessments are necessary in order to track students' progress accurately. Not only is the information used to flexibly group students, but it can be useful also in determining students' grades. The reading skills that are assessed directly correlate with the knowledge the students need to know as outlined in the state standards. The manner in which teachers analyze the assessment results should be the framework for their instructional plan. The success of any reading program rests on the validity, reliability, and systematic use of assessment data.

CHAPTER 7

Managing Small-Group Instruction in Self-Contained and Departmentalized Classrooms

The management aspect of small-group differentiated instruction is the most critical yet often the most difficult part of implementation for many teachers. It requires effective time management and organization of the classroom and instructional materials. However, even with the aforementioned aspects in place, without the appropriate reading material (i.e., leveled texts), the Small-Group Differentiated Reading Model is challenging to implement successfully. This lack of materials hinders students' progress when they are reading independently and when they are reading in small groups.

This chapter examines the two most common intermediate classroom configurations: (1) the self-contained classroom, most frequently seen in grades 3–5, and (2) the departmentalized model, utilized in many upper elementary and middle schools. Each of these classroom configurations can be adapted to include small-group differentiated instruction, although the organization and management will probably look different in order to maximize the instructional efficiency of each environment.

The Self-Contained Classroom

The self-contained classroom that will be discussed in this chapter is one in which the classroom teacher is primarily responsible for teaching all subject areas in his or her own classroom. This does not preclude students who may be pulled out to receive services such as speech and language, special education, Title I, English as a second language (ESL), or other specialized instructional programs. This self-contained classroom allows teachers the flexibility to plan for and implement both whole- and small-group instruction in a manner that maximizes instructional time for both the teacher and the students.

Typically, self-contained classrooms are organized in blocks of time, especially with regard to reading and math instruction. Table 10 is an example of a fourth-grade self-contained classroom. We have also taken into consideration general curriculum guidelines as they pertain to time allocations for each subject area.

Planning for the Reading Block

A two-hour literacy block is common in most upper elementary classrooms. It also is quite common to have four reading groups at various instructional levels in any given

TABLE 10
Sample Daily Schedule for the Self-Contained Classroom

Time		
8:00–8:15	Students arrive	Morning announcements, classroom business (lunch, attendance, homework collection) Students read independently leveled text to promote fluency.
8:15–10:15	Reading block	Whole-group instruction/Small-group instruction (Basal—read-aloud, shared reading)
10:15–11:00	Special classes	Art, music, physical education, computer, library
11:00–12:00	Math	
12:00–12:25	Lunch	
12:25–12:55	Recess	Bathroom, water, etc.
1:00–1:45	Process writing/Grammar	
1:45–2:45	Social studies/Science	Rotate every two weeks, depending on unit of study
2:45–3:00	Wrap-Up	Prepare for dismissal

TABLE 11
Sample Daily Reading Block Schedule for the Self-Contained Classroom

Time		
8:15–8:55 M–W 8:15–8:45 Th–F	Whole class	Read-aloud, shared reading (with basal if district mandated or use content-related text). During this time, instruction will focus on specific comprehension strategy instruction and vocabulary development.
8:55–9:25 (30 minutes)	Small group A (two years below)	Complete small-group lesson plan
9:25–9:55 (30 minutes)	Small group B (two years below)	Complete small-group lesson plan
9:55–10:15 (20 minutes)	Small group C (grade level or above)	Word study only
	Small group D (above grade level)	Independent work day

classroom. This is particularly common in classrooms with 25 or more students. In this fourth-grade classroom (see Table 11), there are four different groups of readers within the class, each of which is included in a rotational model that reflects more support for the below grade-level readers and more independent work for those readers who are at or above grade level.

All groups do not meet with the teacher daily. In our experience, we have found that it is unrealistic for an intermediate teacher to provide quality, small-group reading instruction to 25 students per day. Therefore, we feel the rotational schedule is necessary (see Table 12) and must be driven by the classroom assessment data. For example, the students who are performing two grade levels below average in reading must receive small-group instruction at least four times per week in the regular classroom, whereas the above grade-level students may meet for small-group instruction two or three times per week. In some schools, the below grade-level readers are often "shipped out" of the classroom for their primary reading instruction. More often than not, this instruction is boxed, programmed, scripted in nature, and does not support the total reading process. There is little attention given to the literacy needs of the individual student. Regardless, the first line of defense for these students is the instruction they receive from the regular classroom teacher. Any additional reading support should supplement what the classroom teacher is providing.

Description of the Groups

Group A

This group consists of six students who are transitioning into the evolving reader stage. As such, they are currently reading about two years below grade-level expectations. These students meet with the teacher four times per week for small-group reading instruction and an additional 20 minutes for just the comprehension portion of the lesson plan.

Group B

This group consists of seven students who are in the middle of the evolving reader stage. They are currently performing about one year below grade level. This group of students meets with the teacher three times per week for small-group reading instruction and an additional 20 minutes on another day to focus on the comprehension portion of the lesson plan.

TABLE 12
Sample Weekly Schedule for Small-Group Instruction in the Self-Contained Classroom

Monday	Tuesday	Wednesday	Thursday	Friday
80 minutes for small-group reading 8:55–9:25 9:25–9:55 9:55–10:15			90 minutes for small-group reading 8:55–9:25 9:25–9:55 9:55–10:25	
A	C	D	C	A
B	A	B	B	C
D (reading only) Word study activities completed out of group	B (reading only) Word study activities completed out of group	A (reading only) Word study activities completed out of group	A	D

Group C

This group consists of seven students who are currently at the end of the evolving reader stage. These students are able to read grade-level material. They meet with the teacher three times per week for small-group instruction.

Group D

This group consists of five students who are currently at the beginning of the maturing reader stage. These students are reading above grade-level material; therefore, the teacher meets with these students two times per week for a complete lesson and an additional 15 minutes on another day for word study, if necessary.

Additional Support Personnel

This reading block configuration does not take into consideration the supplemental reading instruction that must be provided for the below grade level students. These students need a "double dose" of reading instruction that is consistent with the instruction that the classroom teacher is providing. In most schools, this double dose of instruction is very different from the classroom teacher's instruction. This often results in the already struggling reader feeling more confused and frustrated with the reading process. A true double dose of reading instruction involves the classroom teacher and the additional support teacher (e.g., Title I teacher) focusing on the same skills simultaneously. For example, if the students are reading a level 21 text and working on long *a* vowel patterns in their small-group instruction in the classroom, they should be reading a book at a comparable instructional level and working on long *a* vowel patterns with the additional support teacher. This allows students to read another instructionally appropriate book. It is really quite simple—more time with instructionally appropriate material yields better readers.

Whole-Group Instruction

Although the focus of this book is to provide guidance for small-group reading instruction, we cannot ignore the usefulness of whole-group reading instruction with the intermediate reader. Whole-group instruction allows the opportunity for teacher read-alouds and shared readings. Both of these activities are rich experiences for all students to build and increase vocabulary and comprehension skills. So how can the teacher provide meaningful instruction in the context of the whole group? This question becomes more complex when coupled with district mandates for basal instruction. Thus, we have included information about basal reading instruction because we recognize that 95% of school districts are mandating the use of these basal programs.

What About the Basal Program?

Because the basal story for the week is not an appropriate leveled text for all the students in the class, it is best utilized as a shared reading in which the teacher is primarily responsible for reading the story while the students follow along in their own books. The teacher uses this shared reading as a way to guide comprehension instruction through modeling his or her thought processes and monitoring student understanding by engaging them in meaningful questioning activities that focus on literal, inferential, and application questions.

Although the basal format is specific with regard to weekly lesson plans, many of the suggested activities are not appropriate for all students in a given classroom. Therefore, they must be modified. For example, the excessive number of workbook pages that many basal reading programs include do not give students an opportunity to express themselves in writing—filling in the blanks on a worksheet will not help develop students' critical thinking or writing skills. Teachers must pick and choose the basal activities that hold the most value for whole-group student learning. (See Table 13 for a suggested modifications of basal program activities.) This discrimination process frees up more time for small-group instruction as well as focused content area instruction in the reading block.

You will notice on the sample daily reading block schedule (see Table 11, page 112) that we have provided more time in the beginning of the week for whole-group basal instruction so that the story can be introduced and read together. Although the basal might suggest that the story be read two or three times during the week, this is probably not the best use of instructional time. Rather, this time can be utilized engaging students in grade-level content information that meets the required curriculum standards. This can also be time allotted for student reading in independent leveled text to build fluency. (See Figure 30.) Rereading the basal story numerous times over the course of the week will not increase fluency for those students who are reading below grade level. The text is simply too difficult. Further, although many basal reading programs are accompanied by one lower level and one higher level book to supplement weekly instruction, these books may or may not be at the students' instructional reading level. Clearly, a wider variety of text selections is critical to the overall reading program in any given classroom.

The Departmentalized Classroom

As students transition from upper elementary to middle school, the complexities in teaching reading become more apparent. In most middle schools, there is a 90-minute block of time dedicated to literature, writing, and grammar instruction in the departmentalized classroom. *Departmentalized* refers to an organizational structure whereby teachers are assigned to teach specific subject areas (e.g., language arts, math, science, social studies). As a result, the Small-Group Differentiated Reading Model is modified to balance the reading needs of those students within the middle school structure. (See Table 14.)

Planning for the Language Arts Block

Similar to the self-contained classroom, the 90-minute block in the middle school should contain both whole- and small-group instruction. (See Table 15 for an example of a seventh-grade departmentalized language arts classroom.) In reality, the grouping configurations will be larger than that of the upper elementary classroom because of time

TABLE 13
Suggested Basal Program Modifications

Day	Required Basal Program Activities	Alternative Activities
Monday	• Build background knowledge • Preview story vocabulary • Predict • Focus skill in phonics and comprehension • Workbook pages	**Keep** • Build background knowledge • Preview story vocabulary • Predict **Modify** • Substitute workbook with varied vocabulary and comprehension activities • Omit phonics focus skill, which is taught systematically and explicitly in the word study portion of the small-group lesson plan
Tuesday	• Review story vocabulary • Reading of the story (may include independent, partner, or shared reading) • Workbook pages	**Keep** • Review story vocabulary **Modify** • Shared reading in a whole-group setting (the teacher is responsible for the majority of the reading) • Substitute workbook pages with varied vocabulary and comprehension activities
Wednesday	• Book on tape • Use leveled reader to support higher/lower readers • Workbook pages	**Modify** • Use book on tape as a literacy center activity • Follow up with a comprehension activity • Substitute workbook for partner discussion or an authentic writing activity
Thursday	• Partner read the story for fluency • Workbook pages	**Modify** • Reread other appropriate leveled text for fluency practice with a partner • Partners complete a common comprehension activity based on fluency read or • Shared reading or read-aloud of expository text to support content area standards • Engage students in meaningful comprehension and vocabulary activities
Friday	• Selection assessment	**Modify** • Shared reading or read-aloud of expository text to support content area standards • Engage students in meaningful comprehension and vocabulary activities

FIGURE 30
Students Reading Independently in the Self-Contained Classroom

constraints. A sample rotation schedule has been provided to demonstrate an efficient way to maximize small-group instruction in a limited amount of time (see Table 16). Unlike that of the upper elementary school, the language arts block in the middle school includes reading, writing, and grammar instruction. The text used in the language arts block is generally focused on literature that supports grade-level standards.

Reading in content area text will need to be supported in the respective content area classroom. Although not addressed in this book, effective content area instruction must be supplemented with leveled text to support the varying reading levels of students. They will not become more proficient reading in the content areas without texts they can read. The expository lesson plans that are provided in this book could be adapted to support the content area teachers with the wide variety of readers they have in their class, especially those reading below grade level.

Description of the Groups

The needs of these intermediate students can be met most effectively if all students in a particular grade level are grouped according to ability. There really is no other way to effectively and efficiently meet the needs of all students. We realize however that this model is being utilized only on a limited basis. As such, we have geared our example to the traditional, homogenously grouped language arts class.

TABLE 14
Sample Daily Schedule for the Middle School Classroom

Time		
8:00–8:15	Homeroom	Morning announcements Classroom business (lunch, attendance)
8:15–9:45	Language arts block	Whole-group instruction/Small-group instruction
9:50–11:20	Math block	
11:20–12:00	Lunch	
12:00–1:30	Science/social studies (rotational basis)	
1:30–2:15	Elective class	Art, music, physical education, theater on a rotational quarter basis
2:15–3:00	Elective class	Health/computer

TABLE 15
Sample Daily Reading Block Schedule for the Middle School Classroom

Time		
8:15–8:45 M–W 8:15–9:15 Th–F	Whole class	**Reading** • Read-aloud, shared reading (with basal if district mandated) • Focus on specific comprehension strategy instruction and vocabulary development through **Writing/Grammar** • Process writing instruction • Grammar instruction • Writing conferences
8:45–9:15	Small group A (two years below)	Complete small-group lesson plan
9:15–9:45	Small group B (two years below)	Complete small-group lesson plan
	Small group C (grade level or above)	Independent work day

TABLE 16
Sample Weekly Schedule for Small-Group Instruction in the Middle School Classroom

Monday	Tuesday	Wednesday	Thursday	Friday
60 minutes for small-group reading 8:45–9:15 9:15–9:45			30 minutes for small-group reading 9:15–9:45	
A	C	A	B	A
B	B	C		

Group A

This group consists of nine students who are currently reading two years or more below grade level. They are late in the evolving stage of reading development. This group meets with the teacher three times per week for small-group instruction.

Group B

This group consists of 10 students who are currently reading at or slightly below grade level. They are nearing the end of the maturing reader stage and are well within the meaning level of spelling development. This group meets with the teacher three times per week for small-group instruction.

Group C

This group consists of six students who are in the advanced reader stage. These students are able to read above grade-level expectations. Advanced readers meet with the teacher two times per week for small-group instruction; therefore, the majority of their reading is done independently.

Additional Support Personnel

Unfortunately, there is not a lot of additional support for below grade-level readers in middle schools. This exemplifies the need for small-group differentiated instruction in the language arts block. At-risk students need to have some form of additional reading intervention. The support teacher (special education, ESL, Title I) can utilize the small-group model as part of their daily intervention program. We have found that many intervention programs for struggling readers consist of a computer program or "homework help"—neither of which teaches students how to read.

Whole-Group Instruction in the Middle School Language Arts Block

Clearly, there is a need for whole-group instruction in the middle school language arts block. When you examine the grade-level standards and realize what the students are required to learn, it becomes clear that there is simply not enough time. Further, there is even less time for students to read appropriate level material to practice reading and apply their knowledge.

We are very mindful of the time constraints and curriculum mandates in the middle school classroom. As such, we have provided a sample schedule that breaks down the 90-minute block. (See Table 16, page 118.) You will see that during this time frame, the teacher needs to provide exposure to the information that will appear on the state mandated assessments. This includes both knowledge of information related to reading (i.e., text structure, elements of narrative and expository text) and information related to writing (i.e., writing process, types and purposes of writing, grammatical structure).

Independent Activities

What are the rest of the students doing during small-group reading instruction? This is the question most frequently asked by teachers when implementing the Small-Group Differentiated Reading Instruction Model. As such, we have devoted an entire section to answer this question. We believe these activities can be used in both the self-contained and departmentalized classroom configurations. In addition, we believe these are only a sampling of quality activities that will engage students and facilitate their further development in reading and writing, rather than simply having them fill in the blanks.

First, we have to think about what are meaningful, independent activities that will successfully promote increased reading and writing abilities. Second, we have to think about the time frame in which we are asking students to work independently. Last, we have to think about how these activities best support and extend both small-group and whole-group instruction. In consideration of the research-based components that support effective reading instruction, these activities are categorized according to the components on the lesson plan.

As with other curricular activities, teachers should plan first to model and discuss the expectations for each activity. We believe it is essential that teachers practice with students before asking them to complete any of these activities on their own.

Fluency

Reading fluency can be developed only by reading and rereading independent level text. Some independent activities that promote reading fluency include the following:

Readers Theatre—This activity requires students either to prepare a script or read a premade script based on a text they have read. During the independent work time, students practice and execute the reading of the script. Each student takes a part; however, unlike a typical theatre performance, Readers Theatre does not require props, costumes, or even an audience.

Poetry Alive!—This individual or choral reading activity provides students the chance to practice their intonation, use of voice, pitch, and stress using dramatic presentations.

R & R (Record & Reflect)—This activity uses a fluency rating scale, so students record themselves reading a short passage (no more than 150 words) and then reflect on their own fluency ability. Students then listen to themselves and record their own performance on the R&R rating scale. The student should do this two or three times. (See R&R rating scale in Appendix C and Figure 31.)

Read With Me—This activity allows students to choose three times per week different partners who will listen to them read the same short passage. The listening partner uses the Read With Me rating scale to rate his or her partner's oral reading. (See Read With Me rating scale in Appendix C.)

FIGURE 31
Student Recording and Reflecting on a Short Reading Passage

Word Study

The following activities are designed to support small-group instruction only. These activities should be used as follow-up activities that utilize the same features studied in a given time frame.

Word Hunts—Students search for words with the feature(s) they are currently studying, such as homographs, and keep track of them in their word study notebooks. Students can receive points for each word found.

Sort and Stick—With a partner, students sort the words they are currently studying in their word study notebooks. Then, each student explains his or her sorting to a partner, and the partner checks for accuracy. Finally, students glue the words into their word study notebooks, so they can be used for future reference.

Spelling Sort—In this activity, students work with a partner from their small group and take turns dictating the words they are currently studying and writing the sort.

Define Me!—With a partner, students turn their word study cards face down and choose three words. Then, the students fill out a Vocabulary Word Map for each word. Finally, in their own words, students have to verbally define the word for their partner. (See Vocabulary Word Map in Appendix C.)

Extension Games—Teachers can also create their own word study games, such as Suffix Rummy and Homophone Rummy, using a simple game board and word cards.

Vocabulary

Vocabulary activities are used primarily as a follow-up to support whole-group instruction. They should relate to the read-aloud and shared reading experience. They can also support content area vocabulary when appropriate.

Vocabulary Word Map—This activity allows students to use a graphic organizer to visually define a given word using examples, illustrations, sentences, and student-generated definitions that demonstrate their understanding. (See Vocabulary Word Map in Appendix C and Figure 32.)

Vocabulary Headbands—For this activity, students write story vocabulary words (or content specific words) on sentence strips. Then, they staple the sentence strips together to make a headband. Each student puts on a headband without looking at the word on it. Finally, students go around the room and ask their classmates questions that have only

FIGURE 32
Completed Vocabulary Word Map

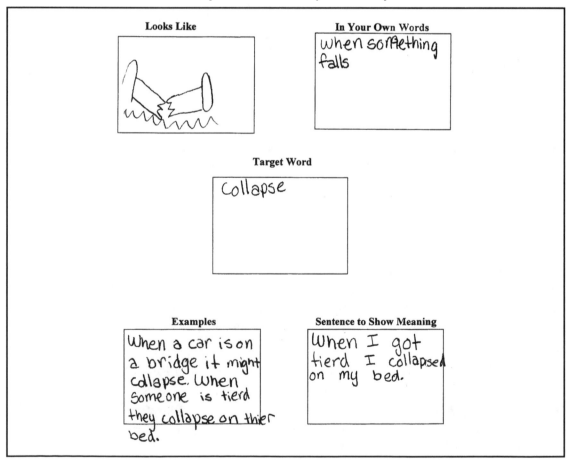

a yes or no answer. For example, Is the word a noun? or Does the word have anything to do with losing sleep? Students keep rotating around the classroom until they guess the word.

Find Me, Define Me—In this activity, the teacher gives the students a list of words they will come across in their assigned reading. When the students find the words in the text, they should write the definitions in their own words. Then, teachers should review the definitions.

Comprehension

The following activities can be a connection to or extension of the text used in either small-group or whole-group instruction. These comprehension activities support questioning, visualizing, summarizing, and examining text structure.

Questioning

Question Maker—As a follow-up activity to either small-group or whole-group reading instruction, students make up their own questions in each of the three following categories: literal, inferential, and application. Students write one question for each category. Then, the students exchange questions with a partner and answer their partner's questions. (See Question Maker in Appendix C.)

Interrogation—In this activity, students create a series of generic questions that allow them to find out more about a text they have not read. Students ask another student who has read the text their questions. If the student who has read the text does not know the answer to a question, he or she has to return to the text to find the answer.

Visualizing

Story Snapshots—This activity should be done after a teacher read-aloud. During the read-aloud, the teacher stops at strategic points and discusses with the students what she is visualizing. Then, during independent time, students draw a picture (using the top half of the paper) of something they visualized during the read-aloud. Next, students write a paragraph (using the bottom half of the paper) describing their visualization. Finally, the students share their illustrations (top half) with a partner, and the partner has to guess which part of the story the first student visualized. (See Story Snapshots in Appendix C.)

Picture Perfect—For this activity, students listen to a story on tape (without picture support), then they draw a scene they visualized as they listened to the tape. Finally, students write a descriptive paragraph about that part of the story. (See Picture Perfect in Appendix C.)

Summarizing

You're the Reporter—In this activity, students write a summary of a story for a newspaper article. The summary must answer the questions who, what, when, where, and why. (See You're the Reporter in Appendix C.)

Fact or Fib—For this activity, students write three facts and one fib about information they learned while listening to or reading a text. Students exchange this information with one another and see if they can "trick" their friends. The student who tricks the most people is the classroom winner. (See Fact or Fib? in Appendix C.)

Top 10 List—For this activity, students listen to or read a selection independently. Then, students create their own top 10 lists about the reading, such as the top 10 most important details of the story or top 10 most important facts about a given topic. (See Top 10 List in Appendix C.)

Text Structure

The Perfect Setting—In this activity, students write a descriptive paragraph of the setting of the story. The description must include the time, place, and three descriptive details. Students also should include a drawing of the setting. (See The Perfect Setting in Appendix C.)

Secret Sequence—As a follow-up to small- or whole-group reading, this activity calls for students to write a list of five events in the story in random order and create an answer key. The students exchange their lists of events with a partner and then place the events in the proper sequence. Then, students check their final products against the answer key. (See Secret Sequence in Appendix C and Figure 33.)

FIGURE 33
Student Working on Secret Sequence

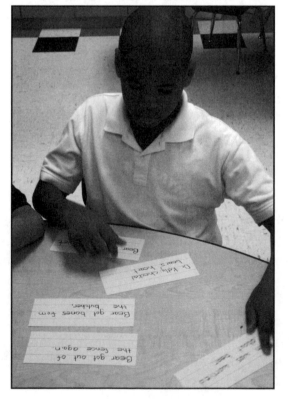

Character Counts—For this activity, students identify a particular character trait of one of the main characters and give two examples of how this character trait is exhibited in the story. For example, in the *Wizard of Oz* (Baum, 1900/1993), Dorothy exhibits caring when the Wicked Witch of the West melts after being splashed with water and when the wizard is revealed to be a regular man hiding behind curtains pretending to be something that he was not. (See Character Counts in Appendix C.)

Conclusion

Effectively managing small-group and whole-group instruction, as well as independent reading activities, is not a task that should be taken lightly. In fact, this is a pivotal point in which a teacher can make the difference between the successful transformation of readers and status quo reading ability. Striking a balance among small-group, whole-group, and independent activities is crucial to the management of the total reading program. Embracing changes in instructional practices takes time, patience, and an understanding of the change process itself. However, the reward of more proficient readers far outweighs the effort needed to make these changes a reality.

The challenge of teaching reading does not diminish after the completion of the primary grades. Rather, the challenge continues throughout the intermediate grades as students develop and refine critical reading skills. Clearly, all intermediate teachers must be competent teachers of reading, capable of meeting the needs of a wide variety of readers. Differentiated reading instruction based on the needs of the readers must become the standard if we are to provide opportunities for growth for all students.

Students who enter the intermediate grades with deficits in reading face unique challenges and need focused, effective instruction based on their individual needs. These reading deficits create a multitude of issues as students attempt to master grade-level standards. For intermediate-grade students, reading is the centerpiece for learning across the content areas. Intensive reading instruction that reflects students' specific needs must be a priority if students are to make the necessary curriculum gains. Foundational reading knowledge that relates to fluency, phonics, vocabulary, and comprehension must be learned and mastered during the intermediate grades. In most instances, this will be the last opportunity for students to participate in focused reading instruction.

Although there are certainly struggling readers who must be provided with instruction that will enhance their critical reading skills as they face more complex text, there also are proficient readers who need this instruction as well. These students also will need instruction that addresses their instructional needs. Reading cannot be successfully taught in the context of all whole-class instruction. Whole-class instruction alone will not provide the scaffolding essential to the development of good readers. Striking a balance between whole-class and small-group instruction will allow all students the opportunity to maximize their learning. Differentiated reading instruction geared to the needs of all readers is no longer a luxury in an age of high-stakes assessment and teacher accountability. It is vital.

Teachers in the intermediate grades readily admit they are overwhelmed by the curricular mandates established by the district, state, and even federal government. Unfortunately, without solid reading competencies in place, students and teachers will continue to fall short of these standards. All intermediate teachers must become teachers of reading—that is, knowledgeable about the reading process and those assessments that will guide instruction. Further, they need to know how to effectively implement research-based strategies and activities in their classrooms.

There is much to be optimistic about as we begin the 21st century. We know a great deal about the teaching of reading, and we also know what works and how to make it happen in a classroom. Our hope is that this book will be a tool to assist teachers as they strive to take the research base and apply it in practical classroom situations. Reading practices for students in the 20th century will no longer suffice in our increasingly complex society where a much higher level of literacy is necessary for the survival of each individual. If we are serious about "leaving no child behind," intermediate teachers must be committed to the continuation of differentiated reading instruction.

Assessment Materials

4 x 4 Oral Reading Fluency Rating Scale

Name_____ Grade_____ Teacher_____

Assessment 1 (Pretest) Date_____	Assessment 2 Date_____	Assessment 3 Date_____	Assessment 4 (Posttest) Date_____
Phrasing ❑ Word by word ❑ Some word by word, some phrases ❑ Reads mostly in phrases ❑ Uses appropriate phrasing consistently	**Phrasing** ❑ Word by word ❑ Some word by word, some phrases ❑ Reads mostly in phrases ❑ Uses appropriate phrasing consistently	**Phrasing** ❑ Word by word ❑ Some word by word, some phrases ❑ Reads mostly in phrases ❑ Uses appropriate phrasing consistently	**Phrasing** ❑ Word by word ❑ Some word by word, some phrases ❑ Reads mostly in phrases ❑ Uses appropriate phrasing consistently
Punctuation ❑ Little attention to punctuation ❑ Inconsistent use of punctuation ❑ Generally efficient use of punctuation ❑ Consistent attention to punctuation	**Punctuation** ❑ Little attention to punctuation ❑ Inconsistent use of punctuation ❑ Generally efficient use of punctuation ❑ Consistent attention to punctuation	**Punctuation** ❑ Little attention to punctuation ❑ Inconsistent use of punctuation ❑ Generally efficient use of punctuation ❑ Consistent attention to punctuation	**Punctuation** ❑ Little attention to punctuation ❑ Inconsistent use of punctuation ❑ Generally efficient use of punctuation ❑ Consistent attention to punctuation
Rate ❑ Slow, laborious reading rate ❑ Rate varies (some slow, some faster) ❑ Rate does not interfere with comprehension ❑ Consistently uses appropriate rate according to text type	**Rate** ❑ Slow, laborious reading rate ❑ Rate varies (some slow, some faster) ❑ Rate does not interfere with comprehension ❑ Consistently uses appropriate rate according to text type	**Rate** ❑ Slow, laborious reading rate ❑ Rate varies (some slow, some faster) ❑ Rate does not interfere with comprehension ❑ Consistently uses appropriate rate according to text type	**Rate** ❑ Slow, laborious reading rate ❑ Rate varies (some slow, some faster) ❑ Rate does not interfere with comprehension ❑ Consistently uses appropriate rate according to text type
Expression ❑ Monotone, no expression ❑ Mostly monotone, occasional expression ❑ Appropriate expression generally used ❑ Appropriate expression and intonation consistently used	**Expression** ❑ Monotone, no expression ❑ Mostly monotone, occasional expression ❑ Appropriate expression generally used ❑ Appropriate expression and intonation consistently used	**Expression** ❑ Monotone, no expression ❑ Mostly monotone, occasional expression ❑ Appropriate expression generally used ❑ Appropriate expression and intonation consistently used	**Expression** ❑ Monotone, no expression ❑ Mostly monotone, occasional expression ❑ Appropriate expression generally used ❑ Appropriate expression and intonation consistently used
CWPM _____ New Read: _____ Reread: _____ Comments _____	CWPM _____ New Read: _____ Reread: _____ Comments _____	CWPM _____ New Read: _____ Reread: _____ Comments _____	CWPM _____ New Read: _____ Reread: _____ Comments _____

CWPM = Correct Words Per Minute

Grade 3 Fluency Profile

Teacher: _____

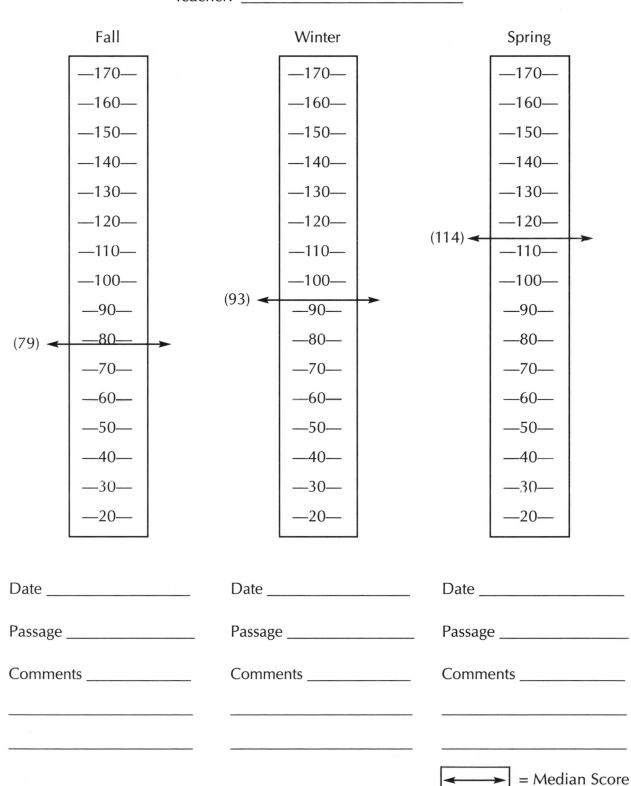

Fall	Winter	Spring
—170—	—170—	—170—
—160—	—160—	—160—
—150—	—150—	—150—
—140—	—140—	—140—
—130—	—130—	—130—
—120—	—120—	—120—
—110—	—110—	—110—
—100—	—100—	—100—
—90—	—90—	—90—
—80—	—80—	—80—
—70—	—70—	—70—
—60—	—60—	—60—
—50—	—50—	—50—
—40—	—40—	—40—
—30—	—30—	—30—
—20—	—20—	—20—

(79) ⟵⟶   (93) ⟵⟶   (114) ⟵⟶

Date _____   Date _____   Date _____

Passage _____   Passage _____   Passage _____

Comments _____   Comments _____   Comments _____

_____   _____   _____

_____   _____   _____

⟵⟶ = Median Score

Grade 4 Fluency Profile

Teacher: _____

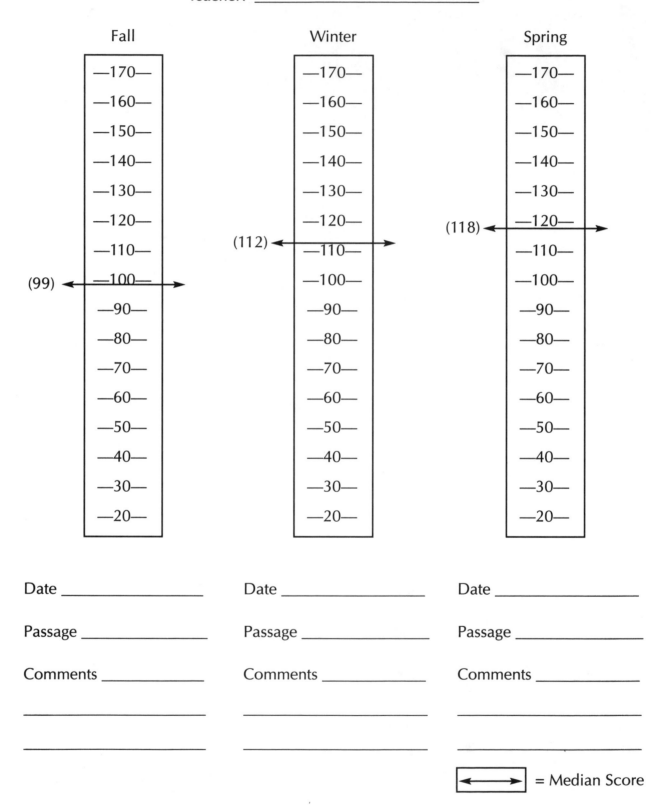

Fall	Winter	Spring

Fall
—170—
—160—
—150—
—140—
—130—
—120—
—110—
(99) ◄—100—►
—90—
—80—
—70—
—60—
—50—
—40—
—30—
—20—

Winter
—170—
—160—
—150—
—140—
—130—
—120—
(112) ◄—110—►
—100—
—90—
—80—
—70—
—60—
—50—
—40—
—30—
—20—

Spring
—170—
—160—
—150—
—140—
—130—
(118) ◄—120—►
—110—
—100—
—90—
—80—
—70—
—60—
—50—
—40—
—30—
—20—

Date _____

Passage _____

Comments _____

_____

_____

Date _____

Passage _____

Comments _____

_____

_____

Date _____

Passage _____

Comments _____

_____

_____

◄———► = Median Score

130

Grade 5 Fluency Profile

Teacher: _____

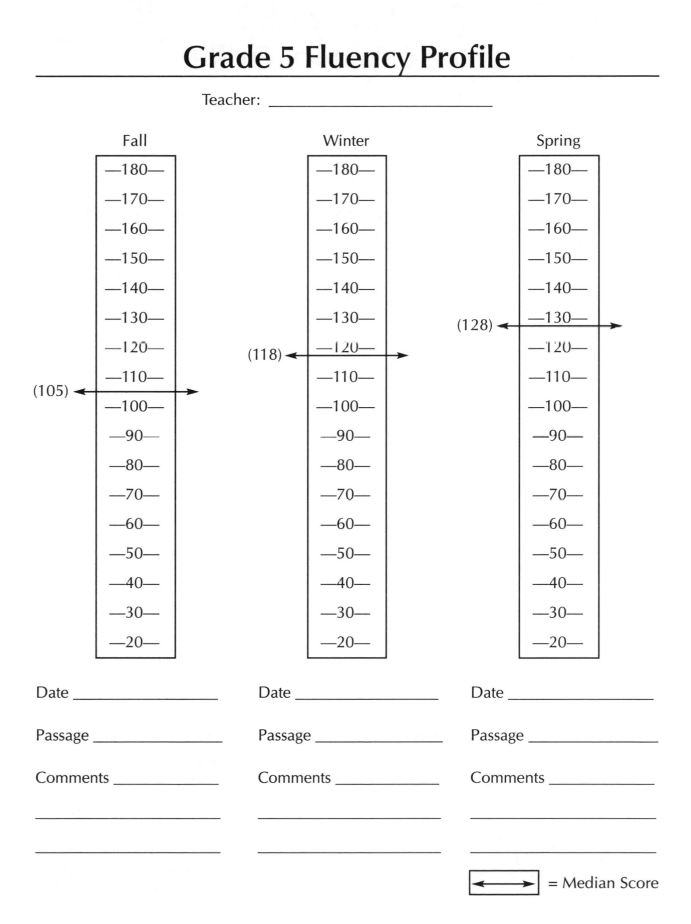

Fall

—180—
—170—
—160—
—150—
—140—
—130—
—120—
—110—
(105) ←—→ —100—
—90—
—80—
—70—
—60—
—50—
—40—
—30—
—20—

Winter

—180—
—170—
—160—
—150—
—140—
—130—
(118) ←—→ —120—
—110—
—100—
—90—
—80—
—70—
—60—
—50—
—40—
—30—
—20—

Spring

—180—
—170—
—160—
—150—
—140—
(128) ←—→ —130—
—120—
—110—
—100—
—90—
—80—
—70—
—60—
—50—
—40—
—30—
—20—

Date _____   Date _____   Date _____

Passage _____   Passage _____   Passage _____

Comments _____   Comments _____   Comments _____

_____   _____   _____

_____   _____   _____

←———→ = Median Score

131

Grade 6 Fluency Profile

Teacher: _____

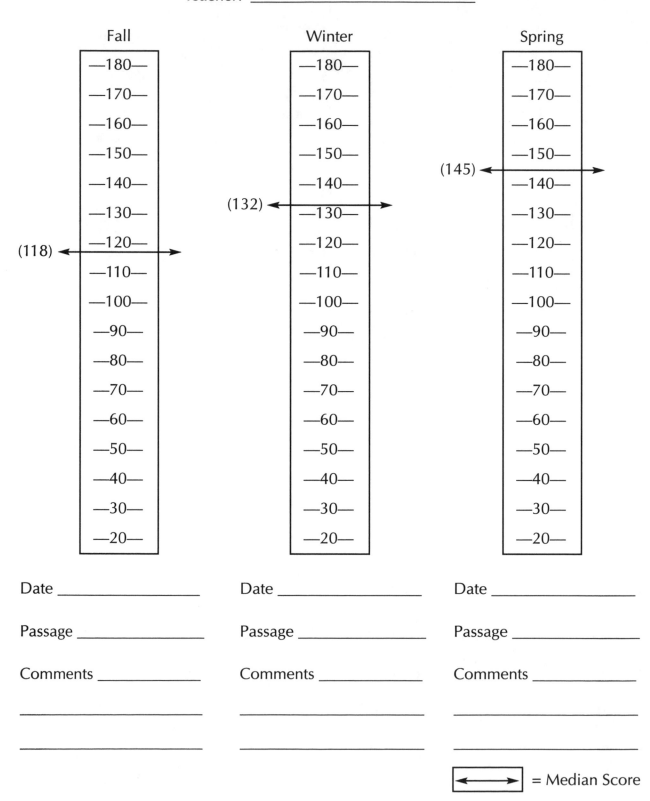

Fall	Winter	Spring
—180—	—180—	—180—
—170—	—170—	—170—
—160—	—160—	—160—
—150—	—150—	—150—
—140—	—140—	—140—
—130—	—130—	—130—
—120—	—120—	—120—
—110—	—110—	—110—
—100—	—100—	—100—
—90—	—90—	—90—
—80—	—80—	—80—
—70—	—70—	—70—
—60—	—60—	—60—
—50—	—50—	—50—
—40—	—40—	—40—
—30—	—30—	—30—
—20—	—20—	—20—

(118) ← Fall median
(132) ← Winter median
(145) ← Spring median

Date _____   Date _____   Date _____

Passage _____   Passage _____   Passage _____

Comments _____   Comments _____   Comments _____

_____   _____   _____

_____   _____   _____

←———→ = Median Score

Grade 7 Fluency Profile

Teacher: _____

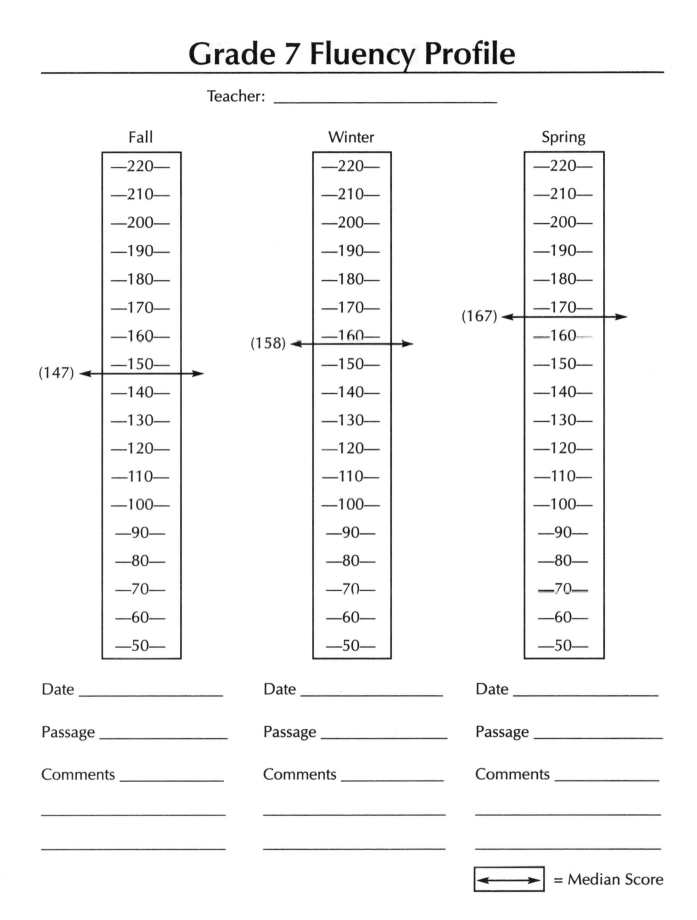

Fall	Winter	Spring

Date _____   Date _____   Date _____

Passage _____   Passage _____   Passage _____

Comments _____   Comments _____   Comments _____

_____   _____   _____

_____   _____   _____

⟷ = Median Score

Grade 8 Fluency Profile

Teacher: _____

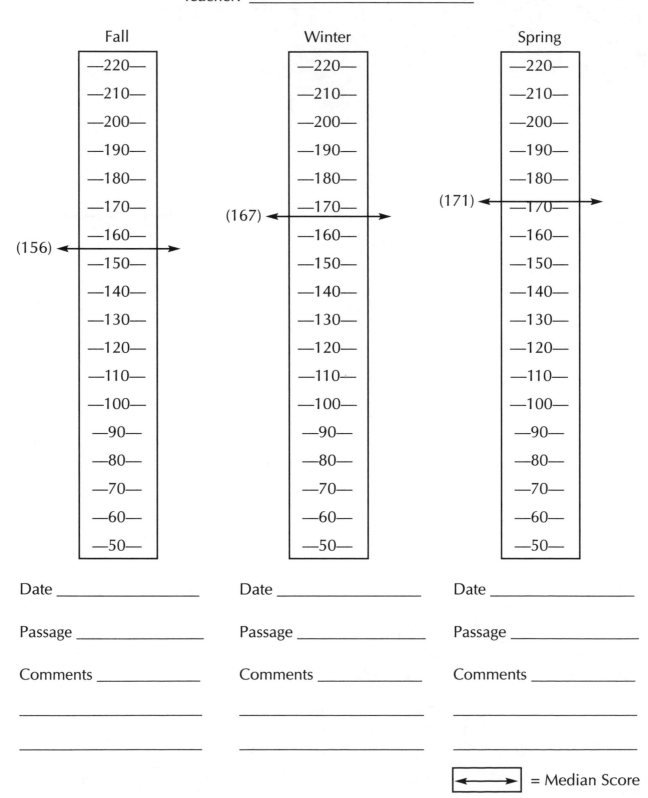

Fall	Winter	Spring
—220—	—220—	—220—
—210—	—210—	—210—
—200—	—200—	—200—
—190—	—190—	—190—
—180—	—180—	—180—
—170—	—170—	—170—
—160—	—160—	—160—
—150—	—150—	—150—
—140—	—140—	—140—
—130—	—130—	—130—
—120—	—120—	—120—
—110—	—110—	—110—
—100—	—100—	—100—
—90—	—90—	—90—
—80—	—80—	—80—
—70—	—70—	—70—
—60—	—60—	—60—
—50—	—50—	—50—

(156)   (167)   (171)

Date _____   Date _____   Date _____

Passage _____   Passage _____   Passage _____

Comments _____   Comments _____   Comments _____

_____   _____   _____

_____   _____   _____

◄——————► = Median Score

Evolving Reader Word Study (Spelling)
Pre- and Postassessment

	Evolving: Year 1				Evolving: Year 2	
	Pretest	Posttest			Pretest	Posttest
1	plane	chunk	Cycle 1	1	charm	flair
2	close	page		2	your	source
3	flute	white		3	dear	heard
4	stray	trust		4	hurt	surf
5	plain	play		5	gym	grape
6	teeth	wait		6	stretch	twitch
7	night	beach		7	judge	smudge
8	cloak	mule		8	screw	scrunch
9	fruit	sky	Cycle 2	9	squint	squeeze
10	crowd	phone		10	you'd	they'd
11	couldn't	bruise		11	heck	shook
12	square	hadn't		12	gnat	wrench
13	veil	chore		13	sprung	strength
14	pride	neigh		14	unkind	miscount
15	host	wind		15	headstone	background
16	bruise	comb		16	overview	underline
17	brief	suit	Cycle 3	17	how's	where's
18	nightgown	grief		18	they're	wagged
19	anytime	input		19	whizzed	treated
20	recharge	anyone		20	dotted	whining
21	clerk	germ		21	riding	blew
22	should	crook		22	know	whole
23	hoist	point		23	bravest	boldest
24	cloud	scowl		24	lawful	peaceful
25	caught	pause	Cycle 4	25	speechless	knight
26	we've	haven't		26	humid	emptiness
27	preheat	recall		27	napkin	blizzard
28	boxes	worries		28	mammal	market
29	carries	girls		29	migrate	improve
30	monkeys	glasses		30	construct	mourning

Maturing Reader Word Study (Spelling)
Pre- and Postassessment

	Maturing: Year 1				Maturing: Year 2	
	Pretest	Posttest			Pretest	Posttest
1	everything	waterfall	Cycle 1	1	scholar	molten
2	overhead	underground		2	snuggle	rumor
3	who'd	should've		3	harbor	rarely
4	disclose	pretest		4	jerky	spearhead
5	louder	cheapest		5	thirsty	virtue
6	garden	lantern		6	formal	stormy
7	ginger	lobster		7	murky	endure
8	rabbit	traffic		8	tattoo	rookie
9	punish	medal	Cycle 2	9	aloud	colonel
10	purchase	candle		10	except	patience
11	resist	prevent		11	edition	principle
12	bicycle	biweekly		12	catalogue	circumscribe
13	decade	decameter		13	breakable	tangible
14	elbow	writer		14	affordable	digestible
15	encourage	foreground		15	brilliant	agent
16	postpone	postscript		16	consistent	prominent
17	purple	person	Cycle 3	17	fountain	garden
18	cabbage	chapter		18	rotten	pumpkin
19	enter	welcome		19	nasal	nostril
20	ignore	winter		20	metal	jewel
21	desert	rebel		21	feature	rancher
22	seller	boulder		22	pasture	trencher
23	supermarket	intercom		23	hornet	habit
24	transplant	transfer		24	garbage	porridge
25	automobile	multilateral	Cycle 4	25	malice	lettuce
26	bridal	vital		26	trolley	beauty
27	sequel	pebble		27	fasten	resignation
28	tremor	soldier		28	definition	pleasure
29	generic	physique		29	delusion	intuition
30	persuade	traitor		30	celebrity	chronology

Advanced Reader Word Study (Spelling) Pre- and Postassessment

Advanced: Year 1

	Pretest	Posttest	
1	construction	inspection	Cycle 1
2	disruption	disruption	
3	confrontation	pigmentation	
4	transmission	reversion	
5	possession	compression	
6	physician	magician	
7	communication	graduation	
8	decision	comprehension	
9	mandible	preferable	Cycle 2
10	measurable	excitable	
11	respectable	perishable	
12	reality	feasible	
13	presumption	extremity	
14	publicize	presumption	
15	essential	ethnicity	
16	initiate	residential	
17	associate	separate	Cycle 3
18	vertebra	certificate	
19	nuclei	larvae	
20	inferred	cacti	
21	existing	inferred	
22	identifying	preventing	
23	conceiving	classifying	
24	aggression	insisting	
25	corruption	allow	Cycle 4
26	dissatisfied	combine	
27	efficiency	different	
28	immobile	efficiency	
29	surreal	sufficient	
30	archaeology	apologize	

Advanced: Year 2

	Pretest	Posttest
1	aerobic	aeronautics
2	archipelago	hierarchy
3	astronaut	astrophysics
4	dispose	impose
5	biography	biology
6	concentric	egocentric
7	chronometer	synchronize
8	germicide	homicide
9	cosmic	cosmos
10	crisis	diacritical
11	demagogue	epidemiology
12	comfort	perforce
13	condominium	predominate
14	equable	equilateral
15	abdicate	dictionary
16	abduct	deduce
17	emission	omission
18	demote	motel
19	dispense	pendulum
20	millipede	pedicure
21	audiometer	inaudible
22	inscribe	script
23	despicable	prospectus
24	convert	traverse
25	primeval	principal
26	microphone	saxophone
27	scope	telescope
28	telegram	prejudice
29	hydraulic	illiterate
30	judiciary	conspire

Word Study (Spelling) Pre- and Postassessment Student Recording Form

Name: _____

Date: _____

Stage: _____

Year (circle one)   1   2

Pre   Post   (circle one)

		Word	Student Spelling	Number of Errors Per Cycle
	1			
	2			
	3			
	4			
	5			
	6			
	7			
	8			
		Cycle 1		
	9			
	10			
	11			
	12			
	13			
	14			
	15			
	16			
		Cycle 2		
	17			
	18			
	19			
	20			
	21			
	22			
	23			
	24			
		Cycle 3		
	25			
	26			
	27			
	28			
	29			
	30			
		Cycle 4		
Total Number of Errors		Score (% correct)		

Evolving Reader Word Study (Spelling) Cycle Assessments

Evolving Stage Year 1 Cycle Assessment 1	Evolving Stage Year 1 Cycle Assessment 2	Evolving Stage Year 1 Cycle Assessment 3	Evolving Stage Year 1 Cycle Assessment 4
1 camp	1 cry	1 drew	1 ground
2 rude	2 live	2 cruel	2 draw
3 fast	3 spoke	3 brief	3 yawn
4 grade	4 cloak	4 fleet	4 wand
5 mule	5 drove	5 inside	5 she's
6 graph	6 cute	6 outlaw	6 hadn't
7 phone	7 fruit	7 anyone	7 insane
8 plump	8 bread	8 everlast	8 prefix
9 quaint	9 she'll	9 burst	9 relive
10 quake	10 flight	10 perch	10 recall
11 skunk	11 bark	11 chirp	11 heir
12 speck	12 chore	12 brook	12 maize
13 steam	13 strait	13 should	13 eaves
14 stray	14 beige	14 soil	14 style
15 swell	15 hind	15 ploy	15 chute
16 teeth	16 stride	16 shoot	16 chances
17 theft	17 cold	17 town	17 rulers
18 tilt	18 tomb	18 fowl	18 carries
19 waist	19 bolt	19 know	19 pennies
20 white	20 woe	20 ground	20 girls'
21 teeth	21 scare	21 sire	
22 street	22 veil	22 cure	
23 deal	23 slight	23 tear	
24 quote	24 doe	24 yearn	
25 spruce	25 carve	25 steer	

(continued)

Evolving Reader Word Study
(Spelling) Cycle Assessments *(continued)*

Evolving Stage Year 2 Cycle Assessment 1	Evolving Stage Year 2 Cycle Assessment 2	Evolving Stage Year 2 Cycle Assessment 3	Evolving Stage Year 2 Cycle Assessment 4
1 branch	1 backside	1 boldest	1 pare
2 bridge	2 distaste	2 breezy	2 pear
3 church	3 footstep	3 chased	3 browse
4 coach	4 gnat	4 cheerful	4 brows
5 court	5 knock	5 dusty	5 endless
6 cycle	6 misguide	6 eight	6 speechless
7 earth	7 overlook	7 funniest	7 merciless
8 fare	8 scream	8 here's	8 basket
9 glad	9 she'd	9 hopeful	9 happy
10 hire	10 smoke	10 know	10 human
11 hoarse	11 sprain	11 peaceful	11 famous
12 patch	12 squeak	12 popping	12 garden
13 peer	13 strange	13 quicker	13 parent
14 sage	14 they'd	14 right	14 vacant
15 scrunch	15 thick	15 shading	15 desert
16 shrew	16 thrive	16 stopped	16 police
17 smudge	17 undermine	17 tripped	17 giraffe
18 stair	18 unpack	18 walked	18 project
19 switch	19 update	19 where's	19 morning
20 throw	20 wrench	20 write	20 mourning

Maturing Reader Word Study (Spelling) Cycle Assessments

Maturing Stage Year 1 Cycle Assessment 1	Maturing Stage Year 1 Cycle Assessment 2	Maturing Stage Year 1 Cycle Assessment 3	Maturing Stage Year 1 Cycle Assessment 4
1 flaking	1 because	1 cabbage	1 autograph
2 breaking	2 bimonthly	2 chapter	2 profile
3 boiling	3 border	3 complete	3 semifinal
4 crying	4 complain	4 content	4 polygraph
5 popping	5 confuse	5 cradle	5 multiple
6 anything	6 decagon	6 interlock	6 pentameter
7 cheerful	7 encourage	7 intramural	7 quadrant
8 cleanest	8 foreground	8 intrapersonal	8 squad
9 discomfort	9 intuitive	9 lizard	9 pencil
10 everywhere	10 monopoly	10 malady	10 neutral
11 granddaughter	11 octagon	11 malign	11 eagle
12 hammock	12 paddle	12 mermaid	12 morsel
13 helmet	13 pentagon	13 profit	13 calendar
14 napkin	14 pilot	14 prophet	14 jogger
15 overflow	15 preparatory	15 rebel	15 juror
16 prepay	16 preschool	16 reverse	16 toxin
17 shouldn't	17 pretend	17 supermarket	17 sermon
18 smaller	18 proficient	18 transparent	18 tropic
19 that'll	19 riot	19 welcome	19 chronic
20 there'd	20 trilogy	20 window	20 plague
21 there's			
22 uncommon			
23 underground			
24 village			
25 waterproof			

(continued)

Maturing Reader Word Study
(Spelling) Cycle Assessments *(continued)*

Maturing Stage Year 2 Cycle Assessment 1	Maturing Stage Year 2 Cycle Assessment 2	Maturing Stage Year 2 Cycle Assessment 3	Maturing Stage Year 2 Cycle Assessment 4
1 adopt	1 adolescent	1 bandit	1 academic
2 barrel	2 allow	2 cartridge	2 addendum
3 bony	3 chili	3 catcher	3 admission
4 fireplace	4 chilly	4 comet	4 composition
5 floral	5 circumscribe	5 cousin	5 criminal
6 future	6 employ	6 denture	6 democracy
7 marble	7 hesitant	7 fresher	7 design
8 murky	8 laughable	8 gerbil	8 explosion
9 normal	9 laundry	9 giggle	9 geometric
10 obscure	10 lawsuit	10 global	10 guilty
11 pouring	11 morning	11 hostile	11 hockey
12 promote	12 mourning	12 jewel	12 induction
13 raccoon	13 perimeter	13 lemon	13 intuition
14 rookie	14 prominent	14 metal	14 lettuce
15 sirloin	15 remarkable	15 orphan	15 menace
16 snuggle	16 stationary	16 oxen	16 millennia
17 storefront	17 stationery	17 package	17 pleasure
18 surgeon	18 tangible	18 pressure	18 prairie
19 veneer	19 terrible	19 thicken	19 preparation
20 verdict	20 tower	20 torture	20 resignation

Advanced Reader Word Study (Spelling) Cycle Assessments

Advanced Stage Year 1 Cycle Assessment 1	Advanced Stage Year 1 Cycle Assessment 2	Advanced Stage Year 1 Cycle Assessment 3	Advanced Stage Year 1 Cycle Assessment 4
1 associate	1 admissible	1 alga	1 adhesive
2 collection	2 commercial	2 algae	2 aggression
3 comprehension	3 conception	3 animate	3 approach
4 compression	4 confidential	4 associate	4 attain
5 disruption	5 criticize	5 committing	5 biology
6 division	6 distinguishable	6 digested	6 collect
7 educate	7 essential	7 enforcing	7 combine
8 electrician	8 extravagant	8 entering	8 different
9 expansion	9 extremity	9 explaining	9 dissatisfied
10 expression	10 impatient	10 graduated	10 efface
11 importation	11 irritate	11 identifying	11 effectual
12 invasion	12 legible	12 inferred	12 excommunicate
13 inversion	13 liability	13 inserting	13 illiterate
14 navigate	14 pentathlon	14 insisting	14 immeasurable
15 pediatrician	15 predictable	15 intimidate	15 inefficient
16 presentation	16 racial	16 measuring	16 irrigation
17 protrusion	17 reduction	17 nuclei	17 occupancy
18 statistic	18 substantial	18 nucleus	18 pathology
19 suggestion	19 transcription	19 nucleuses	19 suffix
20 transmission	20 vegetable	20 omitting	20 surreal

(continued)

Advanced Reader Word Study
(Spelling) Cycle Assessments *(continued)*

Advanced Stage Year 2 Cycle Assessment 1	Advanced Stage Year 2 Cycle Assessment 2	Advanced Stage Year 2 Cycle Assessment 3	Advanced Stage Year 2 Cycle Assessment 4
1 aerate	1 aqueduct	1 audiometer	1 primate
2 aerobic	2 benediction	2 auditory	2 primordial
3 antibiotic	3 cosmic	3 conspicuous	3 principle
4 archbishop	4 criterion	4 convert	4 stereophonic
5 astronomy	5 criticize	5 demise	5 phonetic
6 biography	6 deduct	6 demobilize	6 headphone
7 centrifugal	7 democracy	7 dependent	7 kaleidoscope
8 chronicle	8 dictionary	8 describe	8 stereoscope
9 chronometer	9 domain	9 millipede	9 telephone
10 compose	10 endemic	10 missionary	10 telecourse
11 concentric	11 enforcement	11 motel	11 televise
12 disaster	12 equality	12 pediatrician	12 hydroplane
13 ethnocentric	13 equidistant	13 pendant	13 hydraulic
14 excise	14 equinox	14 promote	14 hydrangea
15 germicide	15 fortress	15 propensity	15 injudicious
16 impostor	16 hypocrisy	16 proscribe	16 judiciary
17 insecticide	17 introduction	17 quadruped	17 prejudice
18 matriarch	18 macrocosm	18 remission	18 literate
19 proposition	19 predominate	19 specimen	19 conspire
20 symbiotic	20 valedictorian	20 versus	20 transpire

Oral Questioning Response Checklist

Teacher: _____

Date(s): _____

Student	Literal		Inferential		Application	
	Asked	Response	Asked	Response	Asked	Response

+ correct response   – incorrect response   ½ partial

Comments:

_____

_____

_____

_____

Narrative Text Comprehension:
Classroom Profile Sheet for Oral Summary

Teacher: _____   Date(s): _____

Student	Main characters				Setting				Problem				Action				Resolution			
Quarter	1st	2nd	3rd	4th	1st	2nd	3rd	4th	1st	2nd	3rd	4th	1st	2nd	3rd	4th	1st	2nd	3rd	4th

Expository Text Comprehension: Classroom Profile Sheet for Written Summary

Teacher: _____   Date(s): _____

Student	Main Idea/Supporting Details				Cause and Effect				Sequencing				Compare/Contrast			
Quarter	1st	2nd	3rd	4th	1st	2nd	3rd	4th	1st	2nd	3rd	4th	1st	2nd	3rd	4th

Expository Text Comprehension Assessment: Cause and Effect

Student: _____

Date: _____

Text: _____

Directions: List four cause-and-effect relationships stated in the text.

Cause   Effect

1. _____ ⟹ _____

2. _____ ⟹ _____

3. _____ ⟹ _____

4. _____ ⟹ _____

The numbers in the scoring rubric indicate the number of correct causes and effects identified on this assessment.

Scoring Rubric:	Mastery	Developing	Deficient
# Correct	6–8	4–5	0–3

Expository Text Comprehension Assessment: Sequencing

Student: _____

Date: _____

Text: _____

Directions: Identify five important events from the selection, and place them in the sequence in which they occurred.

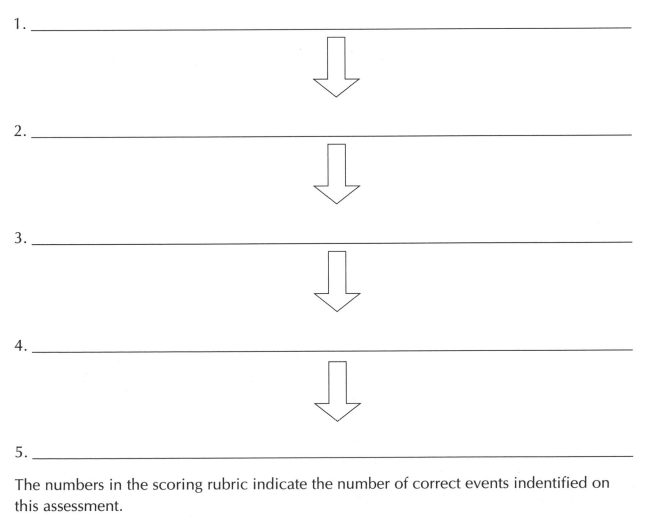

1. _____

2. _____

3. _____

4. _____

5. _____

The numbers in the scoring rubric indicate the number of correct events indentified on this assessment.

Scoring Rubric:	Mastery	Developing	Deficient
# Correct	5	3–4	0–2

Expository Text Comprehension Assessment: Compare and Contrast

Student: _____

Date: _____

Text: _____

Directions: Compare and contrast _____ and _____ by writing distinct features in the outer parts of the circle and similar features in the area where the circles overlap.

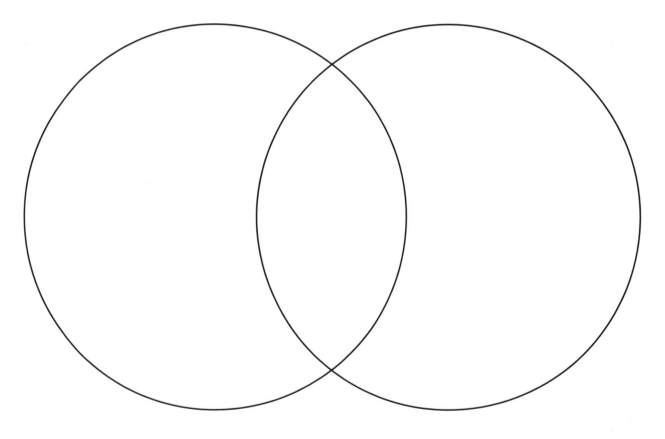

The numbers in the scoring rubric indicate the number of correct features identified on this assessment.

Scoring Rubric:	Mastery	Developing	Deficient
# Correct	8–9	5–7	0–4

Expository Text Comprehension Assessment: Main Idea and Supporting Details

Student: _____

Date: _____

Text: _____

Directions: Identify the main idea of the text you are reading and include three supporting details. Please write in complete sentences.

Main Idea: _____

_____

_____

_____

Supporting Details:

1. _____

_____

2. _____

_____

3. _____

_____

The numbers in the scoring rubric indicate the number of correct components identified on this assessement.

Scoring Rubric:	Mastery	Developing	Deficient
# Correct	4	2–3	1

Word Study Materials

Note: Some sorts include a large amount of words. Teachers may choose to limit the number of word study cards the group uses. We recommend that at least seven cards be included for each feature for sorting purposes.

Glossary of Word Study Terms

This glossary provides definitions of terms specific to the word study component of the Small-Group Differentiated Reading Model. The terms are word study features that are learned throughout the evolving, maturing, and advanced reader stages.

Ambiguous vowel patterns: Vowel combinations that produce a sound other than long, short, or r-controlled. Examples of these patterns include b*oil*, j*oy*, m*ouse*, and h*aul*. These vowel combinations are also known as abstract, vowel digraphs, or diphthongs.

Assimilated prefixes: Prefixes that change in spelling based on the consonant they precede but that retain the meaning of the original prefix. For example, *in* + *legal* = *il*legal. *In* means *not*, but when placed before a word that starts with *l*, the spelling of *in* changes to *il*, typically for the purposes of pronunciation.

Base word: A word that can stand alone. Prefixes and suffixes are often added to this word. For example, in the word *misspelling*, the base word is *spell*, the prefix is *mis*, and the suffix is *ing*.

Closed syllables: Syllable patterns that end in a consonant, typically leaving the vowel short. Examples of these patterns include HABit, BUBble, and COMpose.

Complex consonants or triple blends: Three-letter combinations usually consisting of all consonants. Examples of these patterns include *scr*eam, *thr*ee, *squ*are, and *shr*iek.

Digraph: Two letters that make one sound. For the purposes of this book, digraphs refer only to consonant digraphs. Examples of this feature include *sh*ook, *ch*ip, *th*ink, *wh*ip, and gra*ph*.

Homographs: Words that are spelled the same but have different meanings. For example, RECord (noun) and reCORD (verb).

Homophones: Words that sound the same but are spelled differently. For example, *eight* and *ate* are homophones.

Long-vowel patterns: Vowel combinations that produce long-vowel sounds, such as tr*ai*n, th*ese*, b*oa*t, and s*igh*.

Open syllable: Syllable pattern that ends in a vowel, typically leaving the vowel sound long. Examples include RObot and TUlip.

Prefix: A group of letters attached to the beginning of a word; it has specific meaning and cannot stand alone as a single word. Examples include *un*tie, *re*mind, and *mis*spell.

R-controlled vowel patterns: Vowel combinations that are followed by the letter *r*. Simple r-controlled patterns include st*ar*, m*ore*, s*ir*, f*ur*, h*er*. More complex patterns include ch*eer*, *ear*th, r*oar*. Note: All r-controlled vowel patterns are not listed here.

Root words: A group of letters derived from Latin or Greek that carries specific meaning. Typically, root words cannot stand alone as words and prefixes and/or suffixes are added to them. For example, in the word *visible*, *vis* (meaning to see) is the root word, and *ible* is the suffix.

Schwa: Unaccented vowel sound in a word. Typically, the schwa sound is similar to the short *u* sound. The schwa sound is represented phonetically with the ə symbol.

Suffix: A group of letters attached to the end of a word; it has specific meaning and cannot stand alone as a single word. Examples of suffixes include bad*ly*, great*er*, and worth*less*.

Syllable pattern: The patterns of letters that are found at the point where the syllables joins. Note: At this juncture, digraphs and blends are considered one consonant unit. For example, in the word *monster* the V-C-C-V pattern is as follows: *o* is a vowel, *n* is a consonant, *st* is a blend considered to be one consonant unit, and *e* is the final vowel.

Syllable stress: The syllable that is emphasized the most in pronunciation. For example, in the word aDOPT, the stress is placed on the second syllable.

Word Sort Directions

These word sort directions are to be used in conjunction with the word study scope and sequence for evolving, maturing, and advanced readers.

Evolving Reader

Evolving Reader: Year 1: Cycle 1: 9 weeks

1. Review short vowels with preconsonantal nasals, digraphs, blends.
   Sort Directions: Sort according to vowel sound. Students should pay special attention to how the nasal sounds of /m/ and /n/ change the sound of the vowel. In addition, students can discuss the sound change in the *all* pattern.

2. Review short vowels with preconsonantal nasals, digraphs, blends.
   Sort Directions: Sort according to vowel sound. Students should pay special attention to how the nasal sounds of /m/ and /n/ change the sound of the vowel.

3. Long *A* patterns(a_e, short *A*)
   Sort Directions: Sort by sound first and then pattern. Then, sort both by sound and pattern. Students should pay special attention to the oddball words (e.g., *have*) that change categories when sorted this way.

4. Long *O* patterns (*v_e*, short)
   Sort Directions: Sort by sound and pattern.

5. Long *E* and *I* patterns (*v_e*, short)
   Sort Directions: Sort by sound and pattern.

6. Long *U* patterns (*u_e—yoo/oo*, short)
   Sort Directions: Sort by pattern first and then sound. Students should pay special attention to the two sounds that long *u* makes.

7. Long *A* patterns (*a_e, ay*)
   Sort Directions: Sort by pattern. Students should pay special attention to the placement of the long *a* in the patterns. In the *a_e* pattern, you hear the sound in the middle of the word; with *ay*, you hear the sound at the end of the word.

8. Long *A* patterns (*a_e, ai, ay*)
   Sort Directions: Sort by pattern. Students should pay special attention to the final consonants in the *a_e* and *ai* patterns to see if they can make any generalizations about the pattern (e.g., *ain, ail, aid*).

9. Long *E* patterns (*ee, ea, e*)
   Sort Directions: Sort by pattern. Students should pay special attention to the placement of the long *e* in the patterns. In the *ee* and *ea* patterns, the sound usually is in the middle of the word. In the final single *e* pattern, the sound is at the end of the word.

Evolving Reader: Year 1: Cycle 2: 9 weeks

1. Long and short *E* patterns (*ea*)
   Sort Directions: Sort by sound. Students should recognize that the pattern can be long or short. Further, students should pay special attention to those words that can have either the short or long sound (e.g., *lead*, *read*).

2. Long *I* patterns (*i_e, igh, y*)
   Sort Directions: Sort by pattern. Students should pay special attention to the placement of the long *i* in the patterns. In the *i_e* and *igh* patterns, the sound is usually in the middle of the word; in the final *y* pattern, the sound is at the end of the word.

3. Long *O* patterns (*o_e, oa, ow*)
   Sort Directions: Sort by pattern. Students should pay special attention to the placement of the long *o* in the patterns. In the *o_e* and *oa* patterns, the sound is in the middle of the word; in the final *ow* pattern, the sound can be either in the middle (e.g., *flown*, *blown*, *known*) or at the end of the word (e.g., *grow*).

4. Long *U* patterns (*u_e, ew, ui*)
   Sort Directions: Sort by pattern. Students should pay special attention to the placement of the long *u* in the patterns. In the *u_e* and *ui* patterns, the sound is in the middle of the word. In the final *ew* pattern, the sound is usually at the end (e.g., *grew*, *shrewd*). Note: The *ew* pattern also can be studied with ambiguous vowels.

5. Contractions (*not, will, have*)
   Sort Directions: Sort by contraction. Students should note the number of letters that the apostrophe takes the place of in the given categories.

6. *R*-controlled (*ar, are, oar, ore*)
   Sort Directions: Sort by pattern. Students should note the different patterns that make the same sound for *or*, as well as the change in the sound when an *e* is added onto *ar*.

7. Less common *A* (*ei, ey, ai*)
   Sort Directions: Sort by pattern. Students should pay special attention to the placement of the long *a*. In the *ei* and *ai* patterns, the sound is usually in the middle of the word. In the final *ey* pattern, the sound is at the end of the word.

8. Less common *I* (*iCC, igh, i_e*)
   Sort Directions: Sort by pattern. Students should pay special attention to the word *wind* because it can have a long or short sound.

9. Less common *O* (*oCC, oe, o*)
   Sort Directions: Sort by pattern. Students should pay special attention to the word *tomb* because it has an ambiguous sound, as well as the few words that have the *oe* and final *o* pattern.

Evolving Reader: Year 1: Cycle 3: 9 weeks

1. Less common *U* (*ue, ui, ew*)
   Sort Directions: Sort by pattern. Students should pay special attention to the placement of the long *u*. In the *ue* and *ew* patterns, the sound is usually at the end word; in the *ui* pattern, the sound is in the middle of the word.

2. Less common *E* (*ie, e, ee*)
   Sort Directions: Sort by pattern. Students should pay special attention to the placement of the long *e*. In the *ie* pattern, the sound is in the middle of the word.

3. Compound words (*in, out, night*)
   Sort Directions: Sort by compound word. Emphasis should focus on the meaning of these words.

4. Compound words (*any, every, ever*)
   Sort Directions: Sort by compound word. Emphasis should focus on the meaning of these words.

5. *R*-controlled (*ur, er, ir*)
   Sort Directions: Sort by pattern. Students should pay special attention to the placement of the long *u* in the patterns. In the *ue* and *ew* patterns, the sound is usually at the end word; in the *ui* pattern, the sound is in the middle of the word.

6. *R*-controlled (*eer, ear, ure, ire*)
   Sort Directions: Sort by pattern. Students also can sort by sound and should pay special attention to the different sounds of the *ear* pattern (e.g., *dear, learn*).

7. Ambiguous vowels (*oo, ou*)
   Sort Directions: Sort by pattern. Students also can sort by sound and should pay special attention to the different sounds of the *oo* pattern (e.g., *book, moon*).

8. Ambiguous vowels (*oi, oy*)
   Sort Directions: Sort by pattern. Students should also pay special attention to the placement of the *oi*. The *oi* pattern is found at the beginning or the middle of the word, whereas the *oy* pattern is found at the end of the word.

9. Ambiguous vowels (*ow, ou*)
   Sort Directions: Sort by pattern and then sound. Students should pay special attention to the two sounds each of the patterns make (e.g., *how/grow, soup/cloud*).

Evolving Reader: Year 1: Cycle 4: 8 weeks

1. Ambiguous vowels (*aw, au, wa*)
   Sort Directions: Sort by pattern and then by sound. Students should pay attention to the sound change of the *wa* pattern when an *r* is added (e.g., *swap* as opposed to *warm*).

2. Contractions (*would, had, is, has, not*)
   Sort Directions: Sort by contraction. Students should note the number of letters that the apostrophe takes the place of in the given categories.

3. Introduction to easy prefixes (*in*—in or into, *pre*—before, *re*—again)
   Sort Directions: Sort by the prefix. Emphasis should focus on the meaning of these words.

4. Homophones (single syllable)
   Sort Directions: Students should match up the homophone pairs. Emphasis should focus on the meaning of the words.

5. Homophones (single syllable)
   Sort Directions: Students should match the homophone pairs. Emphasis should focus on the meaning of the words.

6. Introduction to easy suffixes (*s*, *es*)

   Sort Directions: Sort by pattern. Students should be able to articulate when a word needs an *s* versus an *es*. Typically, words ending in *ch*, *sh*, *s*, *ss*, or *x* require *es*.

7. Suffixes—single syllable plurals (*es*, *y* to *i*)

   Sort Directions: Sort by pattern. Students should be able to articulate when a word needs an *s* versus an *es*. Students should also be able to articulate when a word needs to change from *y* to *i* before adding *es*.

8. Possessives (*s*, '*s*, *s*')

   Sort Directions: Students add *s*, '*s*, and *s*' in order to signify words that show plural, possessive, and plural possessive forms.

Evolving Reader: Year 2: Cycle 1: 8 Weeks

1. Complex *r*-controlled (*are*, *air*, *ar*)

   Sort Directions: Sort by pattern and then by sound. Students should pay special attention to the *are* and *air* patterns because they sound the same.

2. Complex *r*-controlled (*ore*, *our*, *oar*)

   Sort Directions: Sort by pattern and then by sound. Students should pay special attention the two sounds the *our* pattern makes (e.g., *hour*, *four*).

3. Complex *r*-controlled (*eer*, *ear*, *er*)

   Sort Directions: Sort by pattern and then by sound. Students should pay special attention to the two sounds the *ear* pattern makes (e.g., *learn*, *dear*) and the addition of the final *e* on other *er* pattern words.

4. Complex *r*-controlled (*ire*, *ure*, *ur*, *ir*)

   Sort Directions: Sort by sound and then by pattern. Students should pay special attention to the additional of the final *e* on the *ire* and *ure* pattern. In addition, students should recognize the two sounds of the *ure* pattern.

5. Complex consonants (*c*, *g*—beginning, ending)

   Sort Directions: Sort by sound. Students should recognize that the consonants make the hard sound when followed by *a*, *o*, and *u*. The consonants make the soft sound when followed by *e*, *i*, and *y*.

6. Complex consonants (*ch*, *tch*, *Cch*)

   Sort Directions: Sort by pattern. Students should recognize that typically, the *ch* pattern contains a long-vowel pattern, the *Cch* pattern contains a short or sometimes *r*-controlled, and the *tch* pattern contains a short-vowel sound.

7. Complex consonants (*ge*, *dge*, *Cge*)

   Sort Directions: Sort by pattern. Students should recognize that typically, the *ge* pattern contains a long-vowel pattern; the *Cge* pattern contains a short, *r*-controlled, or in a few cases, a long-vowel sound (change); and the *dge* pattern contains a short-vowel sound.

8. Complex consonants (*shr*, *thr*, *scr*)

   Sort Directions: Sort by sound and pattern.

Evolving Reader: Year 2: Cycle 2: 8 Weeks

1. Triple-letter blends (*scr, squ, spl*)
   Sort Directions: Sort by sound and pattern.

2. Contractions (*had, would, are*)
   Sort Directions: Sort by contraction. Students should note the number of letters that the apostrophe takes the place of in the given categories.

3. Complex consonants (final *k—ck, ke, VVk*)
   Sort Directions: Sort by sound and then pattern. Students should recognize that the *ck* pattern contains a short-vowel sound, and the *ke* and *V-V-k* patterns contain a long- or ambiguous vowel sound.

4. Silent consonants (*kn, gn, wr*)
   Sort Directions: Sort by sound and then by pattern. Students should recognize that the *gn* and *kn* patterns make the same sound.

5. Triple-letter blends (*str, thr, spr*)
   Sort Directions: Sort by sound and pattern.

6. Intro to easy prefixes (*un, dis, mis*)
   Sort Directions: Sort by prefix. Emphasis should focus on the meaning of these words.

7. Compound words (*back, head, foot*)
   Sort Directions: Sort by the given words. Emphasis should focus on the meaning of these words.

8. Compound words (*over, under, down, up*)
   Sort Directions: Sort by the given words. Emphasis should focus on the meaning of these words.

Evolving Reader: Year 2: Cycle 3: 8 Weeks

1. Contractions (*is, has, us, are, am*)
   Sort Directions: Sort by contraction. Students should note the number of letters that the apostrophe takes the place of in the given categories.

2. Suffixes (*ed*—doubling, e-drop, nothing)
   Sort Directions: Sort by pattern. Students should recognize when you have to drop the final *e*, double the final consonant, or do nothing before you add the *ed* suffix. Note: Typically, if the word has one vowel, ends in one consonant, and has one syllable, you have to double the final consonant before adding *ed*. This is to preserve the short-vowel sound. The knowledge of preserving the short-vowel sound is critical to the study of syllable patterns.

3. Suffixes (sounds of *ed*)
   Sort Directions: Sort by sound. Students should recognize that when *ed* is added to a word, it has three sounds: /ed/ (*treated*), /d/ (*loved*), and /t/ (*baked*).

4. Suffixes (*ing*—doubling, e-drop, nothing)
   Sort Directions: Sort by pattern. Students should recognize when you have to drop the final *e*, double the final consonant, or do nothing before you add the *ing* suffix. Note: typically, if the word has one vowel, ends in one consonant, and has one syllable, you have to double the final consonant before adding *ing*. Again, this is to preserve the short-vowel sound. The knowledge of preserving the short-vowel sound is critical to the study of syllable patterns.

5. Homophones (single syllable)
   Sort Directions: Students should match up the homophone pairs. Emphasis should focus on the meaning of the words.

6. Homophones (single syllable)
   Sort Directions: Students should match up the homophone pairs. Emphasis should focus on the meaning of the words.

7. Suffixes (*er, est*)
   Sort Directions: Sort by pattern. Students should recognize when you have to drop the final *e*, double the final consonant, or do nothing before you add the *er* suffix. Note: Typically, if the word has one vowel, ends in one consonant, and has one syllable, you have to double the final consonant before adding *er*. This is to preserve the short-vowel sound. The knowledge of preserving the short-vowel sound is critical to the study of syllable patterns. The students should also engage in a discussion about the meaning changes as the suffix is added—*er* and *est* are known as comparatives and superlatives, respectively.

8. Suffixes (*ful*—full of/having, *ly*—like/in a like manner, *y*—having)
   Sort Directions: Sort by pattern. Students should discuss the meaning of the suffixes and how that meaning influences the meaning of the words when the suffix is added.

Evolving Reader: Year 2: Cycle 4: 8 Weeks

1. Homophones (single syllable)
   Sort Directions: Students should match up the homophone pairs. Emphasis should focus on the meaning of the words.

2. Suffixes (*less*—without, *ness*—state of being)
   Sort Directions: Sort by pattern. Students should discuss the meaning of the suffixes and how that meaning influences the meaning of the words when the suffix is added.

3. Syllable patterns (VCCV, with first syllable stress)
   Sort Directions: Sort by pattern. Students are introduced to syllable patterns (the pattern at the juncture of the syllables). AF/ter and AT/tic both follow the V-C-C-V pattern with stress on the first syllable. Students should recognize the C-C pattern with single-consonant combinations and doublet (double consonants) combinations. Both of these patterns contain closed syllables. This understanding of syllable patterns allows students to use this knowledge when they encounter unknown words in their reading as well as when spelling or pronouncing words. Note: Blends and digraphs are considered to be one unit rather than two individual letters. A discussion of syllable stress can also occur during the syllable pattern study.

4. Syllable patterns (VCV and VCCV, with first syllable stress)
   Sort Directions: Sort by pattern. Students should recognize the V-C-C-V (MAR/ket) pattern they studied the previous week as having a closed syllable. Further, they compare the VCV (MU/sic) pattern in words with an open syllable and discuss the differences in the vowel sounds (open—long, closed—short).

5. Syllable patterns (VCV open and VCV closed, with first syllable stress)
   Sort Directions: Sort by sound and pattern. Students should recognize the V-C-V pattern they

studied the previous week as having an open syllable (MUsic). This week, they compare and contrast the V-C-V pattern with a closed syllable (CABin). The V-C-V pattern is typically more difficult for students to master because of the nature of the pattern—at times, the consonant stays with the first vowel (CREDit), and other times, the consonant stays with the second vowel (TUlip). Thus, students should be encouraged to complete word hunts to solidify their knowledge of this pattern.

6. Syllable patterns (VCCV and VCV, with second syllable stress)
   Sort Directions: Sort by pattern. Students should compare and contrast the V-C-C-V (adMIT) and the V-C-V (hoTEL) patterns as they both have the second syllable stressed.

7. Homographs—two syllable (noun, first syllable stress; verb, second syllable stress; adjective, first or second syllable stress)
   Sort Directions: Students should say each word and decide which syllable is stressed. As students discover which syllable is stressed, they should also discuss the part of speech the word is used (CONduct—noun, conDUCT—verb).

8. Homophones—two syllable (spelling variation in the stressed syllable)
   Sort Directions: Students should match up the homophone pairs. Emphasis should focus on the meaning of the words as well as the spelling variation that occurs in the stressed syllable.

Maturing Reader

Maturing Reader: Year 1: Cycle 1: 9 Weeks

1. Suffixes (*ing*—doubling, e-drop, nothing)
   Sort Directions: Sort by pattern. Students should recognize when you have to drop the final *e*, double the final consonant, or do nothing before you add the *ing* suffix. Note: Typically, if the word has one vowel, ends in one consonant, and has one syllable, you have to double the final consonant before adding *ing*. Again, this is to preserve the short-vowel sound. The knowledge of preserving the short-vowel sound is critical to the study of syllable patterns.

2. Compound words—three plus syllables (*any, every, water*)
   Sort Directions: Sort by the given words. Emphasis should focus on the meaning of these words.

3. Compound words—three plus syllables (*over, under, grand*)
   Sort Directions: Sort by the given words. Emphasis should focus on the meaning of these words.

4. Contractions (review all)
   Sort Directions: Sort by contraction. Students should note the number of letters that the apostrophe takes the place of in the given categories.

5. Prefix review (*un*—not/opposite of, *re*—again, *pre*—before, *dis*—opposite of)
   Sort Directions: Sort by prefix. Emphasis should focus on the meaning of these words.

6. Suffix review (*ful*—full of/having, *ly*—like/in a manner, *er*—comparative, *est*—superlative)
   Sort Directions: Sort by pattern. Students should discuss the meaning of the suffixes and how that meaning influences the meaning of the words when the suffix is added.

7. Syllable patterns (VCCV—regular/doublet, first syllable stress)
   Sort Directions: Sort by pattern. Students review syllable patterns (the pattern at the juncture of the syllables). AFter and ATtic both follow the V-C-C-V pattern with stress on the first syllable. Students should recognize the C-C pattern with single-consonant combinations and doublet (double consonants) combinations. Both of these patterns contain closed syllables and have first syllable stress.

8. Syllable patterns (VCCV—regular/doublet, first syllable stress)
   Sort Directions: Sort by pattern. Students review syllable patterns (the pattern at the juncture of the syllables). AFter and ATtic both follow the V-C-C-V pattern with stress on the first syllable. Students should recognize the C-C pattern with single-consonant combinations and doublet (double consonants) combinations. Both of these patterns contain closed syllables and have first syllable stress.

9. Syllable patterns (VCCV—doublets, first and second syllable stress)
   Sort Directions: Sort by syllable stress. Students should recognize that both categories have doublets, but syllable stress is different. Also, there are much fewer words with the V-C-C-V doublet pattern with the second syllable stressed.

Maturing Reader: Year 1: Cycle 2: 8 Weeks

1. Syllable patterns (VCV—open [FInal]/closed [HABit], first syllable stress)
   Sort Directions: Sort by sound and pattern. Students should recognize the VCV pattern they studied previously and continue to add more words to their vocabulary as they study this pattern.

2. Syllable patterns (VCCV—regular [MONster] doublet [BUBble], first syllable stress and regular [conFESS] doublet [posSESS], second syllable stress)
   Sort Directions: Sort by pattern. Students should compare and contrast the VCCV pattern with both single consonants and doublets as the diferent syllable is stressed.

3. Syllable patterns (VCV—open [poLITE] closed [exACT] second syllable stress)
   Sort Directions: Sort by sound and pattern. Students should recognize the V-C-V pattern as the second syllable is stressed. Students should also recognize that there are very few V-C-V closed syllable words.

4. Number-related prefixes (*mon/mono, bi, tri*)
   Sort Directions: Sort by prefix. Emphasis should focus on the meaning of these words.

5. Number-related prefixes (*pent, oct/octa/octo, dec/deca*)
   Sort Directions: Sort by prefix. Emphasis should focus on the meaning of these words.

6. Syllable patterns (VV [LIar], VCCV [CACtus], VCV [ROtate])
   Sort Directions: Sort by pattern. Students should recognize the different syllable patterns and be able to discuss which syllable is stressed in each pattern.

7. Prefixes (*in*—in/into, *en*—to put into/make, *fore*—before/in front of)
   Sort Directions: Sort by prefix. Emphasis should focus on the meaning of these words.

8. Common prefixes (*pro*—before/forward, *post*—after, *pre*—before)
   Sort Directions: Sort by prefix. Emphasis should focus on the meaning of these words.

Maturing Reader: Year 1: Cycle 3: 8 Weeks

1. Sensitizing to stress (first or second syllable)
   Sort Directions: Sort according to the stressed syllable.

2. Vowel patterns in the stressed syllable (short *A*, long *A*)
   Sort Directions: Sort according to the short and long *a* patterns in the stressed syllable. Patterns include short *a* (FABric), long *a_e* (creATE), and open *a* (BAsic).

3. Vowel patterns in the stressed syllable (short *E*, long *E*)
   Sort Directions: Sort according to the short and long *e* patterns in the stressed syllable. Patterns include short *e* (ENter, REAdy), long *e* (CHEEtah), and open *e* (BEing).

4. Vowel patterns in the stressed syllable (short *I*, long *I*)
   Sort Directions: Sort according to the short and long *i* patterns in the stressed syllable. Patterns include short *i* (INsect, GYPsy), long *i_e* (adVICE), and open *i* (DIner).

5. Homographs (two syllable with syllable stress)
   Sort Directions: Students should say each word and decide which syllable is stressed. As students discover which syllable is stressed, they should also discuss the part of speech the word is used (CONduct—noun, conDUCT—verb).

6. Homophones (two syllable, spelling variation in both syllables)
   Sort Directions: Students should match up the homophone pairs. Emphasis should focus on the meaning of the words as well as the spelling variation that occurs in the stressed syllables.

7. Common prefixes (*inter*—between/among, *super*—higher/greater, *intra*—within)
   Sort Directions: Sort by the prefix. Emphasis should focus on the meaning of these words.

8. Common prefixes (*trans*—over/across, *mal/male*—bad/evil)
   Sort Directions: Sort by the prefix. Emphasis should focus on the meaning of these words.

Maturing Reader: Year 1: Cycle 4: 8 Weeks

1. Common prefixes (*anti*—against, *auto*—self, *pro*—before forward)
   Sort Directions: Sort by prefix. Emphasis should focus on the meaning of these words.

2. Number-related roots (*multi*—many/much, *poly*—many, *semi*—half/partly)
   Sort Directions: Sort by root. Emphasis should focus on the meaning of these words.

3. Spelling patterns at the end of words (*il, al, ile*)
   Sort Directions: Sort by pattern. Hint: Many al pattern words are adjectives. Students should engage in a conversations about the part of speech for the remaining words. *Il* and *ile* are less common /əl/ endings.

4. Spelling patterns at the end of words (*el, le*)
   Sort Directions: Sort by pattern. Hint: Many more words end in *le* than with *el*. Consonants b, c, d, g, k, p, t, and z typically end with *le*. Also, knowledge of soft- and hard-consonant sounds will also help when deciding on the ending (*angel, circle*).

5. Spelling patterns at the end of words (*or, er, ar*)
   Sort Directions: Sort by pattern. Hint: Words relating to people typically end in *er* or *or*. Adjectives tend to end in *er* or *ar*. Students should also emphasize the meaning of these words while they are sorting.

6. Spelling patterns at the end of words (*en*—noun/adjective/verb—*in*, and *on*—noun)
   Sort Directions: Sort by pattern. Hint: Verbs and adjectives typically end in *en*. Nouns tend to end in *on* or *in*.

7. Final *k* sound (*que, ck, c, k*)
   Sort Directions: Sort by pattern. Hint: The final *c* is the most common in polysyllabic words.

8. Vowel patterns in the stressed syllable (long *A*, short *A*)
   Sort Directions: Sort according to the short and long *a* patterns in the stressed syllable. Patterns include short *a* (CANvas), long *a_e* (esCAPE), open *a* (CRAter), *ai* (FAILure), and *ay* (deCAY).

Maturing Reader: Year 2: Cycle 1: 8 Weeks

1. Vowel patterns in the stressed syllable (long *O*, short *O*)
   Sort Directions: Sort according to the short and long *o* patterns in the stressed syllable. Patterns include short *o* (aDOPT), long *o_e* (aLONE), *oa* (TOASTer), *oCC* (STROLLer), *ow* (beLOW), and open *o* (BOny).

2. Vowel patterns in the stressed syllable (long *U*—u_e, open and short *U*)
   Sort Directions: Sort according to the short and long *u* patterns in the stressed syllable. Patterns include short *u* (BUBble), long *u_e* (aBUSE), and open *u* (TUlip).

3. *R*-controlled vowels in the stressed syllable (*ar, are, air*)
   Sort Directions: Sort according to the *r*-controlled patterns in the stressed syllable. Patterns include *ar* (aLARM, CARry), *are* (aWARE), and *air* (PRAIRie).

4. *R*-controlled vowels in the stressed syllable (*er, ear, eer, ere*)
   Sort Directions: Sort according to the *r*-controlled patterns in the stressed syllable. Patterns include *er* (JERky), *ear* (LEARNer, apPEAR), *eer* (LEERy), and *ere* (adHERE).

5. *R*-controlled vowels in the stressed syllable (*ir, ire*)
   Sort Directions: Sort according to the *r*-controlled patterns in the stressed syllable. Patterns include *ir* (CIRcle) and *ire* (inQUIRE).

6. *R*-controlled vowels in the stressed syllable (*or, ore, oar, our)*
   Sort Directions: Sort according to the *r*-controlled patterns in the stressed syllable. Patterns include *or* (aDORN), *ore* (aDORE), *oar* (aBOARD), and *our* (MOURNful).

7. *R*-controlled vowels in the stressed syllable (*ur, ure*)
   Sort Directions: Sort according to the *r*-controlled patterns in the stressed syllable. Patterns include *ur* (BURden) *ure* (enDURE).

8. Ambiguous vowels in the stressed syllable (*oo, ew*)
   Sort Directions: Sort according to the ambiguous vowel patterns in the stressed syllable. Patterns include *oo* (ballOON, ROOKie) and *ew* (CHEWy).

Maturing Reader: Year 2: Cycle 2: 8 Weeks

1. Ambiguous vowels in the stressed syllable (*oy/oi, ou/ow*)
   Sort Directions: Sort according to the ambiguous vowel patterns in the stressed syllable. Patterns include *oy* (LOYal), *oi* (aVOID), *ou* (COUNsel), and *ow* (FLOWer).

2. Ambiguous vowels in the stressed syllable (*au/aw*)
   Sort Directions: Sort according to the ambiguous vowel patterns in the stressed syllable. Patterns include *au* (FAUCet) and *aw* (AWful).

3. Homophones (polysyllabic, two syllable)
   Sort Directions: Students should match up the homophone pairs. Emphasis should focus on the meaning of the words as well as the spelling variations that occur in the stressed syllable (aLOUD, aLLOWED).

4. Homophones (polysyllabic, two syllable)
   Sort Directions: Students should match up the homophone pairs. Emphasis should focus on the meaning of the words as well as the spelling variation that occurs in the unstressed syllable.

5. Homophones (polysyllabic, three plus syllables)
   Sort Directions: Students should match up the homophone pairs. Emphasis should focus on the meaning of the words as well as the spelling variation that occurs.

6. Prefixes (*cat*—down, *peri*—around/near, *circum*—around)
   Sort Directions: Sort by the prefix. Emphasis should focus on the meaning of these words.

7. Latin suffixes (*ible/able*)
   Sort Directions: Sort according to pattern. Students should also discuss base words and root words as they complete this sort. Hint: Typically, you add *able* to a base word and *ible* to a root word. However, there are some predictable spelling changes (suppress—suppressible).

8. Latin suffixes (*ant, ent*)
   Sort Directions: Sort according to pattern. Students should also attempt to add *ance, ancy,* or

ence, ency to each word respectively. The vowel stays the same in each suffix family. This solidifies student knowledge of these tricky suffixes.

Maturing Reader: Year 2: Cycle 3: 8 Weeks

1. Vowels patterns in the unstressed syllable ('n, schwa n)
   Sort Directions: Sort according to the vowel patterns in the unstressed syllable. Patterns include *ain* (CAPtain), *an* (URban), and *en* (CHILdren). Hint: *an* pattern words tend to be nouns.

2. Vowels patterns in the unstressed syllable ('n, schwa n—*en*/adjective, *in* and *on*/nouns)
   Sort Directions: Sort according to the vowel patterns in the unstressed syllable. Patterns include *en* (MOLTen), *in* (ROBin), and *on* (GALlon). Hint: *en* pattern words tend to be adjectives; *in* and *on* pattern words tend to be nouns.

3. Vowels patterns in the unstressed syllable (*al, il, ile*)
   Sort Directions: Sort according to the vowel patterns in the unstressed syllable. Patterns include *al* (BRIdal), *il* (Evil), and *ile* (FERtile).

4. Vowels patterns in the unstressed syllable (*al, el, le*)
   Sort Directions: Sort according to the vowel patterns in the unstressed syllable. Patterns include *al* (CENtral), *el* (CHAPel), and *le* (GIGgle). Hint: Many more words end in *le* than *el*.

5. Vowels patterns in the unstressed syllable (*ure, cher, sher*)
   Sort Directions: Sort according to the vowel patterns in the unstressed syllable. Patterns include *ure* (CAPture), *cher* (POAcher), and *sher* (USHer).

6. Vowels patterns in the unstressed syllable (ure, cher)
   Sort Directions: Sort according to the vowel patterns in the unstressed syllable. Patterns include *ure* (/chər/ - LECture, /shər/ - CENsure, /zhər / - CLOsure) and *cher* (PREAcher).

7. Vowels patterns in the unstressed syllable (*et, it*)
   Sort Directions: Sort according to the vowel patterns in the unstressed syllable. Patterns include *et* (NUGget) and *it* (HABit). Hint: Many more words end in *et* than *it*.

8. Vowels patterns in the unstressed syllable (*age, edge, idge*)
   Sort Directions: Sort according to the vowel patterns in the unstressed syllable. Students should also discuss that all three endings have the same sound (ĭj). Patterns include *age* (GARbage), *edge* (KNOWLedge), and *idge* (CARTRidge). Hint: Many more words end in *age* than *edge* and *idge*.

Maturing Year 2: Cycle 4: 8 Weeks

1. Vowels patterns in the unstressed syllable (*ace, ice, uce, ise, is*)
   Sort Directions: Sort according to the vowel patterns in the unstressed syllable. Students should also discuss that all of the endings have the same sound (ĭs). Patterns include *ace* (PALace), *ice* (JUSTice), *uce* (LETtuce), *ise* (PROMise), and *is* (TENnis).

2. Vowels patterns in the unstressed syllable (*ey, ie, y*)
   Sort Directions: Sort according to the vowel patterns in the unstressed syllable. Students should also discuss that all of the endings have the same sound (/ē/). Patterns include *ey* (DONkey), *ie* (MOVie), and *y* (ENvy).

3. Consonant alternations (silent vs. sounded consonants—*sign/signal, soft/soften*)
   Sort Directions: Students should match up the derived pairs. Emphasis should focus on the meaning of the words as well as the spelling and pronunciation variation of the consonants that occurs in the pairs.

4. Vowel alternations (long to short—*cave/cavity, please/pleasure*)
   Sort Directions: Students should match up the derived pairs. Emphasis should focus on the meaning of the words as well as the spelling and pronunciation variation of the vowels that occurs in the pairs.

5. Vowel alternations (long to schwa—*compose/composition*)
   Sort Directions: Students should match up the derived pairs. Emphasis should focus on the meaning of the words as well as the spelling and pronunciation variation of the vowels that occurs in the pairs.

6. Vowel alternations (long to schwa—*verify/verification, simplify/simplification*) with predictable spelling changes
   Sort Directions: Students should match up the derived pairs. Emphasis should focus on the meaning of the words as well as the spelling and pronunciation variation of the vowels that occur in the pairs focusing on the predictable spelling changes.

7. Vowel alternations (short to schwa—*excel/excellent, critic/criticize*)
   Sort Directions: Students should match up the derived pairs. Emphasis should focus on the meaning of the words as well as the spelling and pronunciation variation of the vowels that occur in the pairs.

8. Plurals (*sis/ses—analysis/analyses, um/a—addendum/addenda*)
   Sort Directions: Students should match up the derived pairs. Emphasis should focus on the spelling and pronunciation variation as the words become plural.

Advanced Reader

Advanced Reader: Year 1: Cycle 1: 8 Weeks

1. Adding /SHəN/—*ct + ion* (pronunciation changes—*elect/election, restrict/restriction*)
   Sort Directions: Students should match up the related pairs and then discuss the pronunciation (/t/ to /sh/) and meaning changes.

2. Adding /SHəN/—ending blends (*nt, pt, rt, st + ion—invent/invention, suggest/suggestion*)
   Sort Directions: Students should match up the related pairs and then discuss the pronunciation (/t/ to /sh/) and meaning changes.

3. Adding /SHəN/—ending blends (*rt, nt, pt*) + *ation* (pronunciation changes—*import/importation, plant/plantation*)
   Sort Directions: Students should match up the related pairs and then discuss the pronunciation (long *a*) and meaning changes.

4. Adding /SHəN/—predictable spelling and pronounciation changes with /t/ (*it* to *ssion*—*commit/commission, rt* to *sion*—*convert/conversion*)
   Sort Directions: Students should match up the related pairs and then discuss the pronunciation (/t/ to /sh/) and meaning changes.

5. Adding /SHəN/—*ss + ion* (*aggress/aggression, obsess/obsession*)
   Sort Directions: Students should match up the related pairs and then discuss the pronunciation (/s/ to /sh/) and meaning changes.

6. Adding /SHəN/—*c + ian* (*music/musician, politic/politician*)
   Sort Directions: Students should match up the related pairs and then discuss the pronunciation (/k/ to /sh/) and meaning changes.

7. Adding /SHəN/—*e*-drop + *ion* (*calculate/calculation, educate/education*)
   Sort Directions: Students should match up the related pairs and then discuss the pronunciation (/t/ to /sh/) and meaning changes.

8. Adding /SHəN/—*d(e)*-drop + *sion* (*collide/collision, expand/expansion, provide/provision*)
   Sort Directions: Students should match up the related pairs and then discuss the pronunciation (/d/ to /sh/ or /zh/) and meaning changes.

Advanced Reader: Year 1: Cycle 2: 8 Weeks

1. Latin suffixes (*ant/ance/ancy, ent/ence/ency*)
   Sort Directions: Sort according to pattern. Students should also attempt to add *ance, ancy,* or *ence, ency* to each word, respectively. The vowel stays the same in each suffix family. This solidifies student knowledge of these tricky suffixes.

2. Latin suffixes (*ible/able* with *e*-drop—*reuse/reusable, ed/edible*)
   Sort Directions: Sort according to pattern. Students should also discuss base words and root words as they complete this sort. Hint: Typically you add *able* to a base word and *ible* to a root word. However, there are some predictable spelling changes (*suppress/suppressible*)

3. Latin Suffixes (*ible/able* with predictable spelling changes—*adapt/adaptable, aud/audible, access/accessible*)

Sort Directions: Sort according to pattern. Hint: Typically, you add *able* to a base word and *ible* to a root word. In this sort, students will also discover some predictable spelling changes when adding this suffix.

4. Number-related roots (*pent*—five, *quad/quadri*—four, *uni*—one)
Sort Directions: Sort by pattern. Students should engage in conversations and activities related to vocabulary development. Emphasis should focus on the meaning of these words.

5. Latin suffixes (*ity* with base words, *e*-drop, and *ble*—minor/minority, active/activity, able/ability)
Sort Directions: Sort according to pattern. Students should pay special attention to how this suffix attaches to different words.

6. Adding /SHəN/—other predictable changes (pronunciation and spelling changes) (*describe/description, convert/conversion*)
Sort Directions: Students should match the related pairs and then discuss the pronunciation, spelling, and meaning changes. Students should discover predictable spelling changes within patterns of words.

7. Consonant alternations with pronunciation changes (*authentic/authenticity, confident/confidential*)
Sort Directions: Students should match the related pairs and then discuss the pronunciation, spelling, and meaning changes. Students should discover predictable spelling changes within patterns of words.

8. Consonant alternation with pronunciation and spelling changes (*face/facial, influence/influential*)
Sort Directions: Students should match up the related pairs and then discuss the pronunciation, spelling, and meaning changes. Students should discover predictable spelling changes within patterns of words.

Advanced Reader: Year 1: Cycle 3: 8 Weeks

1. Polysyllabic homographs (*graduate/graduate, separate/separate*)
Sort Directions: Students should say each word and decide which syllable is stressed. As students discover which syllable is stressed, they should also discuss the part of speech the word is used. Hint: Verbs have the /āt/, nouns and adjectives have the /ĭt/.

2. Polysyllabic homographs (*estimate/estimate, separate/separate*)
Sort Directions: Students should say each word and decide which syllable is stressed. As students discover which syllable is stressed, they should also discuss the part of speech the word is used. Hint: Verbs have the /āt/, nouns and adjectives have the /ĭt/.

3. Polysyllabic plurals—spelling changes in plurals (*a, ae,* also add *s*)
Sort Directions: Students should match up the derived pairs. Emphasis should focus on the spelling and pronunciation variation as the words become plural.

4. Polysyllabic plurals—spelling changes in plurals (*us, i,* also add *es*)
Sort Directions: Students should match up the derived pairs. Emphasis should focus on the spelling and pronunciation variation as the words become plural.

5. Doubling with polysyllabic base words (*expel/expelled, submit/submitted*)
Sort Directions: Sort by pattern. Students should recognize when you have to drop the final *e*, double the final consonant, or do nothing before you add the *ed* suffix. Note: Typically, if the

suffix begins with a vowel and the syllable before the suffix has one vowel, ends in one consonant, and is stressed, you have to double the final consonant.

6. Doubling with polysyllabic base words (*expel/expelling, submit/submitting*)
Sort Directions: Sort by pattern. Students should recognize when you have to drop the final *e*, double the final consonant, or do nothing before you add the *ing* suffix. Note: Typically if the suffix begins with a vowel and the syllable before the suffix has one vowel, ends in one consonant, and is stressed, you have to double the final consonant.

7. No doubling with polysyllabic base words (final consonant is preceded by two vowels— a*ppear/appeared/appearing*, stress is not on the last syllable—*benefit/benefited/benefiting*, leaving the final *y*—*classify/classifying*, word ends in two consonants—*attend/attended/attending*)
Sort Directions: Sort by pattern. Students should pay special attention to the spelling changes as suffixes are added to the words.

8. Review suffixes with polysyllabic words
Sort Directions: Sort by pattern. Students should review doubling issues they have learned.

Advanced Reader: Year 1: Cycle 4: 8 Weeks

1. Assimilated prefixes (*ad*—to, toward)
Sort Directions: Sort by pattern. Emphasis should focus on the meaning of these words.
Hint: *Ad* changes to *ac* before *c* and *q, af* before *f, ag* before *g, al* before *l, an* before *n, ap* before *p, ar* before *r, as* before *s, at* before *t,* and *a* before *sc, sp,* and *st.*

2. Assimilated prefixes (*com*—with, together)
Sort Directions: Sort by pattern. Emphasis should focus on the meaning of these words.
Hint: *Com* changes to *col* before *l; cor* before *r; con* before *c, d, g, j, n, q, s, t* and *v; co* before all vowels, *h,* and *w.*

3. Assimilated prefixes (*dis*—opposite of, not, apart)
Sort Directions: Sort by pattern. Emphasis should focus on the meaning of these words.
Hint: *Dis* changes to *dif* before *f and di* before *b, d, g, l, m, n, r,* and *v.*

4. Assimilated prefixes (*ex*—out, from)
Sort Directions: Sort by pattern. Emphasis should focus on the meaning of these words.
Hint: *Ex* changes to *ef* before *f, e* before *b, d, g, h, l, m, n, r* and *v,* and often *ec* before *c,* or *s.*

5. Assimilated prefixes (*in*—in, not, toward, together)
Sort Directions: Sort by pattern. Emphasis should focus on the meaning of these words.
Hint: *In* changes to *il* before *l, ir* before *r,* and *im* before *b, m,* and *p.*

6. Assimilated prefixes (*ob*—to, toward, against)
Sort Directions: Sort by pattern. Emphasis should focus on the meaning of these words.
Hint: *Ob* changes to *oc* before *c, of* before *f,* and *op* before *p.*

7. Assimilated prefixes (*sub*—under, lower)
Sort Directions: Sort by pattern. Emphasis should focus on the meaning of these words.
Hint: *Sub* changes to *suc* before *c, suf* before *f, sug* before *g, sum* before *m, sup* before *p, sur* before *r,* and often it changes to *sus* before *c, p,* and *t.*

8. Greek roots (*log/ology*—discourse, study of)
   Sort Directions: Students should engage in conversations and activities related to vocabulary development. Emphasis should focus on the meaning of these words.

Advanced Reader: Year 2: Cycle 1: 8 Weeks

1. Greek roots (*aer*—air)
   Sort Directions: Students should engage in conversations and activities related to vocabulary development. Emphasis should focus on the meaning of these words.

2. Greek roots (*arch*—chief, ruler)
   Sort Directions: Students should engage in conversations and activities related to vocabulary development. Emphasis should focus on the meaning of these words.

3. Greek roots (*aster/astr*—star)
   Sort Directions: Students should engage in conversations and activities related to vocabulary development. Emphasis should focus on the meaning of these words.

4. Latin roots (*pos/pon*[e]—to put, place)
   Sort Directions: Students should engage in conversations and activities related to vocabulary development. Emphasis should focus on the meaning of these words.

5. Greek roots (*bi/bio*—life)
   Sort Directions: Students should engage in conversations and activities related to vocabulary development. Emphasis should focus on the meaning of these words.

6. Greek roots (*centr*—center)
   Sort Directions: Students should engage in conversations and activities related to vocabulary development. Emphasis should focus on the meaning of these words.

7. Greek roots (*chron*—time)
   Sort Directions: Students should engage in conversations and activities related to vocabulary development. Emphasis should focus on the meaning of these words.

8. Latin roots (*cide*—to kill, to cut)
   Sort Directions: Students should engage in conversations and activities related to vocabulary development. Emphasis should focus on the meaning of these words.

Advanced Reader: Year 2: Cycle 2: 8 Weeks

1. Greek roots (*cosm*—universe, world)
   Sort Directions: Students should engage in conversations and activities related to vocabulary development. Emphasis should focus on the meaning of these words.

2. Greek roots (*cris/crit*—judge, separate)
   Sort Directions: Students should engage in conversations and activities related to vocabulary development. Emphasis should focus on the meaning of these words.

3. Greek roots (*dem*—people)
   Sort Directions: Students should engage in conversations and activities related to vocabulary development. Emphasis should focus on the meaning of these words.

4. Latin roots (*fort/forc*—strong)
   Sort Directions: Students should engage in conversations and activities related to vocabulary development. Emphasis should focus on the meaning of these words.

5. Latin roots (*dom*—lord, master; building)
   Sort Directions: Students should engage in conversations and activities related to vocabulary development. Emphasis should focus on the meaning of these words.

6. Latin roots (*equa/equi*—even)
   Sort Directions: Students should engage in conversations and activities related to vocabulary development. Emphasis should focus on the meaning of these words.

7. Latin roots (*dic/dict*—to speak)
   Sort Directions: Students should engage in conversations and activities related to vocabulary development. Emphasis should focus on the meaning of these words.

8. Latin roots (*duc/duct*—to lead)
   Sort Directions: Students should engage in conversations and activities related to vocabulary development. Emphasis should focus on the meaning of these words.

Advanced Reader: Year 2: Cycle 3: 8 Weeks

1. Latin roots (*mis(s)/mit*—to send)
   Sort Directions: Students should engage in conversations and activities related to vocabulary development. Emphasis should focus on the meaning of these words.

2. Latin roots (*mot/mob*—to move)
   Sort Directions: Students should engage in conversations and activities related to vocabulary development. Emphasis should focus on the meaning of these words.

3. Latin roots (*pens/pend*—to hang)
   Sort Directions: Students should engage in conversations and activities related to vocabulary development. Emphasis should focus on the meaning of these words.

4. Latin roots (*ped*—foot), Greek roots (*ped*—child)
   Sort Directions: Students should engage in conversations and activities related to vocabulary development. Emphasis should focus on the meaning of these words.

5. Latin roots (*aud*—to hear)
   Sort Directions: Students should engage in conversations and activities related to vocabulary development. Emphasis should focus on the meaning of these words.

6. Latin roots (*scribe/script*—to write)
   Sort Directions: Students should engage in conversations and activities related to vocabulary development. Emphasis should focus on the meaning of these words.

7. Latin roots (*spect/spec/spic*—to see, look)
   Sort Directions: Students should engage in conversations and activities related to vocabulary development. Emphasis should focus on the meaning of these words.

8. Latin roots (*vers/vert*—to turn)
   Sort Directions: Students should engage in conversations and activities related to vocabulary development. Emphasis should focus on the meaning of these words.

Advanced Reader: Year 2: Cycle 4: 8 Weeks

1. Latin roots (*prim/princ*—first)
   Sort Directions: Students should engage in conversations and activities related to vocabulary development. Emphasis should focus on the meaning of these words.

2. Greek roots (*phon*—sound)
   Sort Directions: Students should engage in conversations and activities related to vocabulary development. Emphasis should focus on the meaning of these words.

3. Greek roots (*scop*—see, view)
   Sort Directions: Students should engage in conversations and activities related to vocabulary development. Emphasis should focus on the meaning of these words.

4. Greek roots (*tele*—far off)
   Sort Directions: Students should engage in conversations and activities related to vocabulary development. Emphasis should focus on the meaning of these words.

5. Greek roots (*hydr*—water)
   Sort Directions: Students should engage in conversations and activities related to vocabulary development. Emphasis should focus on the meaning of these words.

6. Latin roots (*jud*—a judge)
   Sort Directions: Students should engage in conversations and activities related to vocabulary development. Emphasis should focus on the meaning of these words.

7. Latin roots (*lit*—a letter)
   Sort Directions: Students should engage in conversations and activities related to vocabulary development. Emphasis should focus on the meaning of these words.

8. Latin roots (*spir*—to breathe)
   Sort Directions: Students should engage in conversations and activities related to vocabulary development. Emphasis should focus on the meaning of these words.

Evolving Reader Word Study Scope and Sequence

Year 1

Cycle 1 — 9 weeks

	Features
1	Review short vowels with preconsonantal nasals, digraphs, blends
2	Review short vowels with preconsonantal nasals, digraphs, blends
3	Long A (a_e, short)
4	Long O (v_e, short)
5	Long E and I (v_e, short)
6	Long U patterns (u_e, yoo/oo, short)
7	Long A patterns (a_e, ay)
8	Long A patterns (a_e, ai, ay)
9	Long E patterns (ee, ea, e)

Cycle 2 — 9 weeks

	Features
1	Long and short E (ea)
2	Long I patterns (i_e, igh, y)
3	Long O patterns (o_e, oa, ow)
4	Long U patterns (u_e, ew, ui)
5	Contractions (not, will, have)
6	R-controlled (ar, oar, are, ore)
7	Less common A (ei, ey, ai)
8	Less common I (iCC, igh, i_e)
9	Less common O (oCC, oe, o)

Cycle 3 — 9 weeks

	Features
1	Less common U (ue, ui, ew)
2	Less common E (ie, e, ee)
3	Compound words (in, out, night)
4	Compound words (any, every, ever)

Year 2

Cycle 1 — 8 weeks

	Features
1	Complex r-controlled (are, air, ar)
2	Complex r-controlled (ore, our, oar)
3	Complex r-controlled (eer, ear, er)
4	Complex r-controlled (ire, ure, ur, ir)
5	Complex consonants (c, g—beginning, ending)
6	Complex consonants (ch, tch, Cch)
7	Complex consonants (ge, dge, Cge)
8	Complex consonants (shr, thr, scr)

Cycle 2 — 8 weeks

	Features
1	Triple-letter blends (scr, squ, spl)
2	Contractions (had, would, are)
3	Complex consonants (final k—ck, ke, VVk)
4	Silent consonants (kn, gn, wr)
5	Triple-letter blends (str, thr, spr)
6	Intro to easy prefixes (un, dis, mis)
7	Compound words (back, head, foot)
8	Compound words (over, under, down, up)

Cycle 3 — 8 weeks

	Features
1	Contractions (is, has, us, are, am)
2	Suffixes (ed—doubling, e-drop, nothing)
3	Suffixes (sounds of ed)
4	Suffixes (ing—doubling, e-drop, nothing)

5 R-controlled (*ur, er, ir*)
6 R-controlled (*eer, ear, ure, ire*)
7 Ambiguous vowels (*oo, ou*)
8 Ambiguous vowels (*oi, oy*)
9 Ambiguous vowels (*ow, ou*)

Cycle 4 8 weeks Features
1 Ambiguous vowels (*aw, au, wa*)
2 Contractions (*would, had, is, has, not*)
3 Intro to easy prefixes (*in, pre, re*)
4 Homophones (single syllable)
5 Homophones (single syllable)
6 Intro to easy suffixes (*s, es*)
7 Suffixes—single syllable plurals (*es, y* to *i*)
8 Possessives (*s, 's, s'*)

5 Homophones (single syllable)
6 Homophones (single syllable)
7 Suffixes (*er, est*)
8 Suffixes (*ful, ly, y*)

Cycle 4 8 weeks Features
1 Homophones (single syllable)
2 Suffixes (*less, ness*)
3 Syllable patterns (VCCV—first syllable stress)
4 Syllable patterns (VCV and VCCV, first syllable stress)
5 Syllable patterns (VCV open and VCV closed, first syllable stress)
6 Syllable patterns (VCCV and VCV, second syllable stress)
7 Homographs (two syllable)
8 Homophones (two syllable)

Evolving Reader Word Study Lists

HW indicates header words. Teachers can create header word cards by printing out the blank word study card form available at www.reading.org and writing the header words on them.

Evolving Reader: Year 1: Cycle 1

	Week 1	Week 2	Week 3	Week 4	Week 5	Week 6	Week 7	Week 8	Week 9
	Review short vowels with pre-consonantal nasals, digraphs, blends	Review short vowels with pre-consonantal nasals, digraphs, blends	Long A (a_e, short)	Long O (v_e, short)	Long E and I (v_e, short)	Long U (u_e, yoo/oo, short)	Long A patterns (a_e, ay)	Long A patterns (a_e, ai, ay)	Long E patterns (ee, ea, e)
HW	**blast**	**mash**	**race**	**code**	**bell**	**dude**	**wave**	**date**	**green**
HW	**dock**	**grill**	**flag**	**stop**	**sit**	**cube**	**stay**	**fail**	**deal**
HW	**chill**	**prong**			**hive**	**stuff**		**say**	**he**
HW	**swell**	**plump**			**these**				
HW	**duck**	**spend**							
1	bang	blast	hat	broke	these	cube	bake	date	green
2	blimp	blush	Jack	phone	scene	cute	chase	race	wheel
3	bring	check	ask	woke	theme	fume	grade	plane	sheet
4	kept	chest	slap	bold	eve	fuse	haste	wave	street
5	champ	cross	fast	spot	mess	huge	lake	late	bleed
6	chant	cliff	lap	stole	rest	mule	late	tape	teeth
7	chill	clump	flag	cold	bell	muse	quake	bake	mean
8	chop	flush	pass	whole	kept	mute	shade	make	team
9	chunk	graph	path	job	nest	use	shake	sale	deal
10	clamp	grill	glad	stop	shell	brute	space	scale	reach

11 shop	help	name	box	best	crude	tape	blaze	beach
12 dock	hump	date	lock	chime	dude	wave	fail	steam
13 rung	mash	race	got	guide	duke	day	gain	he
14 duck	mock	plane	top	glide	dune	gray	grain	she
15 grand	plump	cake	pose	whine	flute	hay	nail	we
16 felt	prong	cape	quote	prime	June	play	pail	me
17 lamp	shaft	page	throne	prize	plume	pray	plain	be
18 pink	skunk	same	yoke	scribe	prune	say	praise	the
19 clock	strong	safe	zone	size	rule	spray	quaint	deal
20 loft	spend	gave	doze	stick	spruce	stay	rain	reach
21 speck	spent	gate	code	chimp	tube	stray	sail	
22 stomp	block	have	shock	limp	tune	sway	straight	
23 stump	swish		smock	print	plum	tray	waist	
24 swell	snob		blond	spine	slump	way	wait	
25 think	theft		romp	tribe	skunk		stay	
26 sock	twist			twice	must		clay	
27 thump	welt			write	bluff			
28 tilt	with				stuff			
29 truck					cluck			

Evolving Reader Word Study Lists

HW indicates header words. Teachers can create header word cards by printing out the blank word study card form available at www.reading.org and writing the header words on them.

Evolving Reader: Year 1: Cycle 2

	Week 1	Week 2	Week 3	Week 4	Week 5	Week 6	Week 7	Week 8	Week 9
	Long and short *E* patterns (ea)	Long *I* patterns (i_e, igh, y)	Long *O* patterns (o_e, oa, ow)	Long *U* patterns (u_e, ew, ui)	Contractions (not, will, have)	R-controlled (ar, are, oar, ore)	Less common *A* (ei, ey, ai)	Less common *I* (iCC, i_e, igh)	Less common *O* (oCC, oe, o)
HW	**beam**	**fine**	**rope**	**rude**	**won't**	**car**	**vein**	**kind**	**cold**
HW	**dead**	**sigh**	**boat**	**crew**	**we'll**	**scare**	**hey**	**like**	**toe**
HW		**try**	**grow**	**fruit**	**they've**	**more**	**nail**	**high**	**go**
HW						**roar**			
1	beach	bite	drove	rude	can't	star	nail	mind	old
2	beast	fine	home	June	won't	car	train	find	cold
3	beam	hide	rope	cute	didn't	bar	strait	kind	hold
4	cream	kite	broke	dude	hadn't	far	chain	wind	bold
5	dream	like	smoke	truth	wouldn't	bark	said	bind	told
6	ease	bike	croak	flute	I'd	dark	waist	hind	comb
7	flea	line	hope	tune	she'd	square	pain	blind	holt
8	lead	live	poke	fume	he'd	scare	faith	wild	jolt
9	read	dime	woke	cube	I'm	arm	stain	child	colt
10	leash	high	stole	use	couldn't	part	prey	pride	bolt
11	meal	light	vote	new	shouldn't	chore	hey	wife	host
12	mean	night	hose	grew	I'll	more	grey	stride	most
13	peace	flight	spoke	threw	we'll	care	they	wipe	ghost
14	peak	fight	phone	fruit	he'll	soar	eight	crime	foe
15	reach	cry	boat	juice	she'll	stare	freight	sign	doe

16	breast	fly	float	build	don't	oar	veil	flight	hoe
17	breadth	my	sow	clue	they're	roar	beige	thigh	toe
18	dead	sky	cloak	bruise	we're	board	neigh	tight	woe
19	dread	try	grow	knew	you're		reign	knight	no
20	health	why	know	shrew	you'll				go
21	meant	while	blown	shrewd	we've				so
22	realm	spry	known	screw	isn't				know
23	sweat	guy	flown	drew	could've				
24	thread	fry	shown	crew	that'll				
25	wealth		show						
26			throw						
27			thrown						
28			growth						
29			own						
30			mow						

Evolving Reader Word Study Lists

HW indicates header words. Teachers can create header word cards by printing out the blank word study card form available at www.reading.org and writing the header words on them.

Evolving Reader: Year 1: Cycle 3

	Week 1	Week 2	Week 3	Week 4	Week 5	Week 6	Week 7	Week 8	Week 9
	Less common U (ue, ui, ew)	Less common E (ie, e, ee)	Compound words (in, out, night)	Compound words (any, every, ever)	R-controlled (ur, er, ir)	R-controlled (eer, ear, ure, ire)	Ambiguous vowels (oo, ou)	Ambiguous vowels (oi, oy)	Ambiguous vowels (ow, ou)
HW	chew	field	into	anybody	burn	cheer	moon	boil	soup
HW	juice	we	outside	everybody	her	earth	book	joy	cloud
HW	blue	keep	nighttime	evermore	dirt	clear	could		mow
HW						cure			how
HW						hire			
1	new	we	inside	anybody	burn	cheer	book	coin	how
2	grew	she	incomplete	anymore	hurt	peer	took	join	brown
3	drew	he	inadequate	anyone	turn	sheer	look	point	clown
4	brew	be	indecisive	anyplace	curl	steer	cook	soil	town
5	chew	me	input	anything	purr	earl	brook	boil	crowd
6	blew	sweet	into	anywhere	burst	earth	shook	coil	drown
7	pew	sweep	within	anytime	church	heard	foot	foil	plow
8	knew	keep	indifferent	everyone	curd	learn	crook	joint	wow
9	bruise	fleet	inconsistent	everywhere	curb	pearl	moon	hoist	owl
10	juice	week	outside	everything	her	search	root	moist	scowl
11	suit	tee	dugout	everytime	fern	yearn	shoot	joy	fowl
12	fruit	feet	outlook	everybody	nerd	clear	should	boy	vow
13	cruise	see	outcome	evergreen	jerk	ear	could	toy	crown
14	fuel	deep	outdo	evermore	perch	fear	would	ploy	grow

				everlasting					
15	cruel	bee	outdated	everlasting	clerk	near	hook	soy	know
16	clue	flee	outfield		germ	hear	hoof		sow
17	due	meet	outlaw		herb	spear			mow
18	true	grief	nighttime		per	tear			cloud
19	build	brief	nightmare		bird	fire			found
20	built	thief	nightgown		first	hire			ground
21	guide	chief	midnight		girl	tire			out
22	Sue	field	overnight		chirp	wire			shout
23	shrew	piece	nightfall		dirt	sire			proud
24	brew	shriek			shirt	cure			loud
25	crew	niece			third	pure			bound
26		fiend			birth	lure			wound
27		grieve			firm	sure			couch
28		shield							doubt
29		sleeve							mound
30		siege							

Evolving Reader Word Study Lists

HW indicates header words. Teachers can create header word cards by printing out the blank word study card form available at www.reading.org and writing the header words on them.

Evolving Reader: Year 1: Cycle 4

	Week 1	Week 2	Week 3	Week 4	Week 5	Week 6	Week 7	Week 8
	Ambiguous vowels (aw, au, wa)	Contractions (would, had, is, has, not)	Intro to easy prefixes (in, pre, re)	Homophones (single syllable)	Homophones (single syllable)	Intro to easy suffixes (s, es)	Suffixes—single-syllable plurals (es, y to i)	Possessives (use list of words to show possessives, plurals, and plural possessives)
HW	saw	she's	insane			dogs	plays	
HW	fault	you've	precook			glasses	bodies	
HW	wash	I'd	replay				boxes	
1	draw	hasn't	incomplete	air	aisle	bases	babies	girl
2	saw	she's	incorrect	heir	I'll	boxes	berries	child
3	crawl	he's	indecent	ate	isle	chances	bodies	kitten
4	dawn	haven't	indirect	eight	cite	chops	boys	Chris
5	drawn	I've	informal	base	sight	classes	carries	2000
6	law	you've	insane	bass	site	crashes	churches	wife
7	shawl	we've	invalid	flair	stile	dishes	dishes	wolf
8	squawk	they've	invisible	flare	style	gases	donkeys	deer
9	yawn	hadn't	precook	hall	thyme	glasses	enjoys	sheep
10	caught	she'd	predate	haul	time	hurts	fishes	mouse
11	fault	we'd	prefix	maize	knight	lunches	guesses	baby
12	pause	he'd	pregame	maze	night	nurses	monkeys	house
13	sauce	they'd	preheat	rain	brows	rulers	oxes	fox
14	taught		prejudge	reign	browse	sixes	pennies	sock
15	haunt		premature	rein	hoarse	streets	plays	student

16	launch	prepay	cent	horse		ponies
17	watch	relive	scent	your		preys
18	want	rebound	sent	you're		trays
19	wash	recall	eaves	chews		turkeys
20	wand	recapture	eves	choose		worries
21	wasp	recharge	per	chute		
22	watt	reclaim	purr	shoot		
23	swap	recopy	suite	plum		
24	swat	recycle	sweet	plumb		
25			weave	troop		
26			we've	troupe		
27			shear	who's		
28			sheer	whose	trains	

183

Evolving Reader Word Study Lists

HW indicates header words. Teachers can create header word cards by printing out the blank word study card form available at www.reading.org and writing the header words on them.

Evolving Reader: Year 2: Cycle 1

	Week 1	Week 2	Week 3	Week 4	Week 5	Week 6	Week 7	Week 8
	Complex r-controlled (are, air, ar)	Complex r-controlled (ore, our, oar)	Complex r-controlled (eer, ear, er)	Complex r-controlled (ire, ure, ur, ir)	Complex consonants (c, g—beginning, ending)	Complex consonants (ch, tch, Cch)	Complex consonants (ge, dge, Cge)	Complex consonants (shr, thr, scr)
HW	**dare**	**sore**	**cheer**	**hire**	**cent**	**beach**	**sage**	**shriek**
HW	**chair**	**your**	**year**	**cure**	**car**	**patch**	**ledge**	**throat**
HW	**star**	**roar**	**stern**	**curl**	**gym**	**bench**	**cringe**	**scream**
				girl	**gum**			
1	bar	more	cheer	fire	cane	teach	stage	shrink
2	car	store	deer	tire	coach	reach	huge	shriek
3	tar	shore	peer	wire	cub	beach	page	shrew
4	yarn	bore	steer	hire	club	coach	rage	shrunk
5	carve	chore	jeer	sire	city	couch	age	shrank
6	harp	sore	sheer	cure	cent	pouch	wage	through
7	arm	score	near	pure	cake	screech	sage	thrust
8	card	swore	clear	lure	gym	peach	edge	threat
9	jar	tore	fear	burn	gem	catch	ledge	three
10	charm	your	dear	hurt	girl	patch	bridge	throw
11	sharp	course	tear	turn	gum	stretch	judge	screw
12	far	four	year	curl	gloat	clutch	budge	scrape
13	star	pour	gear	purr	grape	ditch	lodge	scramble
14	hair	court	beard	burst	gash	switch	smudge	scrunch
15	fair	fourth	spear	church	grin	twitch	fudge	scream

184

16 chair	mourn	shear	curb	glad	pitch	charge	scratch
17 flair	source	heard	surf	gas	lunch	change	scribble
18 pair	gourd	earth	bird	gate	bench	strange	
19 stair	roar	learn	first	choice	branch	barge	
20 lair	hoarse	earn	girl	lace	march	forge	
21 hare	soar	search	chirp	mice	porch	surge	
22 bare	boar	pearl	dirt	sauce	birch	large	
23 care	coarse	yearn	shirt	trace	search	badge	
24 fare	hour	verse	third	space	arch	hedge	
25 square	our	nerve	birth	juice	stitch	pledge	
26 stare		stern		rage	sketch	cringe	
27 blare		swerve			witch	lounge	
28 glare		perch				sponge	
29 dare						verge	
30 harm						stooge	
31 arch							

185

Evolving Reader Word Study Lists

HW indicates header words. Teachers can create header word cards by printing out the blank word study card form available at www.reading.org and writing the header words on them.

Evolving Reader: Year 2: Cycle 2

	Week 1	Week 2	Week 3	Week 4	Week 5	Week 6	Week 7	Week 8
	Triple-letter blends (scr, squ, spl)	Contractions (had, would, are)	Complex consonants (final k—ck, ke, VVk)	Silent consonants (kn, gn, wr)	Triple-letter blends) (str, thr, spr)	Intro to easy prefixes (un, dis, mis)	Compound words (back, head, foot)	Compound words (over, under, down, up)
HW	screech	we'd	lock	know	street	undone	backache	overhead
HW	square	they'd	lake	gnat	threat	disarm	headrest	underwater
HW	splat	we're	week	wrong	spring	mistake	foothill	downstairs
HW								uphill
1	scream	you'd	deck	knock	sprain	unable	backyard	overhead
2	script	we'd	clock	know	sprawl	unaware	backrub	overdone
3	scrap	I'd	thick	knot	spray	unclean	backward	overdo
4	scram	he'd	slick	kneel	spread	unclear	backside	overlook
5	scratch	she'd	truck	knee	sprig	uneven	backseat	overseas
6	screw	they'd	cluck	knife	sprout	unfair	backbone	overall
7	squawk	we'd	check	gnome	spruce	unfold	background	overcast
8	squint	you'd	heck	gnat	sprung	unkind	headstone	overview
9	squash	we'd	slack	gnarl	thrash	unleash	headache	overcome
10	squeak	I'd	tuck	gnu	thread	unpack	headlight	undergo
11	squeeze	he'd	block	wreck	threw	untie	headband	underground
12	square	she'd	like	wrong	thrive	unwrap	headstrong	undercover
13	squat	they'd	quake	wrist	throne	disable	headboard	underline
14	split	we'd	shake	wrap	through	disarm	football	undermine
15	splat	you're	brake	write	throw	disclose	footstool	understand

186

#								
16	splash	they're	duke	wrench	thrush	discolor	footstep	underwear
17		we're	spike	wreak	thrust	dislike	footprint	underwater
18			smoke	wren	straight	disobey	foothill	downfall
19			woke	gnaw	strait	disorder	foothold	downhill
20			spoke	knelt	strange	distaste		downtown
21			fluke	knot	streak	distrust		downpour
22			shook	knead	strength	miscount		downstairs
23			sleek	known	stretch	misdeal		downstream
24			weak		strict	misfire		upstairs
25			seek		strife	misfit		update
26			book		strive	misguide		uphold
27			took		stroll	misjudge		upright
28			beak		struck	mislead		uproar
29			tweak		strung	misprint		upset
30						misspell		upstream
31						mistake		

Evolving Reader Word Study Lists

HW indicates header words. Teachers can create header word cards by printing out the blank word study card form available at www.reading.org and writing the header words on them.

Evolving Reader: Year 2: Cycle 3

	Week 1	Week 2	Week 3	Week 4	Week 5	Week 6	Week 7	Week 8
	Contractions (is, has, us, are, am)	Suffixes (ed—doubling, e-drop, nothing)	Suffixes (sounds of ed)	Suffixes (ing—doubling, e-drop, nothing)	Homophones (single syllable)	Homophones (single syllable)	Suffixes (er, est)	Suffixes (ful, ly, y)
HW	she's	dropped	treated	clapping			greater	grateful
HW	he's	waved	loved	taking			greatest	likely
HW	let's	checked	baked	spending				happy
1	she's	slipped	mixed	trimming	be	rode	blacker	careful
2	he's	grabbed	stopped	running	bee	road	blackest	cheerful
3	it's	stopped	chased	popping	blew	sail	bigger	colorful
4	that's	wagged	cracked	dragging	blue	sale	biggest	fearful
5	where's	tripped	walked	wagging	I	whole	bolder	graceful
6	what's	knotted	asked	quitting	eye	hole	boldest	harmful
7	here's	rubbed	jumped	diving	no	one	braver	hopeful
8	how's	whizzed	dotted	riding	know	won	bravest	lawful
9	there's	traded	patted	shading	hear	right	closer	peaceful
10	who's	baked	treated	sliding	here	write	closest	playful
11	let's	wasted	traded	driving	hi	son	cleaner	badly
12	I'm	liked	ended	wasting	high	sun	cleanest	barely
13	we're	stared	handed	whining	knew	knot	colder	bravely
14	they're	waved	needed	pushing	new	not	coldest	closely
15		skated	mailed	jumping	see	made	funnier	constantly

16
17
18
19
20
21
22
23
24
25
26
27
28

tasted
picked
called
tracked
peeled
watched
cheered
talked
dreamed

boiled
raised
tried
filled
seemed
yelled

finding
kicking
wanting
munching

sea
their
there
they're
by
buy
bye
dear
deer
ate
eight
plane
plain

maid
male
mail
hare
hair
tale
tail
way
weigh

funniest
louder
loudest
newer
newest
prettier
prettiest
quicker
quickest
sadder
saddest

costly
deadly
directly
breezy
bumpy
chilly
choppy
cloudy
dirty
dusty
easy
frosty
injury

Evolving Reader Word Study Lists

HW indicates header words. Teachers can create header word cards by printing out the blank word study card form available at www.reading.org and writing the header words on them.

Evolving Reader: Year 2: Cycle 4

	Week 1	Week 2	Week 3	Week 4	Week 5	Week 6	Week 7	Week 8
	Homo-phones (single syllable)	Suffixes (*less, ness*)	Syllable patterns (VCCV, with first syllable stress)	Syllable patterns (VCV and VCCV, with first syllable stress)	Syllable patterns (VCV open and VCV closed, with first syllable stress)	Syllable patterns (VCCV and VCV, second syllable stress)	Homographs—two syllable (noun, first syllable; verb, second syllable; adjective, first or second syllable)	Homophones—two syllable (spelling variation in the stressed syllable)
HW		**worthless**	**after**	**music**	**music**	**admit**		
HW		**greatness**	**attic**	**market**	**cabin**	**hotel**		
1	Maine	ageless	after	baby	agent	admit	abstract	allowed
2	main	bottomless	dentist	duty	cozy	afford	address	aloud
3	mane	endless	basket	fever	eager	cartoon	combat	ceiling
4	pair	homeless	center	human	flavor	control	compact	sealing
5	pare	jobless	injure	music	glider	dessert	construct	censor
6	pear	meaningless	master	rival	item	disturb	contest	sensor
7	their	reckless	number	silent	migrate	employ	desert	colonel
8	there	seamless	orbit	tablet	profile	express	export	kernel
9	they're	speechless	pencil	writer	sequel	improve	increase	incite
10	knight	tasteless	signal	famous	spicy	inspect	perfect	insight
11	night	penniless	under	lazy	tulip	observe	project	morning
12	threw	merciless	wonder	legal	vacant	raccoon	record	mourning

#							
13	through	awareness	attic	shiny	camel	sincere	subject	review
14	course	darkness	blizzard	market	decade	surprise		revue
15	coarse	sickness	happy	sunny	edit	until		holy
16	moan	weakness	button	tablet	habit	believe		wholly
17	mown	happiness	pattern	garden	legend	demand		vary
18	browse	emptiness	tunnel	yellow	limit	event		very
19	brows	nosiness	traffic	basket	model	police		since
20	dew	silliness	hollow	fellow	parent	proceed		sense
21	do	ugliness	common	signal	promise	repair		
22	due	weariness	tennis	center	sliver	resume		
23					topic	reveal		
24					wizard	select		
25						unite		
26						exact		
27						exist		
28						giraffe		

Evolving Reader Dictated Sentences

Underlined words are examples of word study features for each week; not all words are included on the word study list.

Evolving Reader: Year 1: Cycle 1: Week 1

1. The <u>chimp</u> ate a <u>chunk</u> of banana and then needed a <u>drink</u>.
2. I brought a <u>lamp</u> to <u>camp</u> so I could see.
3. I <u>think</u> the <u>dish</u> is by the <u>sink</u>.
4. I heard a <u>thump</u> when the <u>blimp</u> landed.
5. There is a <u>clump</u> of dirt by the tree <u>stump</u>.

Evolving Reader: Year 1: Cycle 1: Week 2

1. She heard a big <u>blast</u> from the rocket.
2. <u>Jack</u> <u>spent</u> all the money at the fair.
3. You have a <u>welt</u> on your arm from the bee.
4. The rock <u>went</u> over the <u>cliff</u>.
5. Can you <u>help</u> us with the <u>grill</u>?

Evolving Reader: Year 1: Cycle 1: Week 3

1. <u>Jack</u> flew his fast <u>plane</u> to the <u>Cape</u> to win the <u>race</u>.
2. I'm glad you gave me a <u>hat</u> and <u>cap</u> that are the <u>same</u> color.
3. He <u>made</u> a good <u>pass</u> in the <u>game</u>.
4. I saw the <u>gate</u> with the <u>flag</u> and felt <u>safe</u>.
5. I walked a <u>lap</u> on the <u>same</u> <u>path</u>.

Evolving Reader: Year 1: Cycle 1: Week 4

1. Did I <u>lock</u> the keys in the <u>box</u>?
2. He <u>broke</u> the <u>phone</u> by throwing it in the <u>hole</u>.
3. I <u>broke</u> the egg <u>yoke</u> in the pan.
4. She made the <u>whole</u> thing.
5. I <u>woke</u> up early to go to my <u>job</u>.

Evolving Reader: Year 1: Cycle 1: Week 5

1. The <u>chimp</u> made a <u>mess</u> on the <u>white</u> rug.
2. The <u>tribe</u> won a <u>prize</u> for the <u>best</u> made throne.
3. The <u>bell</u> had a really loud <u>chime</u>.
4. <u>These</u> <u>shells</u> are <u>twice</u> as big as the ones we had before.
5. The kids are not allowed to <u>whine</u> to their mom about the <u>prize</u>.

Evolving Reader: Year 1: Cycle 1: Week 6

1. The <u>huge</u> ice <u>cube</u> is in the tank.
2. The <u>spruce</u> in the yard is quite big.
3. We will need to replace the <u>fuse</u> so the lamp will work.
4. The player was in a <u>slump</u> the entire month of <u>June</u>.
5. She was going to <u>use</u> the <u>flute</u> this week.

Evolving Reader: Year 1: Cycle 1: Week 7

1. I like to lie in the <u>shade</u> on a bright, sunny <u>day</u>.
2. I had to <u>chase</u> my dog around the lake.
3. It was <u>late</u>, so I sent for a <u>tray</u> of food.
4. I always <u>say</u> I love to <u>bake</u>.
5. Let's go <u>play</u> the <u>space</u> <u>game</u>.

Evolving Reader: Year 1: Cycle 1: Week 8

1. I hope it doesn't <u>rain</u> on the day of my <u>game</u>.
2. Please <u>stay</u> and go for a <u>sail</u> with me.
3. The house was very <u>quaint</u>.
4. The <u>nail</u> went <u>straight</u> into the wall.
5. I like my food <u>plain</u>.

Evolving Reader: Year 1: Cycle 1: Week 9

1. He was on a <u>team</u> with a <u>green</u> shirt.
2. Will they <u>reach</u> the <u>street</u>?
3. <u>We</u> took the <u>sheet</u> to the <u>beach</u>.
4. <u>He</u> got hit and it made his <u>teeth</u> <u>bleed</u>.
5. <u>She</u> walked down the <u>street</u> with <u>me</u>.

Evolving Reader: Year 1: Cycle 2: Week 1

1. The <u>dead</u> <u>seal</u> washed up on the <u>beach</u>.
2. He <u>meant</u> to say that he wants world <u>peace</u>.
3. Did you see the <u>leash</u> for the <u>beast</u>?
4. I <u>read</u> last night before I went to sleep.
5. The pencil was out of <u>lead</u>.

Evolving Reader: Year 1: Cycle 2: Week 2

1. The child went to bed at <u>night</u>.
2. Jen will <u>fly</u> down the street on her bike.
3. You need to turn off the <u>light</u> at <u>night</u>.
4. We took a <u>ride</u> through the <u>sky</u>.
5. Have you ever seen a <u>knight</u>?

Evolving Reader: Year 1: Cycle 2: Week 3

1. We <u>drove</u> <u>home</u> after the <u>show</u>.
2. The <u>rope</u> <u>broke</u> when we had to <u>tow</u> the car.
3. It is not safe to <u>smoke</u>.
4. She <u>spoke</u> up on the <u>phone</u>.
5. The ghost wore a <u>cloak</u> so I could see him.

Evolving Reader: Year 1: Cycle 2: Week 4

1. Don't be <u>rude</u> to Aunt <u>June</u>.
2. Did you see the new <u>clue</u>?
3. The <u>flute</u> was not in <u>tune</u>.
4. He <u>threw</u> the <u>cube</u> on the floor.
5. The <u>fruit</u> wasn't good because it had a <u>bruise</u>.

Evolving Reader: Year 1: Cycle 2: Week 5

1. I <u>wouldn't</u> do that if I were you.
2. <u>I'll</u> see you tomorrow.
3. She <u>couldn't</u> pay attention.
4. <u>You'll</u> be sorry if you eat a lot before you go to bed.
5. I <u>don't</u> think we are going to the party.

Evolving Reader: Year 1: Cycle 2: Week 6

1. She <u>said</u> she <u>wore</u> the <u>charm</u>.
2. Did you see the <u>spark</u> <u>far</u> away?
3. We drove the <u>car</u> in the <u>park</u>.
4. Please don't sit on the <u>arm</u> of the chair.
5. We will <u>carve</u> the pumpkin this year.

Evolving Reader: Year 1: Cycle 2: Week 7

1. The horse ate the hay and then said, "<u>Neigh</u>."
2. She wore a <u>beige</u> <u>veil</u>.
3. They put the <u>stain</u> on the couch.
4. Everyone likes to hear <u>praise</u>.
5. The <u>nail</u> came out of the <u>train</u> track.

Evolving Reader: Year 1: Cycle 2: Week 8

1. Keep in <u>mind</u> it is <u>nice</u> to be <u>kind</u>.
2. John has <u>pride</u> in his <u>wife</u>.
3. The <u>child</u> cries at <u>night</u>.
4. The prince went <u>blind</u> because of a curse.
5. Ben had a <u>slight</u> bruise on his <u>thigh</u>.

Evolving Reader: Year 1: Cycle 2: Week 9

1. Mom wanted us to <u>go</u> see the <u>doe</u>.
2. The <u>ghost</u> must have had the toast.
3. The <u>host</u> had the <u>most</u> fun at the ball.
4. The coffee gave me a <u>jolt</u>.
5. I bought a <u>comb</u> last night.

Evolving Reader: Year 1: Cycle 3: Week 1

1. I will <u>chew</u> my blue candy.
2. Sue <u>blew</u> a big bubble.
3. I ate a lot of <u>fruit</u> on the <u>cruise</u>.
4. She had no <u>clue</u> how to play the game.
5. I <u>knew</u> that it was <u>true</u>.

Evolving Reader: Year 1: Cycle 3: Week 2

1. The flea didn't <u>see</u> the <u>bee</u>.
2. He will meet the <u>chief</u> in the <u>field</u>.
3. She will give me a <u>piece</u> of pie.
4. We heard a loud <u>shriek</u> from my <u>niece</u>.
5. I gave a <u>brief</u> talk this <u>week</u>.

Evolving Reader: Year 1: Cycle 3: Week 3

1. She will go <u>inside</u> at <u>nighttime</u>.
2. Her <u>input</u> was needed about the <u>outcome</u>.
3. The players went into the <u>dugout</u> from the <u>outfield</u>.
4. It was <u>midnight</u>, and I was in my <u>nightgown</u>.
5. We need your <u>input</u> on the <u>incomplete</u> data.

Evolving Reader: Year 1: Cycle 3: Week 4

1. <u>Everybody</u> will go to the store.
2. <u>Anytime</u> you need me, I will be there.
3. <u>Everywhere</u> you look there is an <u>evergreen</u>.
4. Does <u>anyone</u> know <u>everyone</u>?
5. <u>Anyone</u> can do anything he or she wants.

Evolving Reader: Year 1: Cycle 3: Week 5

1. She will <u>burst</u> into the <u>church</u>.
2. I saw the <u>clerk</u> in the store.
3. The boy's <u>bird</u> was <u>hurt</u> in the tree.
4. His <u>shirt</u> was covered with <u>germs</u>.
5. She will <u>turn</u> and <u>jerk</u> her head.

Evolving Reader: Year 1: Cycle 3: Week 6

1. He will <u>learn</u> about the <u>earth</u> next <u>year</u>.
2. The <u>pearl</u> was the <u>lure</u> they used to sell the oyster.
3. The crowd let out a big <u>cheer</u> as the team came <u>near</u>.
4. I <u>heard</u> you the first time you said you wanted the <u>fire</u>.
5. You could see the <u>fear</u> in his eyes the first time he saw the <u>spear</u>.

Evolving Reader: Year 1: Cycle 3: Week 7

1. He <u>should</u> turn in the <u>crook</u>.
2. He placed his coat on the <u>hook</u> by the <u>hood</u>.
3. The <u>crooks</u> took what they <u>could</u> get.
4. He wants to <u>shoot</u> the arrow to the <u>moon</u>.
5. They walked by <u>foot</u> to the <u>brook</u>.

Evolving Reader: Year 1: Cycle 3: Week 8

1. She will <u>point</u> to the <u>toy</u>.
2. The <u>boy</u> flipped a <u>coin</u>.
3. <u>Foil</u> will <u>destroy</u> the microwave.
4. I needed to <u>hoist</u> up the rope.
5. She will <u>boil</u> the <u>soy</u> sauce.

Evolving Reader: Year 1: Cycle 3: Week 9

1. They were <u>proud</u> of their <u>town</u>.
2. She <u>shouted</u> because the boy was about to <u>drown</u>.
3. He found the <u>plow</u> for the snow.
4. The <u>clown</u> was too <u>loud</u> for the children.
5. There was a <u>foul</u> smell coming from the <u>couch</u>.

Evolving Reader: Year 1: Cycle 4: Week 1

1. She will <u>yawn</u> after she <u>washes</u> the dishes.
2. At <u>dawn</u>, she will <u>want</u> breakfast.
3. The boy <u>caught</u> the <u>wasp</u>.
4. He will <u>crawl</u> under the <u>wand</u>.
5. She <u>saw</u> a <u>haunted</u> sight.

Evolving Reader: Year 1: Cycle 4: Week 2

1. She <u>hasn't</u> been upstairs.
2. <u>I've</u> been to a spa.
3. <u>They'd</u> be excited to come to the party.
4. <u>He'd</u> be upset with you if you did that.
5. <u>She's</u> not capable of doing this.

Evolving Reader: Year 1: Cycle 4: Week 3

1. The boy will <u>recall</u> his fun <u>pregame</u> activities.
2. There was an <u>informal</u> meeting.
3. She will <u>recopy</u> the <u>prefix</u> words.
4. The <u>insane</u> man escaped and later was recaptured.
5. <u>Recopy</u> your <u>incorrect</u> sentences.

Evolving Reader: Year 1: Cycle 4: Week 4

1. She <u>ate</u> the cookie in the hotel <u>suite</u>.
2. The <u>flare</u> sent sparks in the sky.
3. The <u>scent</u> of him made his cat <u>purr</u>.
4. I want to try to play <u>bass</u> in the band.
5. We need to <u>haul</u> the books into the house.

Evolving Reader: Year 1: Cycle 4: Week 5

1. <u>I'll</u> sit next to you on the end of the <u>aisle</u>.
2. You need to <u>choose</u> your <u>style</u> of dress for the party.
3. The construction <u>site</u> was dirty.
4. The party for the <u>knight</u> was last <u>night</u>.
5. I would like to <u>browse</u> the books.

Evolving Reader: Year 1: Cycle 4: Week 6

1. There are many <u>chances</u> to win the <u>boxes</u>.
2. The <u>dishes</u> in the sink are dirty.
3. The <u>streets</u> on this side of town are slick from the ice.
4. I am teaching <u>classes</u> at both of the schools.
5. The <u>nurses</u> are going to take care of us.

Evolving Reader: Year 1: Cycle 4: Week 7

1. The <u>babies</u> love to play with the <u>monkeys</u>.
2. Don't pick <u>berries</u> from that tree.
3. I will ask the <u>boys</u> to feed the <u>donkeys</u>.
4. Throw your <u>pennies</u> in the well and your <u>wishes</u> will come true.
5. The <u>churches</u> are very close to our house.

Evolving Reader: Year 1: Cycle 4: Week 8

1. <u>Chris's</u> wife is going to get new glasses.
2. The <u>baby's</u> room will be blue and yellow.
3. We are living in the <u>2000's</u>.
4. There are many <u>sheep</u> at his farm.
5. Did you find the <u>students'</u> hats?

Evolving Reader: Year 2: Cycle 1: Week 1

1. The <u>card</u> was blue.
2. The <u>sharp</u> <u>star</u> poked me.
3. I wore the <u>charm</u> around my <u>arm</u>.
4. The <u>arch</u> is far away.
5. At the <u>fair</u>, I bought an <u>armchair</u>.

Evolving Reader: Year 2: Cycle 1: Week 2

1. There are <u>more</u> than <u>four</u> girls.
2. I bought you a <u>gourd</u> at the <u>store</u>.
3. You <u>tore</u> your pants on the stairs.
4. At the <u>shore</u>, you can see the seagulls <u>soar</u> in the sky.
5. The <u>boar</u> can <u>roar</u> like a lion.

Evolving Reader: Year 2: Cycle 1: Week 3

1. The <u>earth</u> is a <u>sphere</u>.
2. My <u>sheer</u> pantyhose have a <u>tear</u>.
3. How will you <u>learn</u> to <u>earn</u> money?
4. This <u>year</u> I will <u>search</u> far and near for a black <u>pearl</u>.
5. I <u>heard</u> you found a <u>pearl</u> in the water.

Evolving Reader: Year 2: Cycle 1: Week 4

1. The <u>fire</u> <u>hurt</u> the <u>girl</u>.
2. I wore my new <u>shirt</u> to <u>church</u>.
3. The cat will <u>curl</u> up and <u>purr</u>.
4. I found the <u>dirt</u> by the <u>curb</u>.
5. The water is <u>pure</u> here at the stream.

Evolving Reader: Year 2: Cycle 1: Week 5

1. The <u>girl</u> is <u>cute</u> and has a <u>nice</u> grin.
2. I am <u>glad</u> to have a <u>cat</u>.
3. The <u>club</u> meets in the garage.
4. The <u>cub</u> was chewing <u>gum</u>.
5. You can't <u>cut</u> the <u>grape</u>.

Evolving Reader: Year 2: Cycle 1: Week 6

1. Sometimes I <u>teach</u> at <u>lunch</u>.
2. The <u>coach</u> made the team <u>stretch</u>.
3. That <u>bench</u> was in the <u>ditch</u>.
4. The <u>branch</u> is too high to <u>reach</u>.
5. <u>Search</u> the kangaroo's <u>pouch</u> for the key.

Evolving Reader: Year 2: Cycle 1: Week 7

1. He fell off the <u>edge</u> of the <u>stage</u>.
2. The <u>large</u> <u>bridge</u> is closed today.
3. I got the same <u>change</u> as my <u>age</u>.
4. What a <u>strange</u> <u>page</u> to have at the end of the book.
5. Mom said you're in <u>charge</u> of me today.

Evolving Reader: Year 2: Cycle 1: Week 8

1. The clothing <u>shrunk</u> after it was washed.
2. She turned <u>three</u> yesterday.
3. I had to <u>scrape</u> the ice off my car.
4. I like to <u>throw</u> baseballs at the wall.
5. When people <u>scream</u>, it hurts my ears.

Evolving Reader: Year 2: Cycle 2: Week 1

1. I need to <u>scratch</u> my back.
2. If you scare me, I will <u>scream</u>.
3. Don't <u>squeeze</u> the baby chick.
4. The water balloon popped and went <u>splat</u>.
5. The cake is in a <u>square</u> pan.

Evolving Reader: Year 2: Cycle 2: Week 2

1. <u>You'd</u> like to do that, wouldn't you?
2. <u>You're</u> so funny; you always make me laugh.
3. <u>I'd</u> been to that store before.
4. <u>They're</u> not at the party yet.
5. <u>She'd</u> be so proud of you for doing that!

Evolving Reader: Year 2: Cycle 2: Week 3

1. When Mom <u>spoke</u>, we all listened.
2. The <u>chick</u> has a yellow <u>beak</u>.
3. Look in the <u>sack</u> for the <u>black</u> <u>clock</u>.
4. The <u>bike</u> is on the <u>rack</u> on the <u>back</u> of the car.
5. Take a <u>look</u> at my <u>book</u> on the Duke of Earl.

Evolving Reader: Year 2: Cycle 2: Week 4

1. We're tying the <u>knot</u> on the rope.
2. <u>Knock</u> before you enter.
3. That was <u>wrong</u> to kill the gnat.
4. The <u>gnome</u> is on the front lawn.
5. Be careful or you'll <u>wreck</u> it.

Evolving Reader: Year 2: Cycle 2: Week 5

1. Last year I had a bad <u>sprain</u> and couldn't move my arm.
2. We have to try to <u>throw</u> the ball through the hoop.
3. <u>Spread</u> the good cheer and give someone a hug this <u>spring</u>.
4. The baby will <u>thrive</u> in their home.
5. I love to <u>sprawl</u> out on the floor.

Evolving Reader: Year 2: Cycle 2: Week 6

1. She is so uncool; I <u>dislike</u> her.
2. <u>Disregard</u> my <u>mistake</u> about the book.
3. Don't <u>mislead</u> that poor girl.
4. You could easily <u>misinterpret</u> that information.
5. Don't <u>misuse</u> your textbook.

Evolving Reader: Year 2: Cycle 2: Week 7

1. The <u>football</u> hit his <u>headlight</u>.
2. His <u>headstone</u> is <u>backward</u>.
3. The ticket is on the <u>headboard</u>.
4. Play in the <u>backyard</u>.
5. I'm going to need a <u>footstool</u> to reach that.

Evolving Reader: Year 2: Cycle 2: Week 8

1. I <u>understand</u> the directions to go <u>overseas</u>.
2. <u>Downtown</u> is a great place to be.
3. Don't <u>overlook</u> the <u>downstairs</u> when you clean.
4. The cat ran <u>upstairs</u> to get away.
5. The <u>overhead</u> projector wasn't working in the classroom.

Evolving Reader: Year 2: Cycle 3: Week 1

1. <u>She's</u> going to find out <u>what's</u> going on there.
2. <u>Who's</u> going to hear the news?
3. <u>How's</u> it going to look when it's done?
4. <u>Let's</u> all see what's at his house.
5. <u>Here's</u> how to find out where the party will be.

Evolving Reader: Year 2: Cycle 3: Week 2

1. John <u>slipped</u> on the ice and <u>scraped</u> his knee.
2. Mom <u>baked</u> me a cake and I <u>tasted</u> the frosting.
3. The teacher <u>called</u> on me for help.
4. The ball <u>whizzed</u> by him on the field.
5. Harp <u>wagged</u> his tail when we went walking.

Evolving Reader: Year 2: Cycle 3: Week 3

1. We <u>mixed</u> up the directions and <u>jumped</u> through the fence.
2. He <u>handed</u> her the glass after it <u>cracked</u>.
3. She <u>tried</u> to run, but the dog <u>chased</u> her home.
4. The water <u>boiled</u> on the stove for dinner.
5. I <u>asked</u> you when you wanted to go there.

Evolving Reader: Year 2: Cycle 3: Week 4

1. I love <u>running</u> and <u>jumping</u> in the pool when I am hot.
2. The teacher said, "No <u>kicking</u> or <u>whining</u> at the park."
3. We were busy <u>munching</u> on our snacks.
4. I came home and told my dad I was <u>quitting</u> that team!
5. During the rope tug, we did a lot of <u>pulling</u> and <u>pushing</u>.

Evolving Reader: Year 2: Cycle 3: Week 5

1. I got stung <u>by</u> the <u>bee</u> in my <u>eye</u>.
2. She <u>knew</u> <u>there</u> would be a <u>deer</u> in her yard.
3. I <u>hear</u> you are going to the watch whales in the <u>sea</u>.
4. I am turning <u>eight</u> this week, you <u>know</u>.
5. I ate my <u>plain</u> pizza on the <u>plane</u>.

Evolving Reader: Year 2: Cycle 3: Week 6

1. We <u>rode</u> all the way home on <u>one</u> tire.
2. The <u>sale</u> should be on the <u>whole</u> thing.
3. My <u>son</u> will <u>write</u> the longest <u>tale</u>.
4. Did you <u>see</u> what happened to the <u>hare's</u> <u>tail</u>?
5. I can tie a <u>knot</u> on the <u>sail</u> to make it go.

Evolving Reader: Year 2: Cycle 3: Week 7

1. This movie is the <u>funniest</u> one I have seen this year.
2. My mom told us to be the <u>bravest</u> kids on the block.
3. The music became <u>louder</u> and <u>louder</u>.
4. You'll have the <u>biggest</u> and <u>newest</u> car on the street.
5. I was the closest one to the <u>biggest</u> dog.

Evolving Reader: Year 2: Cycle 3: Week 8

1. Being <u>playful</u> is fun for the kids.
2. The police keep people <u>lawful</u> and <u>peaceful</u>.
3. I could <u>barely</u> keep up on the <u>bumpy</u> road.
4. His parents were <u>fearful</u> of the <u>injury</u> to his head.
5. We are <u>constantly</u> being closely <u>watched</u>.

Evolving Reader: Year 2: Cycle 4: Week 1

1. The <u>main</u> point is that we make it <u>through</u> the <u>course</u>.
2. The <u>pair</u> of twins stayed awake <u>through</u> the night.
3. <u>They're</u> going to <u>Maine</u> for the break.
4. The morning <u>dew</u> smells so fresh.
5. <u>Their</u> mom wanted their <u>coarse</u> hair brushed.

Evolving Reader: Year 2: Cycle 4: Week 2

1. Life is <u>meaningless</u> without <u>happiness</u>.
2. <u>Darkness</u> came over the night and we were <u>speechless</u>.
3. People who are <u>homeless</u> are often <u>jobless</u> as well.
4. The <u>ugliness</u> of the comments was <u>tasteless</u>.
5. When we get married, we read vows of in <u>sickness</u> and in health.

Evolving Reader: Year 2: Cycle 4: Week 3

1. <u>After</u> we went to the <u>dentist</u>, we went to play <u>tennis</u>.
2. The <u>signal</u> on the <u>traffic</u> light was not working.
3. A <u>common</u> <u>number</u> of bananas in a bunch is six.
4. <u>Under</u> the <u>basket</u> is the key to the <u>attic</u>.
5. The <u>center</u> of the chocolate bunny is <u>hollow</u>.

Evolving Reader: Year 2: Cycle 4: Week 4

1. They are all <u>fellow</u> <u>music</u> lovers.
2. She became <u>famous</u> after the <u>legal</u> battle.
3. I love the <u>lazy</u>, <u>sunny</u> days in the <u>garden</u>.
4. The <u>baby</u> was finally <u>silent</u> when she saw the <u>yellow</u> <u>basket</u>.
5. <u>Shiny</u> coins are my favorite to collect.

Evolving Reader: Year 2: Cycle 4: Week 5

1. I am <u>eager</u> to see the <u>sequel</u> to that movie.
2. The <u>vacant</u> lot was the <u>topic</u> of choice tonight.
3. We love <u>spicy</u> food; it is full of <u>flavor</u>.
4. He fits the <u>profile</u> the police sent out.
5. The <u>legend</u> of the <u>wizard</u> was a <u>model</u> story.

Evolving Reader: Year 2: Cycle 4: Week 6

1. <u>Believe</u> you can and you won't be <u>surprised</u> when you do.
2. The <u>demand</u> for more food should <u>improve</u> the <u>event</u> this year.
3. We found a <u>raccoon</u> near the <u>police</u> station.
4. <u>Dessert</u> was my favorite part of the <u>surprise</u>.
5. <u>Until</u> I see them for myself, I won't <u>believe</u> that aliens <u>exist</u>.

Evolving Reader: Year 2: Cycle 4: Week 7

1. The pay increase is a <u>record</u> for us!
2. In a <u>perfect</u> world, there would be no <u>combat</u>.
3. I hope the <u>address</u> is correct for the <u>contest</u>.
4. I am the <u>subject</u> of the debate.
5. The <u>desert</u> <u>project</u> will be to construct the <u>perfect</u> tower.

Evolving Reader: Year 2: Cycle 4: Week 8

1. The children should be <u>allowed</u> to go for the exam <u>review</u>.
2. The <u>censor</u> will probably <u>incite</u> a riot among the teens.
3. Most people were <u>mourning</u> the loss of the <u>colonel</u>.
4. The toilet overflowed and ruined our <u>ceiling</u> this <u>morning</u>.
5. We shouted <u>aloud</u> at the people below.

Maturing Reader Word Study Scope and Sequence

Year 1

Cycle 1

9 weeks	Features
1	Suffixes (ing—doubling, e-drop, nothing)
2	Compound words (three plus syllables—any, every, water)
3	Compound words (three plus syllables—any, every water)
4	Contractions (review all)
5	Prefix review (un, re, pre, dis)
6	Suffix review (ful, ly, er, est)
7	Syllable patterns (VCCV—regular/doublet, first syllable stress)
8	Syllable patterns (VCCV—regular/doublet, first syllable stress)
9	Syllable patterns (VCCV—doublets, first and second syllable stress)

Cycle 2

8 weeks	Features
1	Syllable patterns (VCV—open/closed, first syllable stress)
2	Syllable patterns (VCCV—regular/doublet—first and second syllable stress)
3	Syllable patterns (VCV—open/closed—second syllable stress)
4	Number-related prefixes (mon/mono, bi, tri)
5	Number-related prefixes (pent, oct/octa/octo, dec/deca)
6	Syllable patterns (VV, VCCV, VCV)
7	Prefixes (in, en, fore)
8	Common prefixes (pro, post, pre)

Year 2

Cycle 1

8 weeks	Features
1	Vowel patterns in the stressed syllable (long O, short O)
2	Vowel patterns in the stressed syllable (long U—u_e, open and short U)
3	R-controlled vowels in the stressed syllable (ar, are, air)
4	R-controlled vowels in the stressed syllable (er, ear, eer, ere)
5	R-controlled vowels in the stressed syllable (ir, ire)
6	R-controlled vowels in the stressed syllable (or, ore, oar, our)
7	R-controlled vowels in the stressed syllable (ur, ure)
8	Ambiguous vowels in the stressed syllable (oo, ew)

Cycle 2

8 weeks	Features
1	Ambiguous vowels in the stressed syllable (oy/oi, ou/ow)
2	Ambiguous vowels in the stressed syllable (au/aw)
3	Homophones (polysyllabic two syllable)
4	Homophones (polysyllabic two syllable)
5	Homophones (polysyllabic three plus syllables)
6	Prefixes (cat, peri, circum)
7	Latin suffixes (ible/able)
8	Latin suffixes (ant, ent)

Cycle 3

8 weeks	Features
1	Sensitizing to stress (first or second syllable)
2	Vowel patterns in the stressed syllable (short A, long A)
3	Vowel patterns in the stressed syllable (short E, long E)
4	Vowel patterns in the stressed syllable (short I, long I)
5	Homographs (two syllable with syllable stress)
6	Homophones (two syllable, spelling variation in both syllables)
7	Common prefixes (inter, super, intra)
8	Common prefixes (trans, mal/male)

Cycle 4

8 weeks	Features
1	Common prefixes (anti, auto, pro)
2	Number related roots (multi, poly, semi)
3	Spelling patterns at the end of words (il, al, ile)
4	Spelling patterns at the end of words (el, le)
5	Spelling patterns at the end of words (or, er, ar)
6	Spelling patterns at the end of words (en, in, on)
7	Final K sound (que, ck, c, k)
8	Vowel patterns in the stressed syllable (long A, short A)

Cycle 3

8 weeks	Features
1	Vowels patterns in the unstressed syllable ('n, schwa n)
2	Vowels patterns in the unstressed syllable ('n, schwa n—en/adjective, in and on/nouns)
3	Vowel patterns in the unstressed syllable (al, il, ile)
4	Vowel patterns in the unstressed syllable (al, el, le)
5	Vowels patterns in the unstressed syllable (ure, cher, sher)
6	Vowels patterns in the unstressed syllable (ure, cher)
7	Vowels patterns in the unstressed syllable (et, it)
8	Vowels patterns in the unstressed syllable (age, edge, idge)

Cycle 4

8 weeks	Features
1	Vowels patterns in the unstressed syllable (ace, ice, uce, ise, is)
2	Vowels patterns in the unstressed syllable (ey, ie, y)
3	Consonant alternations (silent vs. sounded)
4	Vowel alternations (long to short)
5	Vowel alternations (long to schwa)
6	Vowel alternations (long to schwa) with predictable spelling changes
7	Vowel alternations (short to schwa)
8	Plurals (sis/ses, um/a)

Maturing Reader Word Study Lists

HW indicates header words. Teachers can create header word cards by printing out the blank word study card form available at www.reading.org and writing the header words on them.

Maturing Reader: Year 1: Cycle 1

	Week 1	Week 2	Week 3	Week 4	Week 5	Week 6	Week 7	Week 8	Week 9
	Suffixes (ing—doubling, e-drop, nothing)	Compound words (three plus syllables—any, every, water)	Compound words (three plus syllables—over, under, grand)	Contractions (review all)	Prefix review (un, re, pre, dis)	Suffix review (ful, ly, er, est)	Syllable patterns (VCCV—regular/doublet, first syllable stress)	Syllable patterns (VCCV—regular/doublet, first syllable stress)	Syllable patterns (VCCV doublets, first and second syllable stress)
HW	tugging	anybody	overnight	we're	unable	mouthful	elbow	winter	trolley
HW	speeding	everyone	underwater	he'd	recall	badly	dipper	yellow	dessert
HW	shaping	waterfall	grandmother	we've	precook	smarter			
HW				how's	discolor	biggest			
HW				don't					
HW				we'll					
1	puffing	anybody	overall	he'd	disagree	warmer	absent	after	blizzard
2	tugging	anyone	overboard	I'd	disappear	tougher	basket	biscuit	cattle
3	sprinting	anything	overcast	she'd	discolor	sweeter	cactus	canyon	gossip
4	melting	anytime	overcoat	they'd	discomfort	smaller	dentist	distant	trolley
5	popping	anywhere	overcome	there'd	dislike	quicker	elbow	emblem	soccer
6	quitting	everybody	overflow	we'd	discover	meaner	fabric	furnish	simmer
7	sobbing	everything	overhead	who'd	disclose	louder	garden	ginger	rabbit
8	dragging	everywhere	overlook	you'd	precook	blackest	harvest	helmet	worry
9	snowing	everyone	overview	I've	precut	boldest	index	injure	passage
10	loading	watercolor	undergo	could've	preview	brightest	winter	kingdom	battle
11	blaming	waterfall	underground	should've	pretest	cheapest	lantern	lobster	traffic
12	placing	watermelon	undergrowth	they've	premix	cleanest	market	master	sudden

#									
13	screaming	waterproof	underline	we've	prefix	coldest	napkin	nonsense	village
14	speeding		underlying	would've	predate	abruptly	orbit	orchard	wallet
15	shaping		undermine	you've	prepay	avidly	apple	attic	afford
16	driving		understand	here's	react	badly	ballot	battle	balloon
17	spoiling		underwater	he's	readjust	blindly	cabbage	carry	bassoon
18	scarring		grandchildren	how's	rebound	smoothly	dipper	dizzy	dessert
19	chewing		granddaughter	it's	rebuild	shyly	effort	errand	pollute
20	shouting		grandfather	she's	recall	safely	fellow	flutter	possess
21	stirring		grandmothe⁻	that's	reclaim	careful	gallon	getting	raccoon
22	blurring		grandparents	there's	recycle	cheerful	hammock	happen	
23	puffing		grandson	what's	refill	colorful	inning	ladder	
24	tugging			there's	unable	boastful	kitten	tunnel	
25				where's	unafraid	fearful	yellow	puzzle	
26				who's	unaware	forgetful	valley	office	
27				aren't	unbuckle	harmful	spatter		
28				can't	unbutton		narrow		
29				couldn't	uncommon				
30				doesn't	unfold				
31				don't					
32				hadn't					
33				haven't					
34				isn't					
35				shouldn't					
36				wasn't					
37				weren't					
38				wouldn't					
39				I'll					
40				it'll					
41				he'll					
42				she'll					
43				that'll					
44				they'll					
45				we'll					
46				you'll					

Maturing Reader Word Study Lists

HW indicates header words. Teachers can create header word cards by printing out the blank word study card form available at www.reading.org and writing the header words on them.

Maturing Reader: Year 1: Cycle 2

	Week 1	Week 2	Week 3	Week 4	Week 5	Week 6	Week 7	Week 8
	Syllable patterns (VCV—open/ closed, first syllable stress)	Syllable patterns (VCCV, regular/ double— first and second syllable stress	Syllable patterns (VCV, open/ closed— second syllable stress	Number-related prefixes (mon/mono, bi, tri)	Number-related prefixes (pent, oct/ octa/octo, dec/deca)	Syllable patterns (VV, VCCV, VCV)	Prefixes (in, en, fore)	Common prefixes (pro, post, pre)
HW	final	forbid	relief	monorail	pentagon	liar	inside	protect
HW	finish	dessert	exist	bicycle	octagon	cactus	encode	postpone
HW				triad	decathlon	bacon	forefront	preschool
1	cabin	dolphin	around	triangle	octopus	create	interpret	protest
2	planet	laughter	because	triad	octagon	riot	inconsistent	program
3	finish	pilgrim	before	triceps	October	liar	incomplete	proclaim
4	robin	instant	believe	tricycle	octillion	poem	intuitive	proficient
5	magic	complain	beyond	trilogy	octave	diary	inaccurate	prohibit
6	limit	monster	decide	trinity	pentagon	after	inefficient	prophet
7	cousin	orchard	demand	trimester	pentameter	border	insecure	prospect
8	prison	orphan	event	trio	pentathlon	carpet	inoperative	protect
9	habit	public	hotel	triplet	pentatonic	dentist	engage	posterior
10	punish	purchase	resist	bicycle	decade	elbow	encourage	postpone
11	cover	mumble	prepare	bilateral	decagon	cactus	enjoy	postscript
12	manage	sample	pretend	bipolar	decathlon	canyon	encarta	posterity
13	medal	candle	prevent	biweekly	decameter	writer	foreground	postimpressionism

14	promise	pickle	remain	bipartisan	chosen	forefront	postmeridian
15	closet	absorb	repair	bicentennial	bacon	foreman	preschool
16	camel	admire	return	bimonthly	pilot		predict
17	cavern	although	select	monotonous	music		prehistoric
18	evil	complete	exact	monologue	local		prepay
19	future	compose	exist	monastery	human		premedical
20	glider	confess	giraffe	monarchy	meter		preparatory
21	labor	confuse		monopoly	moment		precook
22	major	contain		monorail	rotate		premarriage
23	migrate	disturb		monograph	cottage		
24	robot	enjoy		monotone	gossip		
25	siren	forget			mammal		
26	solar	attach			soccer		
27	spicy	paddle			wrapper		
28	super	bubble			yucca		
29	treason	balloon					
30		dessert					
31		battle					
32		nozzle					

Maturing Reader Word Study Lists

HW indicates header words. Teachers can create header word cards by printing out the blank word study card form available at www.reading.org and writing the header words on them.

Maturing Reader: Year 1: Cycle 3

	Week 1	Week 2	Week 3	Week 4	Week 5	Week 6	Week 7	Week 8
	Sensitizing to stress (first or second syllable)	Vowel patterns in the stressed syllable (short A, long A)	Vowel patterns in the stressed syllable (short E, long E)	Vowel patterns in the stressed syllable (short I, long I)	Homographs (two syllable with syllable stress)	Homophones (two syllable, spelling variation in both syllables)	Common prefixes (inter, super, intra)	Common prefixes (trans, mal/male)
HW	**nervous**	**fabric**	**enter**	**insect**			**interlock**	**transplant**
HW	**prefer**	**create**	**ready**	**gypsy**			**supersede**	**malfunction**
HW		**basic**	**cheetah**	**advice**			**intramural**	
HW			**being**	**diner**				
1	certain	after	rescue	insect	combat	medal	intercept	translate
2	merchant	capture	seldom	injure	conduct	metal	interrupt	transport
3	mermaid	master	sentence	sister	conflict	meddle	intercede	transaction
4	nervous	plastic	twenty	signal	content	bolder	interlock	transparent
5	person	chapter	welcome	winter	contract	boulder	intercom	transfer
6	service	napkin	velvet	window	desert	peddle	interpersonal	transit
7	circle	raptor	message	chimney	extract	petal	Internet	transform
8	dirty	fabric	better	abyss	import	pedal	supernatural	transpose
9	turtle	attic	forget	crystal	insert	cellar	superstitious	transpire
10	purple	cabbage	enter	gypsy	minute	seller	supermarket	transplant
11	gurgle	tablet	evil	rhythm	object	berry	superficial	malnourish

#								
12	plural	traffic	fever	system	permit	bury	superimpose	malleable
13	current	tragic	recent	advice	present	aisle	superintendent	malady
14	alert	happen	legal	beside	project	I'll	supersede	malfunction
15	emerge	agent	veto	excite	protest	isle	supervision	malpractice
16	exert	basic	deafen	precise	rebel	profit	intramural	malaria
17	prefer	cradle	feather	recline	recess	prophet	intrapersonal	malign
18	reverse	fatal	leather	revise	record	beacle	intravenous	malcontent
19	reserve	baby	ready	surprise	subject	beet e	intergalactic	malevolent
20	observe	labor	treasure	biker	transport	bazaar	intradermal	
21	surprise	vapor	weapon	diner		biza're		
22	perhaps	sacred	weather	icy				
23	surround	April	agree	pirate				
24	survive	navy	breezy	rival				
25	pursue	flavor	gleeful	spider				
26		vacant	steeple	timer				
27		embrace	succeed	virus				
28		erase	tweezers	writer				
29		awake	being	ignite				
30		create		revive				

Maturing Reader Word Study Lists

HW indicates header words. Teachers can create header word cards by printing out the blank word study card form available at www.reading.org and writing the header words on them.

Maturing Reader: Year 1: Cycle 4

	Week 1	Week 2	Week 3	Week 4	Week 5	Week 6	Week 7	Week 8
	Common prefixes (*anti, auto, pro*)	Number-related roots (*multi, poly, semi*)	Spelling patterns at the end of words (*il, al, ile*)	Spelling patterns at the end of words (*el, le*)	Spelling patterns at the end of words (*or, er, ar*)	Spelling patterns at the end of words (*en, in, on*)	Final *K* sound (*que, ck, c, k*)	Vowel patterns in the stressed syllable (long *A*, short *A*)
HW	antidote	multiplex	evil	jewel	sailor	kitten	unique	canvas
HW	autopsy	polygon	equal	eagle	voter	raisin	seasick	escape
HW	profile	semicircle	mobile		dollar	pardon	attic	crater
HW							network	failure
HW								decay
1	antibiotic	multicolored	basil	angel	altar	chicken	antique	accept
2	antidote	multicultural	civil	camel	beggar	children	boutique	attic
3	antifreeze	multilateral	evil	easel	calendar	garden	critique	canvas
4	antihistamine	multinational	pencil	gravel	cellar	kitten	mystique	exact
5	antipathy	multiple	tonsil	jewel	dollar	linen	opaque	falcon
6	antithesis	multiplex	vigil	nickel	molar	raven	physique	satin
7	antitrust	multiplication	lentil	sequel	pillar	siren	plaque	tragic
8	antiwar	multitude	facile	tinsel	scholar	warden	unique	amaze
9	autobiography	polychrome	fertile	travel	sugar	blacken	artwork	create
10	autocrat	polygon	fragile	morsel	barber	broaden	benchmark	escape

#							
11	autograph	polygraph	hostile	ankle	jogger	darken	crosswalk	persuade
12	automatic	polynomial	mobile	beetle	printer	deafen	embark	safety
13	automobile	polyp	sterile	buckle	reader	frighten	hallmark	afraid
14	autonomy	polysyllabic	bridal	cable	seller	given	homework	contain
15	autopsy	semiannual	equal	cripple	soldier	listen	network	failure
16	proceed	semicircle	global	crumble	usher	sharpen	aerobic	painter
17	proclaim	semicolon	neutral	dimple	voter	shorten	attic	raisin
18	procreate	semifinal	oval	eagle	beginner	sweeten	chronic	traitor
19	profile	semiprivate	royal	fable	officer	golden	classic	astray
20	progress	semiweekly	vital	gentle	banner	molten	cubic	decay
21	promote		pedal	grumble	boulder	rotten	elastic	layer
22	prospect		signal	juggle	cancer	sunken	fabric	maybe
23	protect		mammal	mantle	coaster	swollen	frantic	player
24	provide		medal	nestle	fender	cabin	garlic	portray
25			rascal	pebble	actor	dolphin	generic	today
26			scandal	puzzle	donor	penguin	logic	agent
27			vandal	sprinkle	juror	raisin	magic	basin
28				struggle	sailor	toxin	metric	crater
29				trouble	sponsor	margin	music	fable
30				turtle	vendor	apron	panic	hatred
31					visitor	bacon	scenic	labor
32					favor	button	static	lazy
33					honor	colon	toxic	navy
34					humor	felon	tropic	raven
35					terror	iron	attack	vapor
36					anchor	lemon	carsick	
37					color	pardon	cowlick	
38					error	person	gimmick	
39					motor	reason	padlock	
40					tremor	ribbon	ransack	
41					vapor	sermon	seasick	
42					equator	treason		

Maturing Reader Word Study Lists

HW indicates header words. Teachers can create header word cards by printing out the blank word study card form available at www.reading.org and writing the header words on them.

Maturing Reader: Year 2: Cycle 1

	Week 1	Week 2	Week 3	Week 4	Week 5	Week 6	Week 7	Week 8
	Vowel patterns in the stressed syllable (long O, short O)	Vowel patterns in the stressed syllable (Long U—open U, and short U)	R-controlled vowels in the stressed syllable (ar, are, air)	R-controlled vowels in the stressed syllable (er, ear, eer, ere)	R-controlled vowels in the stressed syllable (ir, ire)	R-controlled vowels in the stressed syllable (or, ore, oar, our)	R-controlled vowels in the stressed syllable (ur, ure)	Ambiguous vowels in the stressed syllable (oo, ew)
HW	adopt	bubble	alarm	jerky	circle	adorn	burden	balloon
HW	alone	abuse	aware	learner	enquire	adore	endure	rookie
HW	toaster	tulip	prairie	appear		aboard		chewy
HW	stroller		carry	leery		mournful		
HW	below			adhere				
HW	bony							
1	adopt	bubble	alarm	berry	birthday	adorn	burly	aloof
2	bother	bundle	barber	cherub	birthstone	chorus	burden	baboon
3	congress	chuckle	carbon	merit	circle	cordial	curdle	cartoon
4	comment	funny	carpet	perish	circuit	corner	curry	doodle
5	hockey	husband	charcoal	sterile	dirty	floral	furnish	moody
6	monster	muffin	darkness	certain	firmly	florist	further	raccoon
7	profit	publish	gargle	gerbil	sirloin	forest	hurdle	shampoo
8	scholar	snuggle	harbor	jerky	thirsty	formal	murky	tattoo
9	topic	abuse	marble	mercy	twirler	glory	plural	askew
10	yonder	conclude	parsley	perfect	virtue	hornet	purchase	chewy

214

11	alone	excuse	party	person	acquire	horror	rural	dewdrop
12	compose	lukewarm	scarlet	sermon	aspire	mortal	sturdy	jewel
13	hopeful	misuse	starchy	verdict	attire	moral	surgeon	pewter
14	promote	protrude	tardy	versus	entire	normal	turkey	steward
15	coastal	salute	yardage	bleary	firearm	portion	turnip	bookcase
16	soapy	futile	aware	earthworm	fireplace	sorrow	assure	cookout
17	toaster	future	barely	learner	inquire	stormy	endure	footprint
18	enroll	ruby	careful	rehearse	perspire	torture	manure	foothill
19	molten	rumor	rarely	research	rehire	adore	mature	rookie
20	poster	student	sparerib	yearning	tiresome	before	obscure	mistook
21	stroller	super	warehouse	appear	wiretap	deplore	procure	woodchuck
22	below	tulip	aircraft	clearing		galore	purebred	woodland
23	owner	tumor	airmail	fearful		ignore	surely	
24	rowers	tutor	dairy	nearly		restore	unsure	
25	lower		hairbrush	teardrop		scoreless		
26	bony		prairie	spearhead		shoreline		
27	chosen		stairway	yearly		storefront		
28	locate		barrel	career		storeroom		
29	pony		carat	leery		aboard		
30	rotate		carry	sheerest		boardroom		
31			marrow	veneer		coarsely		
32			parent	adhere		hoarseness		
33			parrot	cashmere		courthouse		
34			tariff	merely		foursome		
35				revere		mournful		
36				sincere		pouring		
37						sources		

Maturing Reader Word Study Lists

HW indicates header words. Teachers can create header word cards by printing out the blank word study card form available at www.reading.org and writing the header words on them.

Maturing Reader: Year 2: Cycle 2

	Week 1	Week 2	Week 3	Week 4	Week 5	Week 6	Week 7	Week 8
	Ambiguous vowels in the stressed syllable (oy/oi, ou/ow)	Ambiguous vowels in the stressed syllable (au/aw)	Homophones (polysyllabic, two syllable)	Homophones (polysyllabic, two syllable)	Homophones (polysyllabic, three plus syllable)	Prefixes (cat, peri, circum)	Latin suffixes (ible/able)	Latin suffixes (ant/ent)
HW	**loyal**	**faucet**				**catacomb**	**edible**	**infant**
HW	**avoid**	**awful**				**periscope**	**breakable**	**infancy**
HW	**counsel**					**circumvent**		**dependent**
HW	**flower**							**dependence**
1	annoy	applaud	allowed	accept	addition	catacomb	agreeable	attendant
2	destroy	author	aloud	except	edition	catalogue	breakable	defiant
3	employ	daughter	ceiling	affect	capital	catapult	dependable	dormant
4	joyful	faucet	sealing	effect	capitol	cataract	laughable	hesitant
5	voyage	jaundice	morning	altar	cereal	catastrophe	perishable	important
6	avoid	laundry	mourning	alter	serial	catatonic	predictable	infant
7	exploit	saucer	holy	basal	complement	pericardium	profitable	occupant
8	loiter	sauna	wholly	basil	compliment	perimeter	remarkable	tolerant
9	poison	slaughter	review	chili	principal	period	transferable	resistant
10	toilet	pauper	revue	chilly	principle	periodontal	audible	reliant
11	bounty	awkward	ascent	council	stationary	periscope	edible	adolescent
12	counsel	awning	assent	counsel	stationery	circumference	visible	consistent

convenient
equivalent
independent
intelligent
patient
prominent
repellent
transparent
violent

horrible
tangible
legible
terrible

circumfuse
circumscribe
circumspect
circumstance
circumvent

hostel
hostile
patience
patients
presence
presents
manner
manor
naval
navel
mantel
mantle

aural
oral
colonel
kernel
censor
sensor
incite
insight

brawny
flawless
lawsuit
pawnshop
rawhide

13 devour
14 doubtful
15 mousetrap
16 scoundrel
17 allow
18 brownie
19 chowder
20 dowel
21 drowsy
22 flower
23 prowler
24 rowdy
25 tower
26 vowel

Maturing Reader Word Study Lists

HW indicates header words. Teachers can create header word cards by printing out the blank word study card form available at www.reading.org and writing the header words on them.

Maturing Reader: Year 2: Cycle 3

	Week 1	Week 2	Week 3	Week 4	Week 5	Week 6	Week 7	Week 8
	Vowels patterns in the unstressed syllable ('n, schwa n)	Vowels patterns in the unstressed syllable ('n, schwa n)	Vowel patterns in the unstressed syllable (al, il, ile)	Vowel patterns in the unstressed syllable (al, el, le)	Vowels patterns in the unstressed syllable (ure, cher, sher)	Vowels patterns in the unstressed syllable (ure, cher)	Vowels patterns in the unstressed syllable (et, it)	Vowels patterns in the unstressed syllable (age, edge, idge)
HW	**captain**	**molten**	**bridal**	**central**	**capture**	**lecture**	**nugget**	**garbage**
HW	**urban**	**robin**	**evil**	**chapel**	**poacher**	**censure**	**habit**	**knowledge**
HW	**children**	**gallon**	**fertile**	**giggle**	**usher**	**closure**		**cartridge**
HW						**preacher**		
1	bargain	barren	bridal	central	capture	lecture	banquet	bandage
2	captain	golden	dental	equal	creature	mixture	blanket	cabbage
3	certain	molten	final	fatal	culture	moisture	comet	carriage
4	mountain	often	global	legal	denture	nature	gadget	damage
5	fountain	rotten	nasal	metal	feature	pasture	hornet	garbage
6	organ	sunken	postal	normal	fixture	puncture	jacket	image
7	orphan	wooden	spiral	oval	fracture	rupture	musket	language
8	slogan	spoken	vocal	royal	gesture	sculpture	nugget	message
9	sultan	swollen	mental	tidal	juncture	structure	poet	package
10	titan	open	neutral	vital	bleacher	texture	wallet	sausage
11	turban	basin	anvil	angel	butcher	torture	audit	voyage
12	urban	cabin	April	bagel	catcher	vulture	bandit	knowledge
13	aspen	cousin	council	chapel	pitcher	archer	credit	selvedge

14 chicken
15 children
16 garden
17 heaven
18 oxen
19 raven
20 warden
21 women
22 listen
23 thicken
24 siren
25
26
27
28
29
30

muffin
penguin
pumpkin
robin
satin
toxin
apron
bacon
cannon
dragon
falcon
gallon
iron
lemon
melon
poison

evil
gerbil
nostril
stencil
tonsil
pencil
fossil
docile
facile
fertile
fragile
futile
hostile
missile
mobile
sterile

diesel
flannel
jewel
kernel
label
model
tinsel
ankle
bubble
cattle
dimple
freckle
giggle
hustle
jungle
knuckle
sprinkle

poacher
richer
rancher
teacher
voucher
crusher
flasher
fresher
usher
washer

marcher
preacher
trencher
searcher
stretcher
censure
fissure
pressure
closure
leisure
measure
pleasure
seizure
treasure

digit
exit
habit
hermit
limit
rabbit
vomit

cartridge
partridge
porridge

Maturing Reader Word Study Lists

HW indicates header words. Teachers can create header word cards by printing out the blank word study card form available at www.reading.org and writing the header words on them.

Maturing Reader: Year 2: Cycle 4

	Week 1	Week 2	Week 3	Week 4	Week 5	Week 6	Week 7	Week 8
	Vowels patterns in the unstressed syllable (ace, ice, uce, ise, is)	Vowels patterns in the unstressed syllable (ey, ie, y)	Consonant alternations (silent vs. sounded consonants)	Vowel alternations (long to short)	Vowel alternations (long to schwa)	Vowel alternations (long to schwa) with predictable spelling changes	Vowel alternations (short to schwa)	Plurals (sis/ses, um/a)
HW	palace	donkey	sign	cave	compose	exclaim	malice	analysis
HW	justice	movie	signal	cavity	composition	exclamation	malicious	analyses
HW	lettuce	envy	soft			apply	excel	addendum
HW	promise		soften			application	excellent	addenda
HW	tennis					purify	critic	
HW						purification	criticize	
HW							inform	
HW							information	
1	furnace	alley	align	assume	able	exclaim	academy	analysis
2	menace	chimney	alignment	assumption	ability	exclamation	academic	analyses
3	necklace	donkey	benign	cave	adoration	explain	metal	basis
4	palace	hockey	benignant	cavity	adore	explanation	metallic	bases
5	preface	journey	design	crime	compose	proclaim	vital	crisis
6	surface	kidney	designate	criminal	composition	proclamation	vitality	crises
7	justice	monkey	fast	ignite	define	apply	celebrate	nemesis
8	malice	trolley	fasten	ignition	definition	application	celebrity	nemeses

9 novice	valley	haste	induce	divide	certify	democrat	psychosis
10 notice	cookie	hasten	induction	dividend	certification	democracy	psychoses
11 office	genie	malign	meter	expose	classify	critic	thesis
12 service	movie	malignant	metric	exposition	classification	criticize	theses
13 lettuce	prairie	moist	nation	gene	identify	prohibit	addendum
14 axis	rookie	moisten	national	genetic	identification	prohibition	addenda
15 basis	zombie	oft	nature	invite	imply	chronic	bacterium
16 crisis	angry	often	natural	invitation	implication	chronology	bacteria
17 tennis	beauty	resign	please	major	magnify	geometry	emporium
18 trellis	candy	resignation	pleasure	majority	magnification	geometric	emporia
19 anise	crazy	sign	produce	narrate	multiply	inform	millennium
20 porpoise	cherry	signal	production	narrative	multiplication	information	millennia
21 promise	daily	soft	provide	prepare	notify	system	referendum
22 tortoise	early	soften	provision	preparation	notification	systematic	referenda
23 treatise	envy		revise	reside	personify		
24	guilty		revision	resident	personification		
25	sturdy		wise	stable	purify		
26	treaty		wisdom	stability	purification		
27	trophy				specify		
28	weary				specification		
29	worry				verify		
30					verification		

Maturing Reader Dictated Sentences

Underlined words are examples of word study features for each week; not all words are included on the word study list.

Maturing Reader: Year 1: Cycle 1: Week 1

1. He was <u>sprinting</u> so fast that he became sick.
2. The baby was <u>screaming</u> and it was <u>spoiling</u> our dinner.
3. My dad said he is <u>quitting</u> his job next year.
4. Hopefully, we won't have school because it's <u>snowing</u>.
5. He was <u>dragging</u> his dog along for a walk.

Maturing Reader: Year 1: Cycle 1: Week 2

1. <u>Everybody</u> loves <u>watercolor</u>.
2. <u>Watermelon</u> is a great treat <u>anytime</u>.
3. We went to the <u>waterfall</u> last summer.
4. I will follow you <u>anywhere</u> you go.
5. I always use <u>waterproof</u> sunscreen.

Maturing Reader: Year 1: Cycle 1: Week 3

1. The bathtub will <u>overflow</u> if you leave the water on.
2. The sky is <u>overcast</u> today.
3. My mother is begging for <u>grandchildren</u>.
4. The girl's parents went <u>overboard</u> on her birthday party.
5. The woman needs to <u>undergo</u> surgery for her tumor.

Maturing Reader: Year 1: Cycle 1: Week 4

1. He <u>couldn't</u> go because there <u>weren't</u> any more seats on the bus.
2. <u>Aren't</u> you glad <u>she's</u> here to stay with you?
3. <u>Haven't</u> you thought of that excuse for your homework?
4. <u>There's</u> always tomorrow for what we <u>should've</u> done today.
5. They <u>should've</u> gone to see the kids who <u>weren't</u> going.

Maturing Reader: Year 1: Cycle 1: Week 5

1. The <u>refill</u> is available at the <u>recycle</u> plant.
2. You need to <u>precook</u> the meat before you send it to the cookout.
3. I am <u>unable</u> to help with the <u>pretest</u> for spelling.
4. Our dog is in some <u>discomfort</u> because he ate the chocolate.
5. The item is on the <u>recall</u> list.

Maturing Reader: Year 1: Cycle 1: Week 6

1. The days are getting <u>warmer</u> and <u>longer</u> because spring is near.
2. I was led <u>blindly</u> into the room and then led <u>safely</u> away.
3. The <u>cheapest</u> cereal is <u>sweeter</u> than the others.
4. The men were <u>fearful</u> of the <u>largest</u> bear.
5. Players need to be <u>smaller</u> so they can be <u>quicker</u> on the field.

Maturing Reader: Year 1: Cycle 1: Week 7

1. The hammock was swinging in the yard.
2. The yellow fabric was wrapped around the cactus.
3. The lantern needs to be lit in the winter.
4. The dentist was absent today.
5. With a little effort, you can see the Big Dipper at night.

Maturing Reader: Year 1: Cycle 1: Week 8

1. After eating the biscuit, I was beginning to feel a flutter in my belly.
2. The master bedroom smelled like ginger.
3. The king was talking nonsense about the kingdom.
4. We took a trip to the apple orchard so we could pick apples on the ladder.
5. Her office is so messy; you should wear a helmet so nothing falls on your head.

Maturing Reader: Year 1: Cycle 1: Week 9

1. We cannot afford to gossip about others.
2. The traffic in the village was awful last summer.
3. Students had to read the passage on the history of the bassoon.
4. Leave the soup on the stove to simmer.
5. We shouldn't worry about the trolley being on time.

Maturing Reader: Year 1: Cycle 2: Week 1

1. Going to the cabin is fun.
2. We will travel to a faraway palace.
3. The count used magic to make a rabbit vanish.
4. We saw a robin at our cabin.
5. I want to finish with a gold medal

Maturing Reader: Year 1: Cycle 2: Week 2

1. The fifth graders purchase pickles.
2. The monster would mumble when he would complain.
3. The candle smells like a fresh orchard.
4. The bubble popped and there was instant laughter.
5. The public came to see the dolphins.

Maturing Reader: Year 1: Cycle 2: Week 3

1. The judges went around to repair the carts.
2. In the event that the hotel is closed, we will return home.
3. I believe there is life beyond this.
4. Prevent pollution before it occurs.
5. Select the lottery number because it will win.

Maturing Reader: Year 1: Cycle 2: Week 4

1. Jag gives a <u>monologue</u> in his show.
2. The professor spoke in a <u>monotone</u> voice.
3. The boy rode his <u>bicycle</u> by the duplex.
4. The <u>tricycle</u> is bright red.
5. The <u>triangle</u> has three sides.

Maturing Reader: Year 1: Cycle 2: Week 5

1. I can sing the full <u>octave</u> range.
2. The <u>octopus</u> has eight legs.
3. The U.S. <u>Pentagon</u> got hit by an airplane.
4. The students measured the hallway in <u>decameters</u>.
5. The stop sign is in the shape of an <u>octagon</u>.

Maturing Reader: Year 1: Cycle 2: Week 6

1. We listened to the <u>local</u> <u>music</u> at <u>Cactus</u> <u>Canyon</u>.
2. The <u>pilot</u> had to <u>fuel</u> the plane <u>after</u> he landed.
3. The <u>writer</u> was hoping for a <u>riot</u> to write about in his <u>diary</u>.
4. The <u>carpet</u> smelled like <u>bacon</u>.
5. The rash will <u>create</u> a red spot on my <u>elbow</u>.

Maturing Reader: Year 1: Cycle 2: Week 7

1. The <u>foreman</u> will discuss the plan.
2. You're an <u>intuitive</u> artist.
3. I <u>engage</u> in social events because I <u>enjoy</u> them.
4. I have trouble with <u>inconsistent</u> people.
5. I will <u>encourage</u> the fifth graders to do well tomorrow.

Maturing Reader: Year 1: Cycle 2: Week 8

1. We had to <u>postpone</u> the <u>preschool</u> enrollment.
2. I predict he will be able to attend the <u>program</u>.
3. The school is supposed to <u>protect</u> the students.
4. He was entering the <u>premedical</u> <u>program</u> in college.
5. The teacher had to <u>prohibit</u> touching the <u>prehistoric</u> bones.

Maturing Reader: Year 1: Cycle 3: Week 1

1. She went to <u>observe</u> the circle.
2. <u>Perhaps</u> a <u>mermaid</u> will say hello.
3. A <u>nervous</u> <u>person</u> was <u>surprised</u>.
4. The people on the beach were asked to be on <u>alert</u> for baby sea <u>turtles</u>.
5. I <u>prefer</u> a <u>purple</u> shirt.

Maturing Reader: Year 1: Cycle 3: Week 2

1. There was a <u>tragic</u> <u>traffic</u> accident.
2. Call me <u>after</u> <u>April</u> first.
3. They will <u>capture</u> their <u>master</u>.
4. The <u>cradle</u> was <u>vacant</u>.
5. The <u>fabric</u> was <u>navy</u> blue.

Maturing Reader: Year 1: Cycle 3: Week 3

1. We <u>seldom</u> have more than <u>twenty</u> students.
2. <u>Forget</u> about your <u>fever</u>.
3. Give me a reason to <u>sentence</u> him.
4. That <u>female</u> is an expert.
5. She will compete in the <u>welcome</u> race.

Maturing Reader: Year 1: Cycle 3: Week 4

1. Michael drew a <u>picture</u> of an <u>insect</u>.
2. The <u>children</u> learned about <u>pirates</u>.
3. Is a <u>spider</u> an <u>insect</u>?
4. Ignore the <u>sirens</u>.
5. The <u>chimney</u> gets used in the <u>winter</u>.

Maturing Reader: Year 1: Cycle 3: Week 5

1. <u>Insert</u> <u>recess</u> in the schedule after lunch.
2. The math <u>subject</u> was a <u>minute</u> problem.
3. I will <u>transport</u> the <u>presents</u> to the party.
4. She will <u>extract</u> the cactus in the <u>desert</u>.
5. The <u>rebel</u> caused a <u>conflict</u>.

Maturing Reader: Year 1: Cycle 3: Week 6

1. There were <u>petals</u> down the <u>aisle</u>.
2. She <u>peddled</u> down the mountain.
3. The modern style is silver <u>metal</u>.
4. Mary put the <u>medal</u> in the <u>cellar</u>.
5. The <u>seller</u> had good manners.

Maturing Reader: Year 1: Cycle 3: Week 7

1. She will not <u>interrupt</u> her mother at the <u>supermarket</u>.
2. <u>Superman</u> was on the <u>intercom</u>.
3. There were <u>superficial</u> things on the <u>Internet</u>.
4. <u>Intercept</u> the football pass.
5. She was <u>superstitious</u> and had to change her socks.

Maturing Reader: Year 1: Cycle 3: Week 8

1. <u>Transport</u> the <u>malnourished</u> dog to the vet.

2. He needed a <u>transplant</u> because of his malaria.

3. She will <u>transform</u> into a Power Ranger.

4. He completed his <u>transaction</u> at the bank.

5. The boy will <u>transpose</u> his classical music.

Maturing Reader: Year 1: Cycle 4: Week 1

1. They found the <u>antibiotic</u> to <u>protect</u> the students.

2. The <u>autopsy</u> was performed on the old man.

3. His <u>autobiography</u> was the <u>antithesis</u> of a happy man.

4. I prefer to <u>proceed</u> with the plan as scheduled.

5. My car needs <u>antifreeze</u> so I don't get stuck in the winter.

Maturing Reader: Year 1: Cycle 4: Week 2

1. The <u>semiprivate</u> room was really noisy.

2. A <u>polygon</u> has <u>multiple</u> sides.

3. We live in a <u>multicultural</u> society.

4. The <u>semicolon</u> is one of the conventions we use in writing.

5. I love to study <u>polysyllabic</u> words.

Maturing Reader: Year 1: Cycle 4: Week 3

1. The <u>bridal</u> party decided on a <u>neutral</u> dress for the wedding.

2. I sat on the jury for the <u>civil</u> trial.

3. Taking out your <u>tonsils</u> is a <u>fragile</u> procedure.

4. I would love to attend the <u>royal</u> wedding.

5. Everyone has a <u>mobile</u> phone today.

Maturing Reader: Year 1: Cycle 4: Week 4

1. She had <u>trouble</u> with the <u>puzzle</u> today.

2. We found a <u>beetle</u>, a <u>turtle</u>, and a <u>morsel</u> of food.

3. Can you <u>juggle</u> with the <u>easel</u> in your way?

4. The <u>gravel</u> on the road was beginning to <u>crumble</u>.

5. My <u>ankle</u> hurt after the <u>camel</u> stepped on my foot.

Maturing Reader: Year 1: Cycle 4: Week 5

1. The <u>burglar</u> ran into the <u>jogger</u> and then he got caught.

2. The <u>soldier</u> was an <u>officer</u> in the military.

3. As a <u>reader</u> you should find <u>humor</u> in the comics.

4. We needed to find a <u>donor</u> for the <u>sailor</u>.

5. Do you have the <u>calendar</u> for the <u>cancer</u> walk?

Maturing Reader: Year 1: Cycle 4: Week 6

1. <u>Children</u> love the <u>chicken</u> nuggets from the store.
2. Be careful to not get frightened when you <u>sharpen</u> the knives.
3. The <u>warden</u> listened to the concerns of the inmates.
4. When given a <u>toxin</u>, you need to get to the doctor quickly.
5. You do not need an <u>apron</u> to eat a <u>raisin</u>.

Maturing Reader: Year 1: Cycle 4: Week 7

1. She found the <u>antique</u> at the new <u>boutique</u>.
2. The <u>fabric</u> was <u>elastic</u> and was difficult to sew.
3. I tend to get <u>carsick</u> when we are going on a <u>scenic</u> route.
4. The <u>hallmark</u> event was the <u>unique</u> design of the building.
5. She had a <u>classic</u> case of <u>chronic</u> coughing.

Maturing Reader: Year 1: Cycle 4: Week 8

1. If you <u>accept</u> the money, I'm <u>afraid</u> you'll regret it.
2. It was a <u>tragic</u> case of a lazy <u>painter</u>.
3. The <u>vapors</u> <u>created</u> <u>decay</u> in the <u>attic</u>.
4. <u>Hatred</u> can only cause problems <u>today</u>.
5. <u>Safety</u> is our first concern for the <u>player</u>.

Maturing Reader: Year 2: Cycle 1: Week 1

1. Why should we <u>bother</u> to do this?
2. That was a weird <u>comment</u>.
3. I would like to <u>enroll</u> in that class.
4. The <u>molten</u> lava was a scary sight in the middle of the road.
5. Billy dropped the <u>toaster</u>.

Maturing Reader: Year 2: Cycle 1: Week 2

1. Jack carried the heavy <u>bundle</u> of sticks.
2. The chocolate chip <u>muffins</u> are my favorite.
3. My coffee became <u>lukewarm</u> very quickly.
4. It was <u>futile</u> to explain the reason for speeding to the police officer.
5. I really need an algebra <u>tutor</u>.

Maturing Reader: Year 2: Cycle 1: Week 3

1. We threw a surprise birthday <u>party</u> for Ellen.
2. The couple <u>barely</u> made the train before it <u>departed</u> the station.
3. The <u>warehouse</u> was empty after trucks loaded the boxes.
4. Bob's <u>dairy</u> farm had many cows.
5. My teacher was not happy because I was <u>tardy</u> to her class.

Maturing Reader: Year 2: Cycle 1: Week 4

1. "That idea has <u>merit</u>!" exclaimed the professor.
2. The rainy, dark evening created a <u>bleary</u> environment.
3. We should not have to <u>rehearse</u> any more before the show.
4. I would like to have a <u>career</u> in information technology.
5. <u>Cashmere</u> is my favorite fabric.

Maturing Reader: Year 2: Cycle 1: Week 5

1. Leonardo daVinci could draw a perfect <u>circle</u> freehand.
2. The <u>attire</u> for the ball was black tie.
3. By <u>virtue</u> of my position, I could make the decision.
4. I was very <u>thirsty</u> after my soccer game.
5. The military policeman carried a large <u>firearm</u>.

Maturing Reader: Year 2: Cycle 1: Week 6

1. Sharon hates <u>horror</u> films.
2. The <u>moral</u> of the story is what we usually remember.
3. The <u>boardroom</u> was very intimidating.
4. The <u>foursome</u> played an impressive round of golf.
5. I <u>adore</u> <u>stormy</u> weather.

Maturing Reader: Year 2: Cycle 1: Week 7

1. The <u>surgeon</u> was able to <u>assure</u> the patient that she would be able to <u>endure</u> the procedure.
2. Would you <u>purchase</u> a home in a <u>rural</u> environment?
3. The <u>turkey</u> ate the <u>turnip</u>.
4. The salesman could not <u>furnish</u> enough information about the car to <u>hurdle</u> my suspicions.
5. He was very <u>mature</u> to accept the blame in the <u>murky</u> situation.

Maturing Reader: Year 2: Cycle 1: Week 8

1. The <u>baboon</u> appeared <u>aloof</u> when we walked by the cage.
2. I left the <u>cookout</u> to watch my favorite <u>cartoon</u>.
3. The <u>rookie</u> <u>mistook</u> the <u>shampoo</u> for a bottle of lotion.
4. Kevin asked the <u>steward</u> for some more cashews.
5. Did you find the <u>jewel</u> on the bookcase?

Maturing Reader: Year 2: Cycle 2: Week 1

1. The <u>scoundrel</u> was trying to <u>avoid</u> paying for the <u>voyage</u>.
2. I love to <u>devour</u> clam <u>chowder</u> from the beach.
3. It is <u>doubtful</u> that she ate the <u>brownie</u>.
4. The <u>mousetrap</u> is going to catch the mice.
5. We are always studying <u>vowel</u> patterns.

Maturing Reader: Year 2: Cycle 2: Week 2

1. His <u>daughter</u> spoke in an <u>awkward</u> manner.
2. The <u>laundry</u> was in the washer.
3. The <u>author</u> turned in the <u>flawless</u> manuscript.
4. The <u>lawsuit</u> for the broken <u>sauna</u> was going to be settled.
5. She broke the <u>faucet</u> when she threw the <u>saucer</u> in the sink.

Maturing Reader: Year 2: Cycle 2: Week 3

1. Jack <u>allowed</u> me to sit down on the chair.
2. I could see a brown stain on the <u>ceiling</u>.
3. Dad will be coming home on Tuesday <u>morning</u>.
4. The movie received a very good <u>review</u>.
5. Bill's <u>insight</u> was especially helpful in solving the problem.

Maturing Reader: Year 2: Cycle 2: Week 4

1. Sharon approached the stage to <u>accept</u> her reward.
2. Benjamin's low voice was noted for its <u>basal</u> tone.
3. Kevin stayed at a youth <u>hostel</u> when he hiked across Europe.
4. Every good friendship is rooted in <u>patience</u>.
5. The <u>Naval</u> officer wore a white uniform.

Maturing Reader: Year 2: Cycle 2: Week 5

1. The second <u>edition</u> of the textbook was much harder to understand.
2. "That was a nice <u>compliment</u> you received," said Mom.
3. The <u>principle</u> of the matter was more important than the act.
4. I remained <u>stationary</u> when the strange dog walked in front of my house.
5. In <u>addition</u> to being grounded, my parents withheld my allowance.

Maturing Reader: Year 2: Cycle 2: Week 6

1. The <u>catalogue</u> had some very pretty clothes.
2. The tsunami <u>catastrophe</u> resulted in great devastation.
3. The soldier walked the <u>perimeter</u> of the base as part of his duties.
4. The <u>circumference</u> of the ball was exactly 18 inches.
5. In order to <u>circumvent</u> the impending fight, the teacher kept John in the classroom until Jim caught the bus home after school.

Maturing Reader: Year 2: Cycle 2: Week 7

1. The dog became quite <u>agreeable</u> after I gave him a bone.
2. Because the milk was <u>perishable</u>, we had to put it in the refrigerator as soon as we arrived home from the store.
3. The meteor shower was a <u>remarkable</u> sight.
4. Our scoutmaster did not allow us to eat the berries because he was not sure if they were <u>edible</u>.
5. There were no <u>tangible</u> results from which to make a recommendation.

Maturing Reader: Year 2: Cycle 2: Week 8

1. George remained <u>adamant</u> that he did not eat the last cookie.
2. It is always <u>important</u> to remember to floss after brushing your teeth.
3. It was quite <u>convenient</u> that the barbershop was located next to the dry cleaners because I had to go both places for my mother.
4. The videogame was too <u>violent</u> for small children.
5. The <u>infant</u> had a dirty diaper.

Maturing Reader: Year 2: Cycle 3: Week 1

1. The <u>captain</u> shouted orders.
2. The <u>airman</u> flew over the <u>mountain</u>.
3. The <u>orphan</u> made a wish at the <u>fountain</u>.
4. There was a <u>kitten</u> who lost a <u>mitten</u>.
5. I am going to <u>thicken</u> the <u>chicken</u> soup.

Maturing Reader: Year 2: Cycle 3: Week 2

1. The <u>golden</u> door swung open.
2. The <u>wooden</u> desk was <u>rotten</u>.
3. His eyes were <u>sunken</u> from lack of eating.
4. Our <u>cabin</u> is near a river <u>basin</u>.
5. My mom wears an <u>apron</u> when she cooks <u>bacon</u>.

Maturing Reader: Year 2: Cycle 3: Week 3

1. All of the girls from class are going to the <u>bridal</u> show.
2. Yesterday I had a <u>mental</u> breakdown.
3. We examined the <u>fossil</u> for a long time.
4. It is important for hospitals to use <u>sterile</u> needles.
5. You can use a <u>stencil</u> to trace letters.

Maturing Reader: Year 2: Cycle 3: Week 4

1. Come and meet me at <u>Central</u> Station.
2. The President of the United States works in the <u>Oval</u> Office.
3. The guy driving the <u>diesel</u> truck wore a <u>flannel</u> shirt.
4. Patty's mom loves <u>tinsel</u> on the tree.
5. While getting into a <u>bubble</u> bath, Evan sprained his <u>ankle</u>.

Maturing Reader: Year 2: Cycle 3: Week 5

1. Let's <u>capture</u> the <u>creature</u> in the book.
2. The <u>butcher</u> sliced the meat for me today.
3. I hope to be <u>richer</u> when I have a full-time job.
4. The <u>usher</u> escorted him out of the room.
5. I have a new <u>washer</u> and dryer at my house.

Maturing Reader: Year 2: Cycle 3: Week 6

1. Put the cows out to <u>pasture</u>.
2. I love the <u>texture</u> of the <u>sculpture</u>.
3. The <u>preacher</u> gave a <u>lecture</u> on Sunday.
4. We had to bring out the <u>stretcher</u> for the player who was hurt.
5. We have a lot of <u>pressure</u> this semester.

Maturing Reader: Year 2: Cycle 3: Week 7

1. A famous <u>poet</u> spoke at the <u>banquet</u>.
2. We brought a <u>blanket</u> to the picnic.
3. The <u>vomit</u> in the cage indicated that the <u>rabbit</u> was sick.
4. My friend found a golden <u>nugget</u> in the stream.
5. Please <u>exit</u> out the back door.

Maturing Reader: Year 2: Cycle 3: Week 8

1. I threw the old <u>bandage</u> in the <u>garbage</u>.
2. We had <u>cabbage</u> and <u>sausage</u> on the <u>voyage</u>.
3. A <u>partridge</u> in a pear tree is a symbol of the holidays.
4. Before starting a lesson, we must activate a student's <u>knowledge</u>.
5. I am always hoping to get a <u>package</u> in the mail.

Maturing Reader: Year 2: Cycle 4: Week 1

1. Did you close the door to the <u>furnace</u>?
2. Barry bought the <u>service</u> from the <u>office</u> across the street.
3. How many <u>basis</u> points will the rate increase?
4. Jay is a great <u>tennis</u> player, not a <u>novice</u>.
5. The lettuce looked like it belonged on a <u>trellis</u> instead of on my sandwich.

Maturing Reader: Year 2: Cycle 4: Week 2

1. The <u>alley</u> did not look like a very safe place.
2. I grew <u>angry</u> when I dropped the <u>candy</u> on the floor.
3. Our team won the <u>hockey</u> <u>trophy</u>.
4. Sally felt like a <u>zombie</u> the day after staying up all night studying for her test.
5. When I fell asleep at work I felt <u>guilty</u>.

Maturing Reader: Year 2: Cycle 4: Week 3

1. We had a problem once we realized that our goals were out of <u>alignment</u>.
2. She <u>often</u> wondered what happened to her old boyfriend.
3. It is not fair to <u>malign</u> the teacher when we never took her class.
4. Willie had to <u>resign</u> from his job.
5. The cloth felt very <u>soft</u> on my skin.

Maturing Reader: Year 2: Cycle 4: Week 4

1. I assume you read the meter before you turned the ignition switch?
2. Would you please act natural?
3. Spending time with nature gives me much pleasure.
4. Can he produce or provide me with a wise revision to his statement?
5. My assumption is that we have enough information to make a decision.

Maturing Reader: Year 2: Cycle 4: Week 5

1. I have nothing but admiration for your composition.
2. The majority of the narrative dealt with his preparation for the task at hand.
3. What is the definition of dividend?
4. What was Jeff's ability to expose us to that experience?
5. Where did you reside before you moved here?

Maturing Reader: Year 2: Cycle 4: Week 6

1. I will apply for the position on the application.
2. We are studying personification in English class.
3. Dennis asked Peter to explain his action recommendations for the problem.
4. Did you have notification about the situation?
5. I was never very good at multiplication.

Maturing Reader: Year 2: Cycle 4: Week 7

1. Brian went to the Naval Academy.
2. How did you meet the celebrity?
3. What was the chronology leading up to the accident?
4. We live in a democracy?
5. Jerry always has great information.

Maturing Reader: Year 2: Cycle 4: Week 8

1. Did you complete your analysis of the situation?
2. I felt disappointed because my nemesis won the competition.
3. I wonder if my thesis was any good.
4. The referendum passed successfully in the election.
5. It is important to cover all the bases in your preparation.

Advanced Reader Word Study Scope and Sequence

Year 1

Cycle 1 8 weeks Features

1. Adding /SHəN/—ct + ion (pronunciation changes)
2. Adding /SHəN/—ending blends (nt, pt, rt, st) + ion (pronunciation changes)
3. Adding /SHəN/—ending blends (rt, nt, pt) + ation (pronunciation changes)
4. Adding /SHəN/ with /t/ (spelling and pronunciation changes)
5. Adding /SHəN/—ss + ion (pronunciation changes)
6. Adding /SHəN/—c + ian (pronunciation changes)
7. Adding /SHəN/—e-drop + ion (pronunciation and spelling changes)
8. Adding /SHəN/—d(e)-drop + sion (pronunciation and spelling changes)

Cycle 2 8 weeks Features

1. Latin suffixes (ant/ance/ancy, ent/ence/ency)
2. Latin suffixes (ible/able with e-drop)
3. Latin suffixes (ible/able with predictable spelling changes)
4. Number-related roots (pent, quad/quadri, uni)

Year 2

Cycle 1 8 weeks Features

1. Greek roots (aer—air)
2. Greek roots (arch—chief/ruler)
3. Greek roots (aster/astr—star)
4. Greek roots (pos, pon(e)—to put, to place)
5. Greek roots (bi/bio—life)
6. Greek roots (centr—center)
7. Greek roots (chron—time)
8. Latin roots (cide—to kill, to cut)

Cycle 2 8 weeks Features

1. Greek roots (cosm—universe, world)
2. Greek roots (cris/crit—judge, separate)
3. Greek roots (dem—people)
4. Latin roots (fort/forc—strong)

(continued)

233

Advanced Reader Word Study Scope and Sequence
(continued)

5	Latin suffix (*ity* with base words, e-drop, and *ble*)		5	Latin roots (*dom*—lord, master; building)
6	Adding /SHəN/—other predictable changes (pronunciation and spelling changes)		6	Latin roots (*equa/equi*—even)
7	Consonant alternations with pronunciation changes		7	Latin roots (*dic/dict*—to speak)
8	Consonant alternations with pronunciation and spelling changes		8	Latin roots (*duc/duct*—to lead)

Cycle 3 8 weeks Features · **Cycle 3 8 weeks Features**

1	Polysyllabic homographs (*graduate/graduate, separate/separate*)		1	Latin roots (*mis[s]/mit*—to send)
2	Polysyllabic homographs (*graduate/graduate, separate/separate*)		2	Latin roots (*mot/mob*—to move)
3	Polysyllabic plurals—spelling changes in plurals (*a, ae*, also add *s*)		3	Latin roots (*pens/pend*—to hang)
4	Polysyllabic plurals—spelling changes in plurals (*us, i*, also add *es*)		4	Latin roots (*ped*—foot), Greek root (*ped*—child)
5	Doubling with polysyllabic base words (suffix *ed*)		5	Latin roots (*aud*—to hear)
6	Doubling with polysyllabic base words (suffix *ing*)		6	Latin roots (*scribe/script*—to write)
7	No doubling with polysyllabic base words		7	Latin roots (*spect/spec/spic*—to see/look)
8	Review suffixes with polysyllabic words		8	Latin roots (*vers/vert*—to turn)

Cycle 4 8 weeks	Features
1	Assimilated prefixes (*ad*—to, toward)
2	Assimilated prefixes (*com*—with, together)
3	Assimilated prefixes (*dis*—opposite of, not, apart)
4	Assimilated prefixes (*ex*—out, from)
5	Assimilated prefixes (*in*—in, not, toward, together)
6	Assimilated prefixes (*ob*—to, toward, against)
7	Assimilated prefixes (*sub*—under, lower)
8	Greek roots (*log, ology*—discourse, study of)

Cycle 4 8 weeks	Features
1	Latin roots (*prim/princ*—first)
2	Greek roots (*phon*—sound)
3	Greek roots (*scop*—see, view)
4	Greek roots (*tele*—far off)
5	Greek roots (*hydr*—water)
6	Latin roots (*jud*—a judge)
7	Latin roots (*lit*—a letter)
8	Latin roots (*spir*—to breathe)

Advanced Reader Word Study Lists

HW indicates header words. Teachers can create header word cards by printing out the blank word study card form available at www.reading.org and writing the header words on them.

Advanced Reader: Year 1: Cycle 1

	Week 1	Week 2	Week 3	Week 4	Week 5	Week 6	Week 7	Week 8
	Adding /SHəN/— ct + ion (pronunciation changes)	Adding /SHəN/— ending blends (nt, pt, rt, st) + ion (pronunciation changes)	Adding /SHəN/— ending blends (rt, nt, pt) + ation (pronunciation changes)	Adding /SHəN/ + /t/ (predictable spelling and pronunciation changes)	Adding /SHəN/— ss + ion (pronunciation changes)	Adding /SHəN/— c + ian (pronunciation changes)	Adding /SHəN/— e-drop + ion (pronunciation and spelling changes)	Adding /SHəN/— d(e)-drop + sion (pronunciation and spelling changes)
HW	**elect**	**invent**	**import**	**commit**	**aggress**	**music**	**calculate**	**collide**
HW	**election**	**invention**	**importation**	**commission**	**aggression**	**musician**	**calculation**	**collision**
HW		**except**	**plant**	**convert**				**expand**
HW		**exception**	**plantation**	**conversion**				**expansion**
HW		**insert**	**adapt**					
HW		**insertion**	**adaptation**					
HW		**suggest**						
HW		**suggestion**						
1	affect	adopt	adapt	admit	compress	clinic	calculate	collide
2	affection	adoption	adaptation	admission	compression	clinician	calculation	collision
3	collect	corrupt	confront	commit	confess	electric	associate	comprehend
4	collection	corruption	confrontation	commission	confession	electrician	association	comprehension
5	construct	digest	import	permit	depress	magic	communicate	conclude
6	construction	digestion	importation	permission	depression	magician	communication	conclusion
7	detect	disrupt	indent	transmit	discuss	mathematics	create	decide

#								
8	detection	disruption	indentation	transmission	discussion	mathematician	creation	decision
9	extinct	except	pigment	omit	express	music	demonstrate	divide
10	extinction	exception	pigmentation	omission	expression	musician	demonstration	division
11	inspect	exhaust	plant	convert	possess	pediatric	educate	exclude
12	inspection	exhaustion	plantation	conversion	possession	pediatrician	education	exclusion
13	protect	insert	present	invert	process	physic	graduate	expand
14	protection	insertion	presentation	inversion	procession	physician	graduation	expansion
15	react	invent	tempt	pervert	regress	politic	hesitate	invade
16	reaction	invention	temptation	perversion	regression	politician	hesitation	invasion
17	reflect	prevent		revert	repress	statistic	isolate	persuade
18	reflection	prevention		reversion	repression	statistician	isolation	persuasion
19	subtract	suggest			suppress		navigate	pretend
20	subtraction	suggestion			suppression		navigation	pretension
21								protrude
22								protrusion
23								suspend
24								suspension

Advanced Reader Word Study Lists

HW indicates header words. Teachers can create header word cards by printing out the blank word study card form available at www.reading.org and writing the header words on them.

Advanced Reader: Year 1: Cycle 2

	Week 1	Week 2	Week 3	Week 4	Week 5	Week 6	Week 7	Week 8
	Latin suffixes (ant/ance/ancy, ent/ence/ency)	Latin suffixes (ible/able with e-drop)	Latin suffixes (ible/able with predictable spelling changes)	Number-related roots (pent, quad/ quadri, uni)	Latin suffixes (ity with base words, e-drop, and ble)	Adding /SHəN/— other predictable changes (pronunciation and spelling changes)	Consonant alternations with pronunciation changes	Consonant alternations with pronunciation and spelling changes
HW	ant	reusable	adaptable	pentagon	minority	describe	authentic	face
HW	ance	edible	audible	quadriceps	activity	description	authenticity	facial
HW	ancy		accessible	unicycle	ability	assume	confident	influence
HW	ent					assumption	confidentiality	influential
HW	ence					conceive		
HW	ency					conception		
HW						produce		
HW						production		
1	assistant	desirable	adaptable	pentadactyl	acidity	description	authenticity	commercial
2	brilliant	desire	allowable	pentagon	authority	inscription	criticize	facial
3	compliant	educable	comfortable	pentameter	electricity	prescription	elasticity	financial
4	elegant	educate	favorable	pentathlon	hospitality	subscription	electricity	official
5	extravagant	excitable	distinguishable	pentatonic	legality	transcription	ethnicity	racial
6	ignorant	excite	preferable	quadrangle	minority	assumption	italicize	sacrificial

#								
7	instant	irritable	punishable	quadrant	popularity	consumption	publicity	circumstantial
8	malignant	irritate	readable	quadriceps	reality	presumption	publicize	essential
9	observant	lovable	remarkable	quadrilateral	vitality	concession	specificity	inferential
10	pregnant	love	tangible	quadruple	activity	recession	confidential	influential
11	absent	measurable	gullible	quadruplets	community	secession	consequential	palatial
12	agent	measure	mandible	squad	extremity	conception	partial	residential
13	decadent	navigable	plausible	square	hostility	deception	potential	sequential
14	different	navigate	possible	reunion	opportunity	perception	presidential	spatial
15	excellent	notable	accessible	unicorn	purity	reception	residential	substantial
16	frequent	note	compressible	unicycle	security	deduction	torrential	commerce
17	impatient	tolerable	admissible	uniform	university	induction	authentic	face
18	innocent	tolerate	permissible	unify	ability	introduction	critic	finance
19	present	vegetable	remissible	unilateral	disability	production	elastic	office
20	resident	vegetate	apprehensible	union	impossibility	reduction	electric	race
21	dependent		comprehensible	unison	liability	describe	ethnic	sacrifice
22			reprehensible	unity	responsibility	inscribe	italic	circumstance
23			deductible	universal	sensibility	prescribe	public	essence
24			digestible	universe	visibility	subscribe	specific	inference
25				unique		transcribe	confident	influence
26						assume	consequent	palace
27						presume	part	residence
28						concede	potent	sequence
29						recede	president	space
30						secede	resident	substance
31						conceive	torrent	
32						deceive		
33						receive		
34						deduce		
35						induce		
36						introduce		
37						produce		
38						reduce		
39								
40								

Advanced Reader Word Study Lists

HW indicates header words. Teachers can create header word cards by printing out the blank word study card form available at www.reading.org and writing the header words on them.

Advanced Reader: Year 1: Cycle 3

	Week 1	Week 2	Week 3	Week 4	Week 5	Week 6	Week 7	Week 8
	Polysyllabic homographs	Polysyllabic homographs	Polysyllabic plurals—spelling changes in plurals (a, ae, also add s)	Polysyllabic plurals—spelling changes in plurals (us, i, also add es)	Doubling with polysyllabic base words (suffix ed)	Doubling with polysyllabic base words (suffix ing)	No doubling with polysyllabic base words	Review suffixes with polysyllabic words
HW					_inserted_	_inserting_	_appearing_	_inserting_
HW					_submitted_	_submitting_	_classifying_	_committing_
HW					_promoted_	_promoting_	_attending_	_promoting_
1	advocate	affiliate	alga	alumnus	admitted	conferring	appearing	assisting
2	alternate	approximate	algae	alumni	compelled	embedding	complaining	corresponding
3	animate	associate	alumna	cactus	controlled	equipping	explaining	insisting
4	articulate	certificate	alumnae	cacti	excelled	expelling	repeating	presenting
5	coordinate	desolate	antenna	eucalyptus	inferred	forgetting	retaining	radiating
6	delegate	duplicate	antennae	eucalypti	omitted	omitting	benefiting	tolerating
7	graduate	estimate	antennas	eucalyptuses	permitted	regretting	developing	conceiving
8	initiate	postulate	larva	fungus	referred	transferring	editing	measuring
9	laminate	predicate	larvae	fungi	abbreviated	attending	entering	pronouncing
10	separate	syndicate	larvas	funguses	demonstrated	collecting	exiting	replacing
11	sophisticate		persona	hippopotamus	graduated	existing	limiting	residing
12			personae	hippopotami	operated	preventing	suffering	vacating
13			personas	hippopotamuses	promoted	supporting	certifying	acquitting

14
15
16
17
18
19
20
21

vertebra
vertebrae
vertebras

nucleus
nuclei
nucleuses
octopus
octopi
octopuses
stimulus
stimuli

translated
adopted
digested
inserted
perfected
reacted
subtracted
tempted

inserting
conducting
apprehending
pronouncing
resuming
disposing
enforcing
exploding

classifying
identifying
varying

allotting
beginning
committing
forbidding
forgetting
propelling
referring

Advanced Reader Word Study Lists

Advanced Reader: Year 1: Cycle 4

	Week 1	Week 2	Week 3	Week 4	Week 5	Week 6	Week 7	Week 8
	Assimilated prefixes (*ad*—to, toward)	Assimilated prefixes (*com*—with, together)	Assimilated prefixes (*dis*—opposite of, not, apart)	Assimilated prefixes (ex—out, from)	Assimilated prefixes (*in*—in, not, toward, together)	Assimilated prefixes (*ob*—to, toward, against)	Assimilated prefixes (*sub*—under, lower)	Greek roots (*log/ology*—discourse, study of)
1	addict	commission	disadvantage	exchange	inaccurate	oblong	subcommittee	analogy
2	adhesive	combine	dissatisfied	excommunicate	inefficient	oblige	subdivision	anthology
3	accept	companion	disseminate	eccentric	inoperative	obstruct	subheading	apologize
4	accident	compare	differ	ecclesiastic	insecure	occasion	submarine	archaeology
5	accomplish	collate	diffuse	efface	illegal	occupancy	suffix	audiology
6	affect	collect	different	effect	illegible	occupation	suffice	biology
7	affinity	collide	differentiate	efficiency	illiterate	occur	sufficient	ecology
8	affluence	colloquial	difficulty	effectual	illicit	offend	suggest	geology
9	aggravate	collusion		effuse	illogical	offering	suggestion	logical
10	aggression	correct			illustrate	opponent	supply	meteorology
11	alliance	corrupt			immature	oppose	supplant	mythology
12	allow	corruption			immeasurable	opposite	surreal	pathology
13	ally				immobile	opposition	surrender	prologue
14	announce				immoral	oppress	surround	sociology
15	appeal				immovable		surrogate	technology
16	appear				irritate			theology
17	appetite				irrational			
18	approach				irreconcilable			
19	arraign				irrigation			
20	arrogance				irrelevant			
21	assess				irreversible			
22	assist							
23	associate							
24	assume							
25	attain							
26	attempt							
27	attendance							

Advanced Reader Word Study Lists

Advanced Reader: Year 2: Cycle 1

	Week 1	Week 2	Week 3	Week 4	Week 5	Week 6	Week 7	Week 8
	Greek roots (aer—air)	Greek root (arch— chief, ruler)	Greek roots (aster/astr— star)	Latin roots (pos/pone)— to put, place)	Greek roots (bi/bio—life)	Greek root (centr—center)	Greek root (chron—time)	Latin root (cide—to kill, to cut)
1	aerate	anarchy	aster	apposition	amphibious	center	anachronism	circumcise
2	aerator	archangel	asterisk	compose	antibiotic	centrifugal	chronic	concise
3	aerial	archbishop	asteroid	composite	autobiography	centrist	chronicle	excise
4	aerie	archduke	astrology	compost	biochemistry	concentrate	chronological	fungicide
5	aerobatics	archetype	astronomy	composure	biodegradable	concentric	chronology	genocide
6	aerobic	archipelago	astronaut	dispose	biography	eccentric	chronometer	germicide
7	aerodynamics	architect	astronomical	expose	biopsy	egocentric	synchronize	herbicide
8	aeronautics	hierarchy	astrophysics	impose	biology	ethnocentric		homicide
9	aerosol	matriarch	disaster	impostor	symbiotic			incise
10	aerospace	monarchy		opposite				insecticide
11		oligarchy		pose				pesticide
12		patriarch		position				precise
13				positive				suicide
14				postpone				
15				preposition				
16				proponent				
17				proposition				
18				repose				
19				superimpose				
20				suppose				
21				transpose				

Advanced Reader Word Study Lists

Advanced Reader: Year 2: Cycle 2

	Week 1 Greek roots (cosm— universe, world)	Week 2 Greek roots (cris/crit— judge, separate)	Week 3 Greek roots (dem— people)	Week 4 Latin roots (fort/forc— strong)	Week 5 Latin roots (dom—lord, master; building)	Week 6 Latin roots (equa/equi— even)	Week 7 Latin roots (dic/dict— to speak)	Week 8 Latin roots (duc/duct— to lead)
1	cosmic	crisis	demagogue	comfort	condominium	equable	abdicate	abduct
2	cosmogony	criterion	democracy	enforcement	domain	equality	benediction	adduce
3	cosmography	critic	democratic	force	dominant	equanimity	contradict	aqueduct
4	cosmology	criticism	demographic	fortify	dominate	equation	dedicate	conducive
5	cosmonaut	criticize	endemic	fortitude	domineer	equator	dictate	conduct
6	cosmopolitan	critique	epidemic	fortress	dominion	equidistant	diction	conductor
7	cosmos	diacritical	epidemiology	perforce	predominate	equilateral	dictionary	deduce
8	macrocosm	hypocrisy		reinforce		equilibrate	edict	deduct
9	microcosm					equilibrium	indict	duct
10						equinox	jurisdiction	educate
11						equivalent	predicate	educe
12						equivocate	predict	induct
13							valedictorian	introduction
14							verdict	product
15							vindicate	reduce
16								semiconductor
17								viaduct

Advanced Reader Word Study Lists

Advanced Reader: Year 2: Cycle 3

	Week 1	Week 2	Week 3	Week 4	Week 5	Week 6	Week 7	Week 8
	Latin roots (*mis[s]*/*mit*—to send)	Latin roots (*mot*/*mob*—to move)	Latin roots (*pens*/*pend*—to hang)	Latin roots (*ped*—foot), Greek roots (*ped*—child)	Latin roots (*aud*—to hear)	Latin roots (*scribe*/*script*—to write)	Latin roots (*spect*/*spec*/*spic*—to see, look)	Latin roots (*vers*/*vert*—to turn)
1	admit	automobile	appendage	biped	audible	ascribe	aspect	adverse
2	commit	bookmobile	appendix	centipede	audience	circumscribe	auspicious	advertise
3	demise	commotion	compensate	expedite	audio	conscription	circumspect	anniversary
4	emissary	demobilize	dependent	impede	audiology	describe	conspicuous	controversy
5	emission	demote	dispense	millipede	audiometer	inscribe	despicable	convert
6	intermission	emotion	expend	moped	audit	nondescript	inspector	divert
7	intermittent	immobile	expense	orthopedic	audition	postscript	introspection	diverse
8	missile	locomotion	impending	pedal	auditorium	prescription	perspective	extrovert
9	mission	mob	pendant	pedestal	auditory	proscribe	perspicacious	introvert
10	missionary	mobile	pending	pedestrian	audiovisual	scribble	prospect	reverse
11	omission	motel	pendulum	pedicure	inaudible	script	prospectus	traverse
12	permission	motion	pension	pedigree		scripture	respect	universe
13	promise	motivate	pensive	pedometer		subscribe	retrospect	versatile
14	promissory	motor	propensity	quadruped		transcription	specimen	versus
15	remission	promote	stipend	encyclopedia			spectacle	vertebra
16	submit	remote	suspend	orthopedic			spectator	vertex
17	transmit		suspense	pedagogue			specter	vertical
18				pedagogy			spectrum	vertigo
19				pediatrician			speculate	
20							suspect	
21							suspicion	

245

Advanced Reader Word Study Lists

Advanced Reader: Year 2: Cycle 4

	Week 1	Week 2	Week 3	Week 4	Week 5	Week 6	Week 7	Week 8
	Latin roots (*prim/princ*—first)	Greek roots (*phon*—sound)	Greek roots (*scop*—see, view)	Greek roots (*tele*—far off)	Greek roots (*hydr*—water)	Latin roots (*jud*—a judge)	Latin roots (*lit*—a letter)	Latin roots (*spir*—to breathe)
1	primal	earphone	gyroscope	telecast	anhydrous	adjudge	alliteration	antiperspirant
2	primary	euphony	horoscope	telecommunications	hydra	adjudicate	illiterate	aspirate
3	primate	headphone	kaleidoscope	teleconference	hydrangea	injudicious	literacy	aspire
4	prime	homophone	microscope	telecourse	hydrant	judge	literal	conspire
5	primer	megaphone	periscope	telegraph	hydrate	judgment	literary	dispirit
6	primeval	microphone	scope	telegram	hydraulic	judiciary	literati	inspire
7	primitive	phoneme	stethoscope	telepathy	hydroelectric	judicious	literature	perspire
8	primogeniture	phonetic	stereoscope	telephone	hydrology	prejudice	literate	respiration
9	primordial	phonics	telescope	telephoto	hydrophobia		obliterate	spirit
10	primrose	phonograph		telescope	hydroplane			transpire
11	prince	polyphonic		telethon	hydroponics			
12	principal	saxophone		televise				
13	principality	sousaphone		television				
14	principle	stereophonic						
15		symphony						
16		telephone						
17		xylophone						

Reproducibles

Spelling Sort

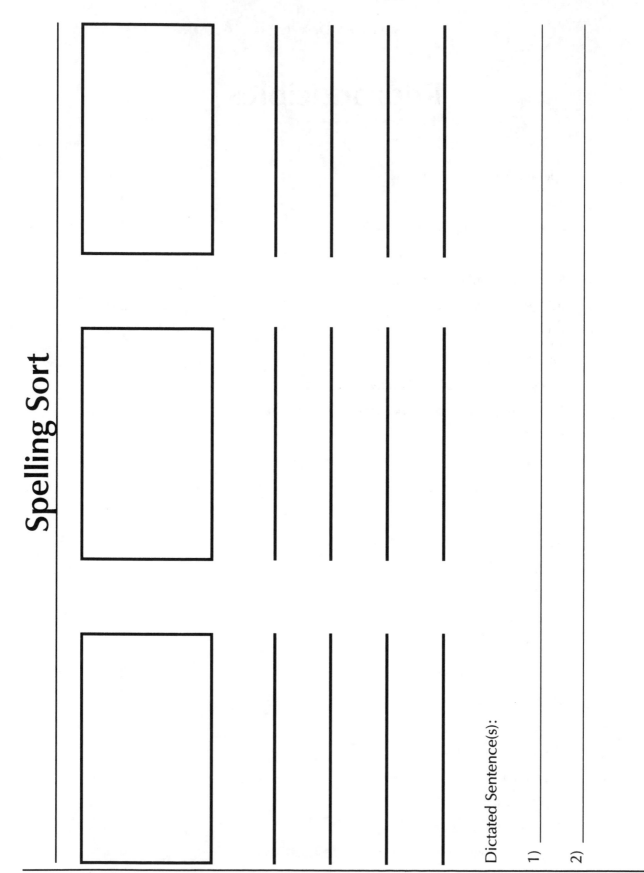

Dictated Sentence(s):

1) _____

2) _____

Root Tree

Root Word

Directed Reading–Thinking Activity Sheet

Name: _____

Story: _____

| What do I think will happen? | ⟶ | What really happened? |

| What do I think will happen? | ⟶ | What really happened? |

| What do I think will happen? | ⟶ | What really happened? |

| What do I think will happen? | ⟶ | What really happened? |

| What do I think will happen? | ⟶ | What really happened? |

Adapted from Vacca et al. (2003)

Very Important Predictions (VIP) Map

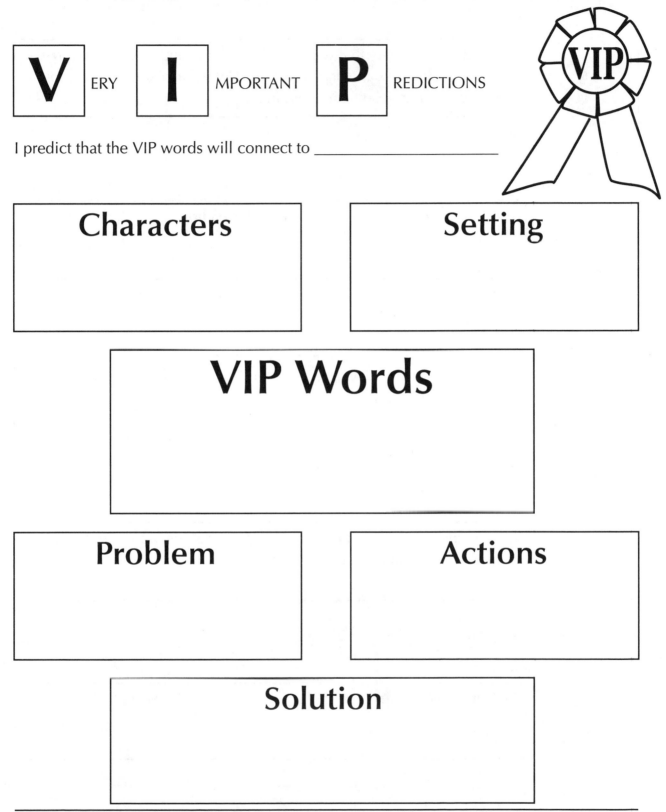

V ERY **I** MPORTANT **P** REDICTIONS

VIP

I predict that the VIP words will connect to _____

Characters

Setting

VIP Words

Problem

Actions

Solution

STARR Vocabulary Development

S Select the vocabulary that will be important for students to recognize and understand. Vocabulary should be selected that students will routinely use in their reading and writing.

T Teach the vocabulary to students prior to reading.

A Activate vocabulary as students read the vocabulary in the selection. Discuss how the word is used in the story.

R Review the vocabulary often. After reading the selection, ask students to use the vocabulary as they summarize the story.

R Revisit the vocabulary routinely over the next few weeks.

ABC Brainstorm

Topic:_____

A _____

B _____

C _____

D _____

E _____

F _____

G _____

H _____

I _____

J _____

K _____

L _____

M _____

N _____

O _____

P _____

Q _____

R _____

S _____

T _____

U _____

V _____

W _____

X _____

Y _____

Z _____

Summary Paragraph

_____

_____

_____

_____

_____

_____

_____

_____

_____

_____

_____

_____

_____

_____

_____

_____

_____

_____

_____

_____

_____

Adapted from Readingquest.org

K-W-L

What I **know**...

What I **want** to know...

What I **learned**...

Question Maker

Partner Names: _____

Date: _____

After reading the text selection, create one of each type of question. Then, exchange papers with your questioning partner and answer each other's questions.

Literal Question

_____

Partner Response:

_____

_____

_____

Inferential Question

_____

Partner Response:

_____

_____

_____

Application Question

_____

Partner Response:

_____

_____

_____

Questioning Guide for Narrative Text (fiction)

Making Connections
- Does this book remind you of another book you have read?
- What does the story title remind you of?
- What do you predict will happen in this story?

Story Structure
Characters
- Who is the most interesting character? Why?
- Who is the most important character? Why?
- Who is the bravest character? Why?
- What other fictional character could be in the story?
- What did you learn from one character in the story?
- How does one of the characters change? Why did the character change?
- How did the characters feel about one another?
- What are some of the choices the characters had?
- Name a character who played a small role in the story. Why is this character important in the story?
- Provide an example of how a character's action affected another character in the story.

Setting
- When and where does the story take place?
- Is the setting important to the story? Why?
- How would the story change if it happened in a different time and place?
- How did the author describe the setting?
- How much time passes in the story?

Plot
- What is the problem in the story? How was it solved?
- What actions were taken to solve the problem?
- What challenges were presented and how were they dealt with?
- Were you able to successfully predict the end of the story?
- What are the important parts of the story?
- What was the most important part of the story?
- What three or four sentences best summarize the story?
- If you were the author, how would you have ended the story? Why?
- How did the story end?

Summary
- In what order did the events take place?
- Do you think that the title is appropriate for the story?
- Who tells the story?
- Whose point of view is presented?
- How would the story change if it were told from another character's point of view?
- What is the story really about?
- Do you have any unanswered questions about the story?
- What lessons does this story tell you about?

Questioning Guide for Expository Text (nonfiction)

Preview

Text Structure

- How is the information organized?
- What does the title tell you about the text?
- How do the headings and subheadings help you find information in the text?
- What information is provided in the illustrations, graphs, diagrams, and so forth?
- Does the text contain reference aids such as a table of contents, index, or glossary?
- Are captions given to explain illustrations, graphs, diagrams, and so forth?

Text Summary

- What are the ways the author shares information on the topic?
- What are the major ideas presented in the text?
- What did you learn about the topic?
- What are some important words related to the topic? What do they mean?
- Are different viewpoints presented on the topic?
- What does this text make you want to learn more about?
- Why is this topic important?

Text Connections

- Does the author present facts or opinions?
- Is the information easy to find?
- Are the illustrations authentic?
- What are the different ways the author presents information on this topic?
- What do you already know about this topic?
- Have you read another book about this topic?
- What have you experienced in your life that might help you to understand the topic?

Story Map

Title: _____

Setting(s): _____

Main Characters   Supporting Characters

_____   _____

_____   _____

_____   _____

Main Problem: _____

_____

Event 1 _____

Event 2 _____

Event 3 _____

Event 4 _____

Solution/Conclusion _____

_____

_____

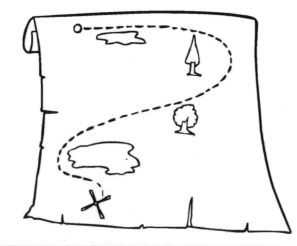

Cause and Effect

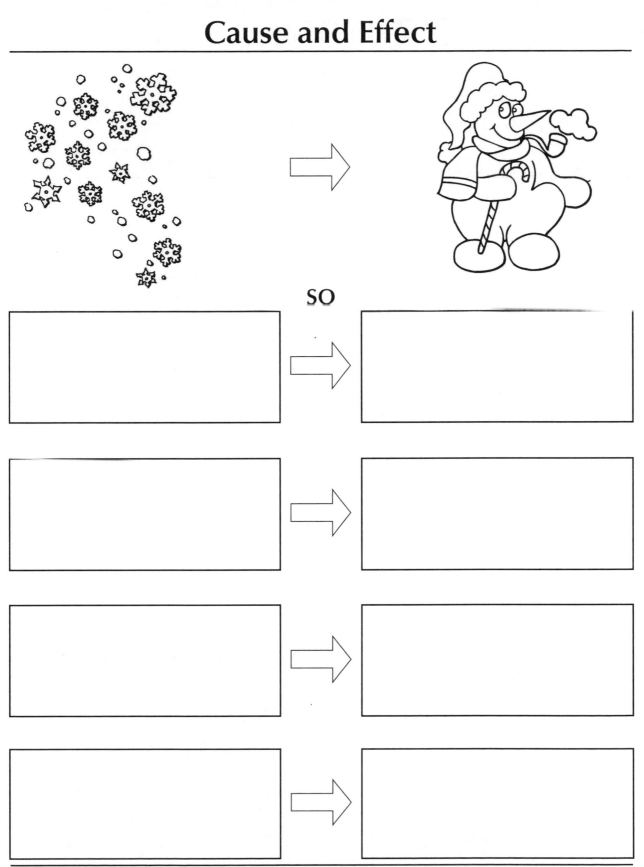

SO

Venn Diagram

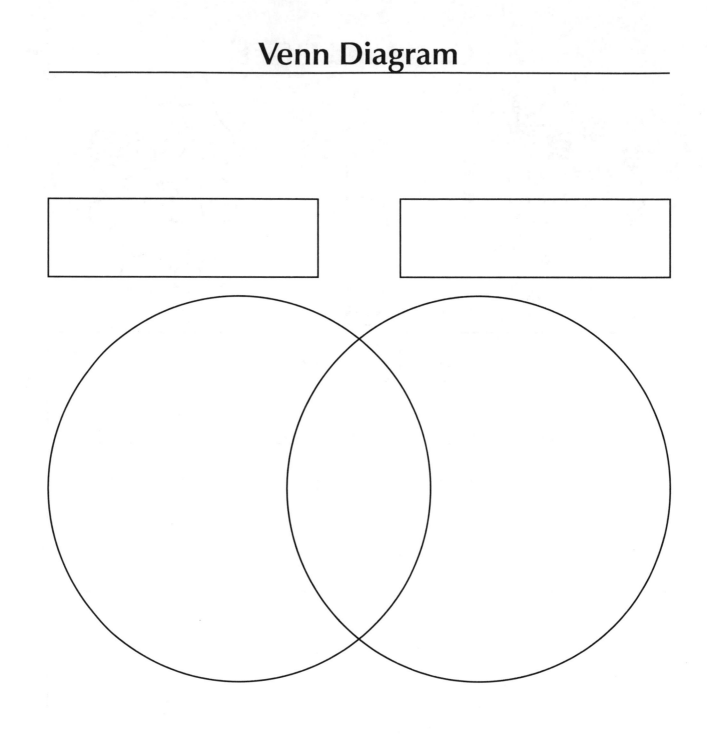

Sequencing

1. [ ]

↓

2. [ ]

↓

3. [ ]

↓

4. [ ]

↓

5. [ ]

Sum It Up

Text: _____

12 9
+5 +9
17 18

1. Read the selection, and come up with main idea or keywords from the text.
2. Review the chosen words, and separate the words that are essential to the summary from the nonessential words.
3. Then, using the essential words, pretend you are writing a classified ad for a newspaper and you get charged for every word you write. Each word costs you $.10.
4. Write a summary paragraph using your main idea words. Be careful, though, because you only have $2.00 to spend!

Main Idea Words

Essential Main Idea Words	Nonessential Main Idea Words

Sum It Up for $2.00

_____ _____ _____ _____

_____ _____ _____ _____

_____ _____ _____ _____

_____ _____ _____ _____

Small-Group Reading Instruction: A Differentiated Teaching Model for Intermediate Readers, Grades 3–8 by Beverly Tyner and Sharon E. Green
© 2005. Newark, DE: International Reading Association. May be copied for classroom use.

What's the Big Idea?

Main Idea: _____

Supporting Details: 1. _____

_____

2. _____

_____

3. _____

_____

Main Idea: _____

Supporting Details: 1. _____

_____

2. _____

_____

3. _____

_____

Main Idea: _____

Supporting Details: 1. _____

_____

2. _____

_____

3. _____

_____

Small-Group Reading Instruction: A Differentiated Teaching Model for Intermediate Readers, Grades 3–8 by Beverly Tyner and Sharon E. Green
© 2005. Newark, DE: International Reading Association. May be copied for classroom use.

Bio-Poem

Line 1: First name _____

Line 2: Four traits that describe #1 _____

_____

_____

Line 3: Related to _____

Line 4: Cares about _____

_____

Line 5: Who feels _____

_____

Line 6: Who needs _____

_____

Line 7: Who gives _____

_____

Line 8: Who fears _____

_____

Line 9: Who would like to see _____

_____

Line 10: Resident of _____

Line 11: Last name _____

Record & Reflect (R & R)

Name: _____

Date: _____

Text: _____

Scoring Rubric	Smoothness	Accuracy	Expression
1	Choppy, long pauses between words	Missed 5 or more words	Monotone voice
2	Some long pauses between words	Missed no more than 4 words	Changes voice sometimes to express meaning but still uses some monotone
3	No long pauses between words	Missed no more than 2 words	Changes voice to express meaning

Recording	Smoothness	Accuracy	Expression
First			
Second			
Third			
Fourth			
Fifth			

Read With Me

Name: _____

Date: _____

Text: _____

Scoring Rubric	Smoothness	Accuracy	Expression
1	Choppy, long pauses between words	Missed 5 or more words	Monotone voice
2	Some long pauses between words	Missed no more than 4 words	Changes voice sometimes to express meaning but still uses some monotone
3	No long pauses between words	Missed no more than 2 words	Changes voice to express meaning

Partners	Smoothness	Accuracy	Expression
1.			
2.			
3.			

Vocabulary Word Map

Name: _____

Date: _____

Looks Like

In Your Own Words

Target Word

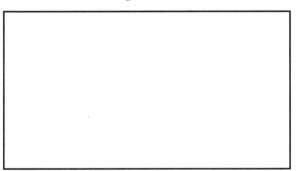

Examples

Sentence to Show Meaning

Story Snapshots

Name: _____

Date: _____

Story: _____

My Visualization

My Summary Paragraph

_____

_____

_____

_____

_____

_____

_____

Picture Perfect

Name: _____

Date: _____

Story: _____

My Picture

My Descriptive Paragraph

_____

_____

_____

_____

_____

_____

_____

You're the Reporter

Name: _____

Date: _____

Story: _____

What's the Story? _____

_____

Who? _____

_____

Did What? _____

_____

Where? _____

_____

When? _____

_____

Why? _____

_____

How? _____

_____

Any other important details? _____

_____

Fact or Fib?

Name: _____

Date: _____

Story: _____

List 3 facts and 1 fib about the text you read.

_____

_____

_____

_____

Fact or Fib?

Name: _____

Date: _____

Story: _____

List 3 facts and 1 fib about the text you read.

_____

_____

_____

_____

Top 10 List

_____'s

Top 10 List about _____

1. _____

2. _____

3. _____

4. _____

5. _____

6. _____

7. _____

8. _____

9. _____

10. _____

The Perfect Setting

Name: _____

Text: _____

Date: _____

_____

_____

_____

_____

_____

_____

_____

_____

_____

_____

_____

_____

_____

Secret Sequence

Name: _____

Date: _____

Story: _____

3...2..1..0

1. _____
2. _____
3. _____
4. _____
5. _____

Secret Sequence Answer Key

Name: _____

Date: _____

Story: _____

3...2..1..0

1. _____
2. _____
3. _____
4. _____
5. _____

Character Counts

Name:_____

Text:_____

Character	Trait

REFERENCES

Allington, R.L. (1983). Fluency: The neglected reading goal. *The Reading Teacher, 36*(6), 556–561.

Allington, R.L., & Cunningham, P.M. (2002). *Schools that work: Where all children read and write* (2nd ed.). Boston: Allyn & Bacon.

Armbruster, B.B, Anderson, T.H., & Ostertag, J. (1989). Teaching text structure to improve reading and writing. *The Reading Teacher, 43*, 130–137.

Armbruster, B.B., Lehr, F., & Osborn, J.M. (2001). *Put reading first: The research building blocks for teaching children to read*. Jessup, MD: National Institute for Literacy.

Bear, D.R. (1989). Why beginning reading must be word-by-word: Disfluent oral reading and orthographic development. *Visible Language, 23*(4), 353–367.

Bear, D.R. (1991). "Learning to fasten the seats of my union suit without looking around": The synchrony of literacy development. *Theory Into Practice, 30*(3), 149–157.

Bear, D.R., Invernizzi, M., Templeton, S., & Johnston, F. (2004). *Words their way: Word study for phonics, vocabulary and spelling instruction* (3rd ed.). Upper Saddle River, NJ: Prentice Hall.

Beaver, J. (1997). *Developmental reading assessment*. Upper Saddle River, NJ: Pearson.

Beck, I.L., McKeown, M.G., McCaslin, E., & Burket, A. (1979). *Instructional dimensions that may affect reading comprehension: Examples of two commercial reading programs*. Pittsburgh, PA: University of Pittsburgh Language Research and Development Center.

Blachowicz, C.L.Z. (1987). Vocabulary instruction: What goes on in the classroom? *The Reading Teacher, 41*, 132–137.

Blachowicz, C.L.Z., & Fisher, P. (2000). Vocabulary instruction. In M.L. Kamil, P.B. Mosenthal, P.D. Pearson, & R. Barr (Eds.), *Handbook of reading research* (Vol. 3, pp. 503–523). Mahwah, NJ: Erlbaum.

Bloodgood, J.W. (1991). A new approach to spelling instruction in language arts programs. *The Elementary School Journal, 92*(2), 203–211.

Bloom, B.S. (Ed.). (1956). *Taxonomy of educational objectives: The classification of educational goals*. New York: Longman.

Burns, P.C., & Roe, B.D. (2002). *Informal reading inventory: Preprimer to twelfth grade* (6th ed.). Boston: Houghton Mifflin.

Carver, R.P. (1990). *Reading rate: A review of research and theory*. San Diego, CA: Academic Press.

Chall, J.S. (1979). The great debate: Ten years later, with a modest proposal for reading stages. In L.B. Resnick & P.A. Weaver (Eds.), *Theory and practice of early reading* (pp. 29–54). Hillsdale, NJ: Erlbaum.

Chall, J.S. (1983). *Stages of reading development*. New York: McGraw-Hill.

Chall, J.S. (1987). Developing literacy in children and adults. In D.A. Wagner (Ed.), *The future of literacy in a changing world* (pp. 65–80). Oxford, UK: Pergamon Press.

Cohen, R. (1983). Students generate questions as an aid to reading comprehension. *The Reading Teacher, 36*, 770–775.

Cudd, E., & Roberts, L.L. (1987). Using story frames to develop reading comprehension in a first grade classroom. *The Reading Teacher, 41*, 71–79.

Daneman, M., & Reingold, E.M. (1993). What eye fixation tells us about phonological recording during reading. *Canadian Journal of Experimental Psychology, 47*, 153–178.

Daniels, H. (1994). *Literature circles: Voice and choice in the student-centered classroom*. York, ME: Stenhouse.

Dowhower, S.L. (1991). Speaking of prosody: Fluency's unattended bedfellow. *Theory Into Practice, 30*(3), 158–164.

Dowhower, S.L. (1999). Supporting a strategic stance in the classroom: A comprehension framework for helping teachers help students to be strategic. *The Reading Teacher, 52*, 672–688.

Ellis, N., & Cataldo, S. (1990). The role of spelling in learning to read. *Language and Education, 4*(1), 1–28.

Fielding, L.G., & Pearson, P.D. (1994). Reading comprehension: What works. *Educational Leadership, 51*(5), 62–68.

Fountas, I., & Pinnell G. (1996). *Guided reading: Good first teaching for all children*. Portsmouth NH: Heinemann.

Fowler, G.L. (1982). Developing comprehension skills in primary students through the use of story frames. *The Reading Teacher, 36*, 176–179.

Ganske, K. (2000). *Word journeys: Assessment-guided phonics, spelling, and vocabulary instruction.* New York: Guilford.

Gill, J.T., Jr. (1992). Development of word knowledge as it relates to reading, spelling, and instruction. *Language Arts, 69*(6), 444–453.

Green, S., & Massengill, D. (2005). *Effective tutoring makes a difference.* Manuscript submitted for publication.

Griffin, C., Malone, L., & Kameenui, E. (1995). Effects of graphic organizer instruction on fifth-grade students. *Journal of Educational Research, 89*(2), 98–107.

Gunning, T.G. (2002). *Assessing and correcting reading and writing difficulties* (2nd ed.). Boston: Allyn & Bacon.

Guthrie, J. (2005, March). *Teaching for engagement: The pathway to reading comprehension.* Paper presented at the George Graham Lecture in Reading, University of Virginia.

Hasbrouck, J.E., & Tindal, G. (1992). Curriculum-based oral reading fluency norms for students in grades 2 through 5. *Teaching Exceptional Children, 24*(3), 41–44.

Henderson, E.H. (1990). *Teaching spelling* (2nd ed.). Boston: Houghton Mifflin.

Henderson, E.H., & Templeton, S. (1986). A developmental perspective of formal spelling instruction through alphabet, pattern, and meaning. *The Elementary School Journal, 86*(3), 305–316.

Hennings, D.G. (2000). Contextually relevant word study: Adolescent vocabulary development across the curriculum. *Journal of Adolescent & Adult Literacy, 44*, 268–279.

Howe, K.B., & Shinn, M.M. (2001). *Standard reading assessment passages (RAPS) for use in general outcome measurement: A manual describing development and technical features.* Eden Prairie, MN: Edformation.

Invernizzi, M., Abouzeid, M., & Gill, J.T. (1994). Using students' invented spellings as a guide for spelling instruction that emphasizes word study. *The Elementary School Journal, 95*(2), 155–167.

Invernizzi, M., & Hayes, L. (2004). Developmental spelling research: A systematic imperative. *Reading Research Quarterly, 39*, 216–228.

Invernizzi, M., Juel, C., & Rosemary, C.A. (1997). A community volunteer tutorial that works. *The Reading Teacher, 50*, 304–311.

Johnston, F.R., Invernizzi, M., & Juel, C. (1998). *Book buddies: Guidelines for volunteer tutors of emergent and early readers.* New York: Guilford.

Kansas Department of Education. (2003, July 8). *Reading Standards: Grade 3.* Retrieved September 4, 2004, from http://www.ksde.org/outcomes/rwstd3g7803.doc

Kansas Department of Education. (2003, July 8). *Reading Standards: Grade 5.* Retrieved September 4, 2004, from http://www.ksde.org/outcomes/rwstd5g7803.doc

Kansas Department of Education. (2003, July 8). *Reading Standards: Grade 7.* Retrieved September 4, 2004, from http://www.ksde.org/outcomes/rwstd7g7803.doc

Keene, E.O. (2002). From good to memorable: Characteristics of highly effective comprehension teaching. In C.C. Block, L.B. Gambrell, & M. Pressley (Eds.), *Improving comprehension instruction: Rethinking research, theory and classroom practice* (pp. 80–105). Newark, DE: International Reading Association; San Francisco, CA: Jossey-Bass.

LaBerge, D., & Samuels, S.J. (1974). Toward a theory of automatic information processing in reading. *Cognitive Psychology, 6*, 293–323.

Leslie, L., & Caldwell, J. (2001). *Qualitative reading inventory—3.* New York: Addison-Wesley Longman.

Menke, D.J., & Pressley, M. (1994). Elaborative interrogation: Using "why" questions to enhance learning from text. *Journal of Reading, 37*(8), 642–645.

Moats, L.C. (2000). *Speech to print: Language essentials for teachers.* Baltimore, MD: Brookes Publishing.

Morris, D. (1999). *The Howard Street tutoring manual: Teaching at-risk readers in the primary grades.* New York: Guilford.

Morris, D., & Slavin, R.E. (2003). *Every child reading.* Boston: Allyn & Bacon.

Morris, D., Tyner, B., & Perney, J. (2000). Early Steps: Replicating the effects of a first-grade reading intervention program. *Journal of Educational Psychology, 92*(4), 681–693.

National Center for Education Statistics. *Reading: Average reading scale scores, grades 4 and 8: 1992–2003.* Retrieved November 8, 2004, from http://nces.ed.gov/nationsreportcard/reading/results2003/natscale score.asp

National Institute of Child Health and Human Development. (2000). *Report of the National Reading Panel. Teaching children to read: An evidence-based assessment of the scientific research literature on reading and its implications for reading instruction* (NIH Publication No. 00-4769). Washington, DC: U.S. Government Printing Office.

Nelson, L. (1989). Something borrowed, something new: Teaching implications of developmental spelling research. *Reading Psychology, 10*(3), 255–274.

No Child Left Behind Act of 2001, Pub. L. No. 107-110, 115 Stat. 1425 (2002).

Ogle, D.M. (1986). K-W-L: A teaching model that develops active reading of expository text. *The Reading Teacher, 39,* 564–571.

Pearson, P.D. (1993). Teaching and learning reading: A research perspective. *Language Arts, 70*(6), 502–511.

Pearson, P.D., & Dole, J.A. (1987). Explicit comprehension instruction: A review of research and a new conceptualization of instruction. *The Elementary School Journal, 88*(2), 151–165.

Pearson, P.D., & Fielding, L. (1991). Comprehension instruction. In R. Barr, M.L. Kamil, P. Mosenthal, & P.D. Pearson (Eds.), *Handbook of reading research* (Vol. 2, pp. 815–860). White Plains, NY: Longman.

Pinnell, G.S., Pikulski, J.J., Wixson, K.K., Campbell, J.R., Gough, P.B., & Beatty, A.S. (1995). *Listening to children read aloud: Data from NAEP's integrated reading performance record (IRPR) at grade 4.* Washington, DC: U.S. Department of Education, National Center for Educational Statistics.

Pitts, L., Jr. (2004, November 7). The wounded must be counted as casualties of war, any war. *Chattanooga Times Free Press,* p. 90.

Pressley, M. (1990). *Cognitive strategy instruction that really improves children's academic performance.* Cambridge, MA: Brookline.

Pressley, M., & Afflerbach, P. (1995). *Verbal protocols of reading: The nature of constructively responsive reading.* Hillsdale, NJ: Erlbaum.

Pressley, M., Symmons, S., Snyder, B., & Cariglia-Bull, T. (1989). Strategy instruction research comes of age. *Learning Disability Quarterly, 12*(1), 16–31.

Rasinski, T.V. (2000). Speed does matter in reading. *The Reading Teacher, 54,* 146–151.

Rasinski, T.V., & Padak, N.D. (1998). How elementary students referred for compensatory reading instruction perform on school-based measures of word recognition, fluency, and comprehension. *Reading Psychology, 19*(2), 185–216.

Rinehart, S.D., Stahl, S.A., & Erikson, L.G. (1986). Some effects of summarization on reading and studying. *Reading Research Quarterly, 21,* 422–438.

Samuels, S.J. (1976). Automatic decoding and reading comprehension. *Language Arts, 53,* 323–325.

Samuels, S.J. (1979). The method of repeated readings. *The Reading Teacher, 32,* 403–408.

Samuels, S.J., Schermer, N., & Reinking, D. (1992). *Reading fluency: Techniques for making decoding automatic. Read all about it.* Sacramento: California State Board of Education.

Santa, C.M., & Hoien, T. (1999). An assessment of Early Steps: A program for early intervention of reading problems. *Reading Research Quarterly, 34,* 54–79.

Snow, C.E., Burns, M.S., & Griffin, P. (Eds.). (1998). *Preventing reading difficulties in young children.* Washington, DC: National Academy Press.

Stevens, K.C. (1982). Can we improve reading by teaching background information? *Journal of Reading, 25*(4), 326–29.

Sweet, A.P., & Snow, C. (2002). Reconceptualizing reading comprehension. In C.C. Block, L.B. Gambrell, & M. Pressley (Eds.), *Improving comprehension instruction: Rethinking research, theory and classroom practice* (pp. 17–53). Newark, DE: International Reading Association; San Francisco, CA: Jossey-Bass.

Templeton, S., & Morris, D. (1999). Questions teachers ask about spelling. *Reading Research Quarterly, 34,* 102–112.

Tierney, R.J., & Pearson, P.D. (1985). Learning to learn from texts: A framework for improving classroom practice. In H.S. Singer & R.B. Ruddell (Eds.), *Theoretical models and processes of reading* (3rd ed., pp. 860–878). Newark, DE: International Reading Association.

Tomlinson, C.A. (1999). *The differentiated classroom: Responding to the needs of all learners.* Alexandria, VA: Association for Supervision and Curriculum Development.

Topping, K. (1987). Paired reading: A powerful technique for parent use. *The Reading Teacher, 40,* 608–609.

Tyner, B. (2004). *Small-group reading instruction: A differentiated teaching model for beginning and struggling readers.* Newark, DE: International Reading Association.

Vacca, J.L., Vacca, R.T., Gove, M.K., Burkey, L., Lenhart, L.A., & McKeon, C. (2003). *Reading and learning to read* (5th ed.). Boston: Allyn & Bacon.

Vygotsky, L.S. (1978). *Mind in society: The development of higher psychological processes* (M. Cole, V. John-Steiner, S. Scribner, & E. Souberman, Eds. and Trans.). Cambridge, MA: Harvard University Press. (Original work published 1934)

Wasik, B.A. (1997). Volunteer tutoring programs: Do we know what works? *Phi Delta Kappan, 79*(4), 282–287.

Webster's Ninth New Collegiate Dictionary. (1984). Springfield, MA: Merriam-Webster.

Webster's Tenth New Collegiate Dictionary. (2000). Springfield, MA: Merriam-Webster.

Wixon, K.K. (1983). Questions about a text: What you ask about is what children learn. *The Reading Teacher, 37*, 287–293.

Wong, B.Y.L. (1985). Self-questioning instructional research: A review. *Review of Educational Research, 55*(2), 227–268.

Woods, M.L., & Moe, A.J. (2003). *Analytical reading inventory* (7th ed.). Upper Saddle River, NJ: Prentice Hall.

Literature References

Anderson, J. (2001). *Deserts*. Barrington, IL: Rigby.

Baum, L.F. (1993). *Wizard of Oz*. New York: Tor. (Original work published 1900)

Lawrence, D.H. (1998). The piano. In X.J. Kennedy & D. Gioia (Eds.), *An introduction to poetry* (9th ed., p. 6). New York: Addison Wesley Longman.

L'Engle, M. (1973). *A wrinkle in time*. New York: Yearling.

Paterson, K. (1987). *Bridge to Terabithia*. New York: HarperCollins.

Randell, B. (1999). *Pandas in the mountains*. Barrington, IL: Rigby.

Randell, B. (2001). *The horse and the bell*. Barrington, IL: Rigby.

Sachar, L. (1998). *Holes*. New York: Yearling.

Spinelli, J. (1999). *Maniac Magee*. New York: Little, Brown.

INDEX

Page numbers followed by *f*, *t*, and *r* indicate figures, tables, and reproducibles, respectively.

N

NAME THAT WORD, 24

NARRATIVE TEXT: comprehension, classroom profile sheet for oral summary, 109, 146; questioning guide for, 256r

NARRATIVE TEXT LESSON PLANS: for Advanced Reader stage, 83–89, 85f, 90f; for Evolving Reader stage, 37–48, 39f, 49f; for Maturing Reader stage, 62–73, 64f, 74f

NATIONAL CENTER FOR EDUCATION STATISTICS, 1

NATIONAL INSTITUTE OF CHILD HEALTH AND HUMAN DEVELOPMENT (NICHD), vii, 17–18, 20, 26

NELSON, L., 20

NO CHILD LEFT BEHIND (NCLB) ACT, 1

NOTEBOOKS: word study, 23

O

ODDBALL WORDS, 41, 52

OGLE, D.M., 9, 30

1-1-1 CHECK, 68

ONGOING ASSESSMENTS, 98; of comprehension, 109–110; of fluency, 102; versus pre- and postassessment, 99t; of word study, 104–106, 106f, 139–144

OPEN SYLLABLES: definition of, 153

OPEN WORD SORT, 23–24

ORAL QUESTIONING RESPONSE CHECKLIST, 109–110, 145

ORAL READING RATES, 100–102, 101t

OSBORN, J.M., 18, 20, 26

OSTERTAG, J., 27

P

PADAK, N.D., 18

PARTNER READING, 19

PATERSON, K., 61, 68

PATTERN LAYER, 21

PEARSON, P.D., 8, 26–28

THE PERFECT SETTING, 124, 273r

PERNEY, J., 20

PHONEMIC AWARENESS, 20

PHONICS, 20

PICTURE PERFECT, 123, 269r

PIKULSKI, J.J., 18

PINNELL, G., 4

PINNELL, G.S., 18

PITTS, L., JR., 94

POETRY ALIVE!, 120

POSTASSESSMENT, 98; of comprehension, 107–109; of fluency, 99–102; versus ongoing assessments, 99t; of word study, 104, 135–138

PREASSESSMENT, 98; of comprehension, 107–109; of fluency, 99–102; versus ongoing assessments, 99t; of word study, 104, 105f, 135–138

PREDICTING, 25; activities for, 29; in Advanced Reader lesson plan, 88; in Evolving Reader lesson plan, 45; in Maturing Reader lesson plan, 69; research on, 26

PREFIX: definition of, 153

PRESSLEY, M., 26, 28

PREVIEWING, 25; activities for, 29; in Advanced Reader lesson plan, 88, 94; in Evolving Reader lesson plan, 45–46, 55; in Maturing Reader lesson plan, 69–70, 76–77; research on, 26

PRIOR KNOWLEDGE. *See* background knowledge

PROBLEM-AND-SOLUTION TEXT STRUCTURE, 27

PROGRESS: tracking, in fluency, 102

PROSODY, 17–18